Pedagogy of English Language

Pedagogy of English Language

Praveen Sharma

SHIPRA

Price: Rs. 1200; US$ 60

ISBN: 978-81-7541-698-7

First Published in India, 2018

Pedagogy of English Language

Published by:

SHIPRA PUBLICATIONS
LG 18-19, Pankaj Central Market, Patparganj,
I.P. Ext., Delhi 110092, India
Ph.: +91 11 22235152/6152, 9810522367
Email: info@shiprapublication.com

Preface

I am grateful to the Teacher-trainees and Teacher-educators for their patronage to my work entitled *Teaching of English Language,* as the same has been printed thrice since its launching in October 2008. Then it was revised in January 2011, entitled *Teaching of English: Skills and Methods* and reprinted in 2014.

The present volume is specially designed keeping in view the revised B. Ed. syllabus of some Universities specifically M.D.U., Rohtak, Haryana. This book *Pedagogy of English Language* may also be seen as revised and enlarged edition of the earlier stated appreciated and accepted work.

The book has been written in a simple, clear and lucid language as per needs of the students of various universities. It should serve as a practical handbook and guide to both – perspective teachers and in-service teachers.

While working on this volume, many other authentic writings on the subject were consulted, I am grateful to all these authors and their publishers. It is all God's blessings that this book could get its shape. I thank my students who have been a continuous source of learning for me during my inter-action with them and all the teachers who taught me. I am thankful to my family members for their support and cooperation. Shipra publications, Delhi also deserves thanks for publishing the book.

An effort is made to keep the book free from linguistic errors, however, I own the responsibility if there is any. The suggestions for the improvement of the book are welcomed.

October 2017 **Parveen Sharma**

Contents

1

Nature of Language

"Language is a set of human habits, the purpose of which is to give expression to thoughts and feelings." —*O. Jesperson*

Concept

Language is a divine gift of God only to the man. A language helps a person in the development of his personality. What distinguishes a man from an animal is the language and provides him the highest honour among all other forms of life. In fact, it is the language which brings the people of different culture and communities closer. Language is a means of communicating thoughts and feelings to others. The purpose of language teaching is to facilitate language learning. A Teacher's task is to teach and learner's task is to learn. It is essential for a teacher to understand the concept of language, teaching and learning because its nature is quite different. Teaching is an art and learning is science. Let us discuss in detail.

Meaning of Language

Language is an essential part of human life. The word 'language' seems to have been derived from the Latin word Lingua which means 'tongue'. It is a specific form of speech that evolved over a period of time. It is a kind of conventional arrangement, a common usage and intelligible patterns of words and idioms which help the group to communicate effectively. Since language has relevance only in a social setting, it is called a social phenomenon. Language undergoes a continuous change.

Some definitions of Language are:

(i) According to B.M.H. Strang, "Language is an articulated system of signs, primarily in the medium of speech".

(ii) John Dewey says, "Language exists only when it is listened as well as spoken. The hearer is an 'indispensable' partner".

(iii) O. Jesperson defines language as, "A set of human habits, the purpose of which is to give expression to thoughts and feelings".

(iv) Block and Trager write, "A language is a system of arbitrary vocal symbols by means of which a social group operates".

(v) H.A. Gleason says, "Language is one of the most important characteristic forms of human behaviour".

(vi) According to Sweet, "Language reveals ideas and feelings through meaningful sound of words".
(vii) Oxford English Dictionary defines language as, "Words and the methods of combining them for the expression of thought".
(viii) According to Ben Johnson, "Language most shows a man, speak that I may see thee".
(ix) R.A. Hall (1964) defined language as, "It is the instruction whereby human beings communicate and interact with each other by means of habitually used oral-auditory arbitrary symbol".
(x) E. Sapir opines that language is "a purely human and non-instinctive method of communicating ideas, emotions and desires by means of voluntarily produced symbols".

Broadly speaking, language includes all those verbal and non-verbal actions of human beings that are related to the communication of ideas. It is a complex system of communication with various levels of complexities involving intricate selection and ordering of meaningful sounds and larger units and arrangements. Language emerges from meaningful sounds. The moment we say something meaningful we are saying it in some language. In this sense, body postures, gestures, written and printed symbols, etc. come within the definition of language.

According to all these definitions, it becomes clear that language is used to give expression to thoughts and feelings of a social group.

Nature of Language

1. Language is Learnt

Learning of language is not instinctive or an automatic process. It requires efforts. It is not the type of behaviour like walking, sitting etc. which are quite natural. But language learning requires specific efforts. The child has to learn it over a long period of time. He/she is exposed to sounds around him. He begins learning of language by making various isolated sounds like ma-ma, pa-pa and later on, he develops his babbling sounds into speech sounds. This he does by imitation. Gradually, the child learns the words and grammatical constructions of his native language. Thus, language is acquired by conscious efforts.

2. Language is System

Language is a complex whole like the human body. The system of the body functions through different organs, such as, the heart, lungs, brain, ears and eyes. These various organs are interconnected and work in coordination. Similarly, the system of a language functions through sounds, words and structures. In the functioning of human body, different organs are of equal importance. Similar is the function of various aspects of a language. It is difficult to say whether speaking or writing is important in a language.

3. Language is a System of Systems

Language is, undoubtedly, a system. That system involves sound (phonology), words (morphology) and structures (syntax). These different elements function in coordination.

Let us be clearer, as the human body has a blood circulation system, a nervous system and a bone structure system; if any of these organs fail to work the whole body will stop functioning properly. In the same way language has three main elements (sounds, vocabulary and structure). If any of these three elements/systems fail to operate individually, the language will not be correct.

4. Language is a System of Symbols

Language is a system of symbols, and every word, phrase or sentence represents some object or idea. Language functions effectively when the symbols used are known to both the speaker and the listener, the writer and the reader. The various symbols of a language are the words. Symbols have sounds and meanings. The language functions through the symbols if meanings are attached to them. For example, the word 'pen' has three sounds PEN. It is a symbol of English language because the person who uses it has given it a meaning. But if we take up the same three sounds like N, P, E, that do form 'NPE' but that is not a symbol of English language as no meaning has been attached to that by the person using the language.

5. Symbols of Language are Vocal

The word language is derived from the Latin word *'Lingua'* which is produced with the tongue. Therefore, in the beginning language is a speech. There are many languages which are only in spoken form, e.g., different symbols used in a language are vocal. There are other kinds of symbols that cannot be called vocal symbols. For example, gestures, flags, green or red light etc. are visual symbols and beating of a drum, ringing of bell etc. are auditory symbols. They do not form language. In language, the sounds are produced through vocal organs. Language and its symbols are primarily meant for speaking; writing and reading are rather the secondary aspects of a language. Thus, the primary form of language is speech. Without the spoken form, the language would have, in fact, died even though vast amount of literature may remain written in the language. But all the sounds produced by the human vocal organs cannot be included in linguistic symbols. For example, sneeze, cough etc. have no symbolic value. They may have some meaning in a particular social group.

6. The Symbols of Language are Arbitrary

By arbitrary symbols, we mean that there is no visual relationship between the word and the object it stands for. Let us take the example of word 'fan'. We have not named it so on the basis of some logic or scientific principles. In English, we say 'fan', in Hindi we say Pankha (ia[kk]). Actually we call a fan 'fan' because when the language was originated, people agreed to use it in that sense.

7. Language is Unique

Each language is unique because it has its own style of functioning. The sounds, vocabulary and structures of every language have their own speciality. There are geographical and cultural diversities, and, that is the main reason why one language differs from the other.

8. Language is for Communication

Ben Johnson says, "Speech is the instrument of society".

Only through language we can pass on our ideas to others. Without language, we shall not be able to express ourselves. That way, whatever is in our minds, will remain with us. If we use the language correctly only then our ideas will be communicated to others accurately. So, it becomes essential on the part of a person that he/she should have a right type of pronunciation.

9. Language is related to Culture

Each language is the product of society. We cannot think of any language existing in a vacuum. Human language is transmitted from one individual to another not by physical inheritance but by learning. It has meaning only in relation to a particular culture and society. This is so because cultures are different. Language changes its shape and model according to the needs of the people in a particular society. In this regard, G.C. Fries says, "The only basis for correctness in a language is the usage of its native speakers".

Language develops in a cultural context and, therefore, meets the needs of the society (culture) in which it develops.

It may be useful to point out that standard British English (R.P.) and standard American English differ both in spellings and pronunciation, yet each one is correct in its own culture but not in the other.

10. Language is Ever Changing

Change is the law of nature. No language on this earth is static. Every language is undergoing a change with the passage of time. Languages change in all their aspects, in their pronunciation, word forms, syntax and word meanings. These changes are mostly very gradual in their operation, becoming noticeable only cumulatively over the course of several generations. But, in some areas of vocabulary, particular words closely related to rapid cultural change are subject to equally rapid, and, therefore, noticeable changes within a generation or within a decade. In the 20th century, the change in the vocabulary of science and technology is an outstanding example of change in the language. Even the meanings of the words undergo a change with the passage of time, for example, earlier the word *fakir* usually meant 'a saint' but in present scenario it is used for 'shabbily dressed'.

Thus, we can say that language is never static. It undergoes changes' with the passage of time.

Varieties of Language

One may find difference in the English used in official documents, English of classical literature and the spoken English. If we want to understand English language and learn its uses for various purposes we will have to develop a clear idea about the varieties of language which can be divided in following four parts:

1. Idiolect,
2. Dialect,
3. Isogloss, and
4. Standard language or Register language.

Idiolect

Although the members of a speech community may have extreme uniform attitude to their language, their actual individual language behaviour is very variable. In fact, no two people speak the same variety of a language. Each human speaker has his own idiosyncratic and indexical features. The speech of each individual is different in some variable degree from every other speaker of his language. The language of each individual is thus, unique and peculiar to him. This language of the individual is called his/her idiolect.

Idiolect is an individual's personal variety of the community language system and is, thus, identifiable pattern of speech of the individual in its totality. Your idiolect is your total command or knowledge of your language.

A dialect is made up of the idiolects of a group of speakers in a social, regional or temporal sub-division of a speech community.

Dialect

Language learning is not an inherent quality or innate skill, it is acquired in the society. It is reshaped according to the learned behaviour. So, it is quite natural that language behaviour of one individual differs from another.

Language changes due to the influence of time, space and social class. Even within the same community, socio-economic status and culture bring its own impact on the language. A regional, temporal and social variety within a single language is called a dialect. A dialect is a variety of language but not a separate language.

Pie and Gaynor opine that dialect is a specific form of a given language spoken in a certain locality or geographical area, showing sufficient differences from the standard literacy form of that language, as to pronunciation, grammatical construction and idiomatic use of words, to be considered a distinct entity yet not sufficiently distinct from other dialects of the language as to be regarded as a different language.

The study of peculiarities within a language is called Dialectology or Linguistic Geography.

A language is a complex network of its dialects just as a dialect is a complex network of its idiolects.

Isoglosses

An isogloss is a line on a linguistic map that separates the areas in which the language differs with respect to a given feature(s). It is the line(s) that marks the boundaries within which a given linguistic feature or phenomena can be observed. We may think of a bundle of isoglosses that roughly coincide as indicating a dialect boundary. There is no necessary relation between any one isogloss and other. They criss-cross, and diverge and often present a rather bewildering picture.

Standard Language or Register Language

Register indicates the uses to which a language is put: occupational, motive and informative. People working in different walks of life use different kinds of vocabulary. Thus, the occupational vocabulary of a farmer is different from that of a doctor. The technical terms used in commercial, scientific, military and legal literature are different in each case. These provide us with examples of different registers. Besides lexical differences, registers differ on account of phonological and grammatical features also. Speaking to babies, sports commentaries, public speaking, religious discourses and hawking are examples of different registers because of different phonological features. Newspaper headlines and the language of cables and telegrams have a special register because of the grammatical features. It is to be noted that standard language is more correct, more adequate than the dialect.

☛Points to Remember

1. Language has relevance in a social setting.
2. Language is used to give expression to thoughts and feelings of a social group.
3. Language is learnt.
4. Language is a system of systems.
5. Language is unique and ever changing.
6. Symbols of language are vocal and arbitrary.
7. Varieties of language *viz.* idiolect, dialect, isogloss and register language will help the learners to learn language in a better way.

2

Importance of Language

"English is our major window on modern world." —*Pt. Nehru*

Do you remember your first class in English or the first real conversation that you had in the language? Most of us would have memories of making a conscious effort to learn it in an organized school set-up in which it was taught to us as a second language in a very structured way, perhaps, beginning with the alphabet 'a'.

But we have come a long way since then, from being language learners to being language teachers. It, therefore, becomes imperative for us to understand the role of English in general, and, in India in particular, to be able to teach the language not only as a subject but, more importantly, as a life skill which our students need to develop in today's global context.

English has undoubtedly become a global language. It has achieved such a pivotal role today that no other language is likely to take its position in the foreseeable future. Not only does it have a widespread profile ranging from international politics, science and technology, press advertising, education, motion pictures, internet and communications, and much more, it has also become the language of at least a quarter of the world's population. It is the first language of the United Kingdom, the United States of America, Canada and Australia. In addition, it is spoken and read by millions of Europeans, Africans, Chinese, Japanese, Indians, and South Americans as a second language. One person out of every four on earth can be reached through English.

If we look at the media, we find that over 50 per cent of world's newspapers, over 50 per cent of world's scientific and technical periodicals and more than 60 per cent of world's radio stations use English as a medium of communication.

The History of English Education in India

Most of us associate the history of English with the British colonizing our country. However, it is as far back as 1759, which we can call the first phase, that the Christian missionaries with great zeal and enthusiasm initiated the process of establishing English-medium schools in India. The primary desire was to open the doors of Christian faith to the natives in India so that they could come out of the darkness of ignorance and superstition. Although they emphasized the importance of native languages in early education, and the learning of English as something expected to only increase the scope of clerical jobs, English-medium schools remained the preferred choice over the vernacular schools. The majority started to believe in superiority of English language and literature.

The second phase can be said to begin from *Macaulay's famous minutes* of 1835, which laid down the foundation of English emerging as a language of power in India. "We must at present do our best to form a class who may be interpreters between us and the millions we govern—a class of persons, Indian in blood and colour, but English in taste, in opinions, in morals and intellect." English Education was being developed for creating social divisions within our country. English language gradually became the language of government, administration, education and advancement, consolidating its position even further.

In the post-colonial era, the third phase, our national leaders felt that English cannot be eliminated from our soil. English language strengthened its root in almost all spheres, although several attempts were made to give equal importance to the mother tongue and regional languages, by proposing the three-language formula in 1961.

But English language remained on the upward curve in the country. English, in India, today, has assumed overwhelming importance in several domains of Indian society especially in the domain of Education—not only as a subject of study but also as a medium of instruction in many schools. It has specially become the backbone of higher education. Dr. Suniti Kumar Chatterjee's views are enough to highlight the importance of English language. According to him, "A vital contact with English is a fundamental necessity even for the development of our Indian languages, including Hindi and for modernizing them."

IMPORTANCE OF ENGLISH LANGUAGE

(1) English as a Language of Administration

English has been the official language of the country for more than 200 years. It occupies the place even now. It has been declared as the Associate official language of the Union for an indefinite period by an Act of Parliament in 1963. As such, it dominates the administrative business at the Centre as well in the States. Most of the administrative work is done in English throughout the country.

(2) English as a Language of the Court

Cases are presented and verdicts are given in the Apex Court and High Courts in English language only. It continues to be the language of

Court. The documents are prepared, the hearings are held and verdicts are given in Court in English language only.

(3) English in Social Life

English also plays a prominent role in the social life of our country. For example, whenever there is a marriage or other social ceremony, even the invitation cards are mostly printed in English language. Daily routine correspondence is also done in English. Various social groups in the country use English in social and intellectual communications. They put their signature in English most of the times. In this way, English is a unifying force and a unifying factor in the inter-state social life of the country. English has been mingled in such a manner in our day-to-day communication that even the illiterate people use words of English like 'television', 'Radio', 'gas', 'sorry', 'please', 'thank you', 'nut', 'bolt' etc. The list is always on the upward direction as the listener is exposed to newer words.

(4) English as a Language of Trade, Commerce and Industry

English plays an important role in the industrial and commercial life of the country. All correspondence is done in English. National and International trade development of industry and the working in commercial establishments have taken place in English. Efficiency and success in these fields depends upon an adequate knowledge of English. The maintenance of accounts, issuing of instructions and correspondence with others are conducted mainly in English language.

(5) English as a Link Language

English is a link language in India. It is the only language which is understood in all states. Though Hindi is our national language, yet it has not been successful in taking the place of English. In the absence of English language, a person from Tamil Nadu is not able to communicate with a person from Punjab.

Apart from being a unifying force within the country, English is our link with the countries of the world. It is only through English language that we have established social, economic, cultural and political relations with other countries of the world.

(6) English as a Window on the Modern World

It has been rightly remarked by Pt. J.L. Nehru that English is 'our major window on the modern world'. English is a vista through which we see at the scientific, technological, agricultural, commercial, social and political developments taking place in the world. F.G. French has rightly observed, "A traveller who can speak English will find somebody who can understand him wherever he may go, anyone who can read English can keep in touch with the whole world without leaving his own house."

Today the world is coming closer. People travel back and forth to other distant places. People from other countries visit our country. They interact with each other and come close. That is why English language has been called a window through which we can peep and see the whole world. If we shut it, we will be isolated from the whole world. And we want interaction with the whole world, not the isolation.

(7) English in Education

English language has been crucially woven in our education system. It is essential for a child to study English language at high school level. It is the medium of instruction in the public schools, technical, medical, law and other institutions. More and more English medium schools are coming up, as the parents prefer to send their wards for education in the English medium schools only.

(8) English as a Library Language

According to Kothari Commission, "No student will be considered to have qualified for a degree unless he has acquired a reasonable proficiency in English (or in some other library language)". This has two-fold implication:

(a) All teachers in higher education should be essentially bilingual. They should be able to teach in the regional language as well as in English.

(b) All students, particularly post-graduate students, should be able to follow lectures and use reading materials in the regional language as well as in English.

English is the key to the storehouse of knowledge. Most of this knowledge is not yet available in Indian language. It is in this context that the role of English as a library language becomes important in India. It is the only language through which maximum knowledge can be imparted to students. We shall have to retain English as library language if we want to keep abreast with the latest knowledge in various fields, such as, science, law, medicine, technology, space etc.

Learning English as a Library language does not imply that the students would not learn the skills of listening, speaking and writing English. It only implies that the skill of reading would be paid much more attention than the other skills. It enables students to have an access to the latest information in their subject of study. However, equal importance should be given to all the four skills: listening, speaking, reading and writing.

(9) English as an International Language

English is one of the major languages of the world. The UNO has given English the status of being an official language. The number of people speaking this language is 350 million. Even M.K. Gandhi had to say, "English is a language of international commerce, it is the language of diplomacy and it contains many a rich literary treasure, it gives us an introduction to Western thought and culture."

With the help of this language we are able to study the culture and civilization of other nations. A person knowing and speaking English is able to have opportunities of employment almost in every country of the world. It acts as a bridge or link between two languages.

These days every country needs other countries' help in political, social, economic and cultural matters. There comes English as a rescue. In this connection, Gatak opines, "It would be rash to cut ourselves from the English language which keeps us in continuous contact with the latest thoughts in Europe, in every field of life and culture."

English is being learnt and used all over the world not out of imposition but through the realization that it has certain inherent advantages. Today, the compulsion of learning English are no longer political, but keeping in view the scientific and technological advancement. And no longer is English the language of Great Britain only, it is the language required by the world for greater understanding.

(10) English in Communication

The fact that India is a multilingual country with a large number of mutually unintelligible, prestigious and developed languages tends to encourage people to use English in inter-regional communicative contexts. People tend to speak English even when they perceive the same common language, Hindi or regional language.

Future of English in India

In this context, it becomes imperative to quote C. Rajagopalachari when he says, "We, in our anger against the British people, should not throw away the baby (English language) with the bath water (English people)".

English, in India, is like Phoenix, the mythical bird which after living hundreds of years in the Arabian Desert, burnt itself on a funeral pyre and rose from the ashes once again, to live for another cycle. English has been with us for more than 200 years, and will remain with us for times to come. Before independence, English language enjoyed a very prominent and privileged position in Indian education and life. After independence, there was a reaction against the study of English. For a time it seemed to be on its last legs. But, today again, English is on the upward curve in our country. In free India, the importance of English is more than what it used to be in British India. On the basis of past and present, we can foresee a very bright future of English language in India as a link language, a window on the modern world and a library language.

Conclusion

It should be clear that people use English not due to linguistic barrier only but prefer to speak in English as their own choice. The youth, especially, seem to be favourably inclined towards the English language, as they perceive it as significant for their career advancement. Due to its central role, sometimes it has been considered as a status symbol also. For correct learning pattern, native speakers should be followed. For this English channels and cassettes can also be helpful.

☛Points to Remember

1. English language has become global language.
2. In 1759, Christian Missionaries established the English medium schools with a desire to open the doors of Christian faith.
3. In 1835, Lord Macaulay's famous minutes laid down the foundation of English as a language of power in India.
4. In the post-colonial ear, 1961, our national leaders proposed the three language formula.
5. Today, English has assumed overwhelming importance in several domains of Indian Society, especially in domain of Education. For example:
   (a) English as a language of Administration.
   (b) English as a language of Court.
   (c) English as a language of Trade.
   (d) English as a Link language.
   (e) English as a Library language
   (f) English as an International language.
6. Thus, we can foresee a very bright future of English language.

3

Functions of Language

"Speech is the instrument of the society" —*Johnson*

Language is the foremost requirement of a man. Language plays a very significant role in human life. The truth is that human life has been made better by the use of language. It is a means of communication. Our emotions, desires, feelings and other human qualities are communicated with the help of a language. Without language the human life would have been quite different. The functions of language are briefly explained here as follows:

1. Expressive Function

Every individual has some feelings, emotions, ideas and he/she wants to give an outlet to those experiences of life. Language helps an individual to bring out his/her pent up feelings. Through language, one can evoke desirable feelings among the readers/listeners.

How aptly W.H. Davis said: *"What is this life, if full of care? We have no time to stand and stare."*

He was conveying no information, but was expressing his feelings.

Language helps in the process of expression between two individuals. One individual is understood by the other when they have a common language. Language develops mutual understanding. Johnson has rightly said, *"Speech is the instrument of the society. It is language through which we can pass on our ideas to others and then cooperate with each other."*

Language has its aesthetic aspect also. Sometime an individual may have some feeling, but due to lack of formative and expressive quality, cannot give them concrete shape. Later on, those very feelings are expressed by another individual, may be a poet or an author, then that expression gives him a lot of satisfaction. It is vividly clear that it helps in the proper growth and development of the individual.

2. The Informative Function

We can pass on information to others only through language. Suppose a layman has some ideas in his mind and wants to pass it on to others, he will take help of language only. The history teacher, who is giving details of some battle to the class, is communicating information. In the absence of language, passing on the information will become a difficult task. The storehouse of knowledge being passed to the next generation through books or other media is the informative function of language.

3. Communicative Function

Sharing of ideas in a society is called communication. For communication, language is the first requirement. Without proper and appropriate language the communication may not be meaningful. Communication can be in written form and in oral form. Communicative function may seem similar to informative function. But communication function has a broader scope. All information is communicated to the masses through language either in written form or in oral form. The print media, e.g., newspaper, magazine, textbooks and general books is communicating information in the written form. The T.V., computer, internet, movies, documentaries and radio are providing information orally and visually. In communicative function both the sender and the receiver are equally important.

4. Directive Function

Language is a means of giving direction to others. Language is used to cause or prevent actions when a teacher asks the students to sit quietly or when a major in the army asks his soldiers to march ahead; the intention is not to communicate information or to evoke a particular emotion but to cause action of the indicated type. Let us share some more examples. The police standing at the crossing shows green light to the traffic. It is not just communication of information, he is rather directing the whole traffic to move ahead. A superintendent in the examination hall, a principal in the staff meeting give directions to follow.

5. Interaction Function

Language is not a one-way communication. It has both ways communication. Radio and television are the media of one-way communication but on telephone both way communication takes place. In the classroom also question-answer method is preferred so that teaching-learning process may become interactive. In group discussion or seminars, this is the interactive language which makes the topic lively.

6. Evolutionary Function

Literature is the mirror of the society. Any advancement of a society is basically its language development.

If we talk in the context of English, it is a rich and an international language. Language is always influenced by geographical conditions. All the developments of today have been made possible due to evolutionary function of the language.

7. Preservation Function

C. Rajagopalachari has rightly said, "English language is the greatest gift of Goddess Saraswati to India". It is species specific, as no other creature other than man can use it.

Man can preserve his knowledge, observation and experiences in written form. Thus, acquired knowledge and experiences are formed edifice of human knowledge. Through the use of media, we can preserve the knowledge and pass on to the next generation.

☛**Points to Remember**

1. Expressive Function: Language helps an individual to give outlet to his/her feelings and thoughts.
2. Informative Function: It is due to language that information/knowledge is passed on to the next generation.
3. Communicative Function: Language helps in the communication; either in written form or in oral form.
4. Directive Function: Through language directions can be given.
5. Interaction Function: Language is a both way communication which makes the process interactive.
6. Evolutionary Function: Today's language is influenced by geographical conditions.
7. Preservation Function: Media has made it possible to preserve the language.

4

Linguistic Principles

"Important principles may and must be flexible." —*Washington*

Linguistics is a science, a systematic body of knowledge and theory. Charles C. Fries defines linguistics or linguistic science as, "A body of knowledge and understanding concerning in nature and functioning of human language, built up out of information about the structure, the operation, and the history of a wide range of very diverse human languages by means of those techniques and procedures that have proved most successful in establishing verifiable relationship among linguistic phenomenon."

In India, English is taught both as a second language and as a foreign language. The term 'second language' is used because it has become a *lingua franca* between speakers of widely diverse languages. By English as a 'foreign language' is meant that English is taught as a school subject or at an adult level solely for giving students a foreign language competency. For both, it is essential for English Teacher to teach in such a manner that desired goals can be achieved because, in the words of Wren, "In the teaching of class-subjects the actual work of mind-training is being performed. In the early English lessons he/she (the teacher), is being the soil that it may be able to receive the seed."

Therefore, a sound knowledge of the principles of Teaching English language is needed. The general principles of learning a language have been derived by the language experts through their hard work, careful and intense study, good observation and experimentation. These principles are simple in nature and are of great help and importance for language teachers.

To teach a language effectively, the teacher should bear in mind the following important principles of language teaching:

1. Correct Language Standards

Teach the language as it is used by its native speakers and not as somebody thinks what the language ought to be. The only basis of correctness in a language is the use by its native speakers.

2. Principle of Selection and Gradation

No one knows the whole of the language. One does not know all the words even in his own native language. Mastery over a language does not mean knowledge of all the words in it. A person can be said to have learnt a language when he has learnt its essential vocabulary and basic sentence patterns. For this purpose, selection and gradation of language material is required. Moreover, it is expected when a student passes higher secondary class, he must have knowledge of 250 structure and 2,500 words in English. Selection of language should be done keeping in view its usefulness, frequency, structural value, availability, simplicity, productivity, teach-ability and learn-ability. Further, gradation means, putting language items in sequence. Gradation can be done keeping in view the various grouping patterns as phonetic, lexical, grammatical, semantic and structural.

3. Multiple Line of Approach

In the teaching of a foreign language, Multiple Approach plays an important role. Let us see what a Multiple Approach is. It simply means attacking a question from many sides. For example, if a teacher wants his students to learn new sentences and structures, he may first use oral method, then display on the board, asking the students to imitate and later, he may ask the students to cram the spellings present in context of different kinds of sentence structures.

New structures should be taught with the help of old vocabulary already known and new vocabulary should be taught with the help of old structures already known.

4. Structural Approach to Language Teaching

A foreign language should be taught in situations, which is the natural way by which a child learns his mother tongue. Items of vocabulary and structures should be taught in appropriate situations. The teacher should show the various objects either by presenting them actually before the class or by bringing pictures, or by drawing on the chalkboard. He/she should be fully conscious of his surroundings and should make full use of them. The teacher can perform actual actions like sitting, walking, reading and writing for teaching action words. The quality words such as big, small, cold, hot etc. may be similarly demonstrated. Conversation should be encouraged. It is the best way to learn a language.

5. Principle of Imitation

In fact, imitation is natural to man. It is very true in the case of small children. Whatever they see all around them, they imitate those things in the same way. Language is also learnt through natural imitation. A student learns or acquires the style of speaking and writing as demonstrated by his/her teacher. It is very essential that teacher's pronunciation, spelling and use of grammar is correct.

6. Principle of Accuracy

Accuracy is very important in learning a language especially foreign language. Wrong habits once acquired are very difficult to eliminate. So, it becomes imperative that a language teacher should emphasise on accuracy.

7. Principle of Naturalness

A language is learned in a natural way. Natural order of learning a language is listening, speaking, reading and writing. Listening is the basis of learning a language. So, it is the duty of the teacher to make the child listen attentively. Jesperson says, "The very first lesson in a foreign language ought to be devoted to initiating the pupils into the world of the sounds."

8. Maintenance of Interest

Mere verbal lecture will not suffice to motivate the students. The teacher of language should make the lesson interesting, use of audio-visual aids like charts, tape-recorder, flash-cards, pictures, overhead projector, chalkboards, and involvement of the pupils in various activities to create teaching situations, organizing games for teaching vocabulary and innovative strategies in instructional task are some of the ways to make the teaching-learning process interesting. There should be appropriate scope for listening, speaking, reading and writing. The teacher will decide which skill in the lesson should be emphasised for creation of interest.

9. Principle of Motivation

Motivation to use a language plays a very important role in learning a language. Child learns his/her mother tongue to get his needs fulfilled. For learning of a foreign language, like English, students should have some motivation closely related to their life, so that, they have a desire to learn English. Therefore, the atmosphere of learning should be congenial.

10. Principle of Habit-formation and Intensive Practice

Palmer says, "Language learning is essentially a habit forming process, a process during which we acquire new habits. When the child learns a foreign language, he/she has acquired the habit of speaking his/her mother tongue and his/her muscles are set in a particular way. Since the sounds of new language are different from the sounds of his mother tongue, the child has to keep at bay the habits of his mother tongue and has to cultivate a fresh set of habits. To fulfill this purpose, the child needs sufficient practice and drill. All the aspects of language learning, i.e., listening, speaking, reading and writing can be acquired after a lot of practice". In fact, language is a skill—subject and not a knowledge—subject. Like other skills as swimming and cycling, sufficient practice is needed in language learning. Otto Jesperson says, "He who gets the tip of his finger dipped in the water three times in twenty weeks will never learn how to swim". There is a need of continuous practice for acquisition of every skill.

11. Balanced Approach

While teaching the language, the teacher should see that the different aspects of it are fully taken care of. Listening, speaking, reading and writing should be equally emphasised. Each aspect has its own importance. It is not fair to emphasise on one aspect at the cost of another. In this regard Palmer says, "The principle of proportion does not necessarily imply equality of treatment or even a fixed standard of region; it simply means that all items in the whole range of subjects and aspects must receive an appropriate degree of attention so that the students' knowledge of them may ultimately form a harmonious whole."

Conclusion: There should be proper coordination in teaching different aspects of the foreign language. Thus in teaching a prose lesson, grammar portion may be discussed side by side, while during written composition, oral aspect can be covered. So that a kind of balance among the different aspects of language can be maintained.

Maxims of Teaching

According to Advanced Learners' Dictionary, 'Maxims' means a well-known phrase that expresses which is true or that people think is a rule for sensible behaviour."

Various maxims are discussed below:

1. *From simple to complex*: During teaching-learning process, simple things should be presented in the beginning and then the complex things can be taken.
2. *From known to unknown*: It means we can start our teaching after knowing the previous knowledge of a student. For example, if a child knows and identifies alphabets, then help them in learning the words, not a complex sentence abruptly.
3. *From concrete to abstract*: "Our" lessons ought to start in the concrete and end in the abstract. —*Froebel*
   Concrete objects can be seen and touched. Abstract things are imaginary and can be felt only. So, the teacher should forward from concrete to abstract.
4. *From whole to part*: According to this the teacher should introduce the whole lesson first and then tell about its various parts.
5. *From definite to indefinite*: The teaching-learning process should involve definite things to be taught first because the learners can easily have faith in them. Gradually, knowledge about indefinite things can be given.
6. *From near to far*: The things which are near to child can be taught

in the beginning very easily which will facilitate in learning about the things which are far.

These are general maxims and principles of learning a language. But these are only guidelines. Considerable research on second language learning the world over has shown that a learner needs to be psychologically ready to learn another language just the way he/she approaches the task of learning other skills. Her/his attitudes, motivation, personality, aptitude and age, socio-economic status exposure, schooling along with the teacher's beliefs and expectations can contribute significantly to her/his success in learning a second language.

☛Points to Remember

1. Correct language standards should be adopted.
2. Proper selection and gradation of words is must.
3. Attacking a question from many sides is helpful in better learning.
4. Appropriate situations must be created for effective learning.
5. Child always learn by imitating, so better model of pronunciation and writing etc. should be presented before them.
6. Accurate language in a natural and interesting way should be presented.
7. Language learning is a habit formation process.
8. Balanced approach with maxims of teaching should be adopted.

5

Aims and Objectives of Teaching English

"In teaching it is highly desirable to know exactly what one is hoping to achieve."
—Gurrey

Aims are very important in the teaching-learning process as they give direction. But it is really deplorable that these days passing examination and acquiring degrees is given more emphasis. Neither the teachers nor the students seem to be bothered about the aims of teaching English.

Teaching of any subject becomes much more effective and systematic only when the teacher is fully aware of the aims and values of teaching of that subject. Because the basic principle of teaching is "know what you do and only do what you know". Hence we have to understand the aims of teaching English.

Regarding aim of teaching English, Thompson and Wyatt say, "It is necessary that the Indian people should not only understand English when it is spoken or written, but also that they should themselves be able to speak and write it". The teacher of English should aim at linguistic aims only.

According to Palmer, "To aim at literature is to miss the way to language. To aim at language is to pave the way to literature".

After fixing the goals the efforts should be made to achieve them. The aim should be linguistic and practical rather than literary and aesthetic. Aims give direction to activity and help in taking important decisions regarding syllabus, course and methods for teaching and learning language. Gurrey says, "With careful thought, puzzling out precisely what he wants to achieve and what are the immediate needs of his pupils, a language teacher can soon become expert in noting the objective that he should strive for, and once he is aware of the advantage, he very soon forms the habit of directing his efforts and those of his pupils' on to selective objectives".

In this context, two important aims for teaching English language are:

1. Reception
2. Expression

First a child listens, he starts comprehending the language and then expresses it. In the acquisition of a language four steps/skills are involved: listening, speaking, reading and writing. When a child gives response to sound or language it is called comprehension or reception and when he starts using it, it is called expression. At the first stage, the learner gives meanings to language symbols, spoken or written. In the second case, the learner has to produce both meanings and symbols.

In India, English now exists as a second language and it should be taught as a language not as a literature. The aim of teaching English in India is to help students to acquire practical command over English, i.e., students should be able to understand spoken English, speak English, read English and write English.

Thus, these are the four basic aims of teaching English.

According to Thompson and Wyatt, the four specific aims of teaching English at school level are:

(a) To understand spoken English
(b) To speak English
(c) To read English
(d) To write English

(a) To Understand Spoken English

In the learning of a language, listening is the basis of everything. Even in the case of learning mother tongue, listening skills come first. In the teaching of English as a foreign language, the students should be given a lot of listening practice. Because language is first received then expressed. At school level, the students should be enabled to understand spoken English, required in ordinary conversation, exchange of greetings, receiving orders or directions and listening to lectures, talks, running commentaries of matches and news bulletins, etc. on the radio and participation in school debates and dramas.

The learners should be helped to recognise the sounds correctly. Preferably the native speakers should be the listening model. This way the listeners would be able to follow the correct model of listening.

Correct listening is the basis for effective language learning.

(b) To Speak English

The second basic skill in learning a language is to speak the language. Speaking English is easier than reading with comprehension and writing of English. But speaking with correct pronunciation is far more challenging. It requires the ability to produce sounds and to speak with proper stress and intonation. Language is basically speech and the basis of learning all languages. However, skill in speaking is not evaluated in examination that is why it is being neglected. English is required in every sphere of life. It is a language of day-to-day communication. A fair amount of practice should be given to students and the error in pronunciation and stress should be corrected by the teacher. Remedial classes can be arranged.

But it is sad that when a (B.A., B.Ed.) teacher teaching at primary level does not have knowledge of phonetics. They themselves do not speak correct English, how can it be expected that the students' foundation of speaking English will be effective and correct. So, it is suggested that a teacher who teaches English should have knowledge of phonetics.

(c) To Read English

Reading is an important skill to be acquired. But mere reading does not take one towards acquisition of language. The reader must comprehend the meaning of written material. It is only through reading that one gets information and latest knowledge. At the very early stage children should be helped to read in a correct manner. It requires habit formation. For this a teacher can play significant role by guiding the students to read newspapers and magazines daily. A teacher can encourage the students to get pleasure out of reading. It is to be noted in the beginning that they read well with correct pronunciation, proper stress and intonation, appropriate speed and proper understanding.

(d) To Write English

Writing correct English is the most important aspect of English language learning. Through writing, a person is able to express himself/herself. The teachers teaching language should emphasise on this aspect. But students cram the material and express. To improve their writing skill, due weightage should be given to the original ideas. This may include writing letters, applications, formal and informal invitations, personal letters, diary entries and paragraphs on general topics.

Each skill is important in its own way. The teacher should give training for all the skills. He should teach the language in such a way that the learners are able to achieve the aims of teaching English. It is not correct to say that one aim is more important than the other. In language learning reception as well as expression ability are needed.

Michael West opines that Indian children do not get much opportunity to speak, so for them more emphasis should be given on speaking than writing.

So, whenever we are teaching English and in whatever situation we may be, we should try for linguistic aims.

P. Gurrey says, "Our chief concern should not be about the difficulties of pronunciation growth, vocabulary, grammar and structure, but with language abilities".

It depends on the efficiency of the teacher how he/she makes the language learning interesting. V.K. Gokak has said rightly, "Language teaching is not such an unpleasant task as it is imagined to be, with proper training and equipment, it can even be delightful".

It can be said that teacher should be intelligent to choose the aim for particular lesson as this will be a better aid for teaching.

Aims of Teaching English at the Junior Level

(1) To understand spoken English.
(2) To acquire ability to read.
(3) To acquire a limited vocabulary which is enough to help him in the use of the language.
(4) To develop conversational ability, our purpose in the beginning should be to help the student acquire a command over spoken form or conversational English rather than the text-book English.
(5) To enable them to make simple statements in English language.
(6) To follow correct pronunciation, stress and intonation.
(7) To write English legibly and coherently.
(8) To respond in English to directions, calls and greetings.

Aims of Teaching English at the Senior Level

(1) To enable the students to speak English fluently and accurately.
(2) To make them able to express their ideas in English.
(3) To enable them to compose their ideas independently and present them in speech and writing.
(4) To enable them to acquire a vocabulary of about 2,500 words which should include commonly used phrases and idioms.
(5) To enable them to use reference material, *viz.*, dictionaries, encyclopaedia, reference books etc. whenever needed.

Some other Aims of Teaching English at the Senior Secondary Level

(1) A student at the end of the secondary stage should be able to speak English fluently and accurately. Fluency implies acquisition of reasonable standards in speech habits which means speaking with an acceptable pronunciation and intonation. Accuracy means use of the accepted usages.
(2) S/He should be able to speak freely. He should think in English and speak at ease.
(3) S/He should be able to react to situations.
(4) S/He should acquire the ability to understand the native speakers.
(5) S/He should be able to compose freely and independently.
(6) S/He should acquire vocabulary of 2,500 to 3,000 words.
(7) S/He should be able to use resource material, e.g., dictionaries, reference books etc.

Difference between Aims and Objectives

The aim has wider scope, in the sense, that it covers a larger area of study. The scope of objectives is narrow, i.e. it covers a limited area of study. Aims are attained with the help of school, society and nation. Timetable of the school depends upon the needs of the society and nation. Aims deal with various problems. It is not very easy to achieve those aims. To achieve aims, much time is needed. It takes years to achieve a single aim.

The scope of objective is narrow, i.e. it covers a limited area of study. To achieve the objectives, the teacher and the teaching material, both are significant. Objectives are not ideals, they are behavioural. They can be achieved easily. Objectives can be achieved in a shorter time.

The aims are the ultimate goals, the destination, the target but the objectives are immediate. They are the immediate concern of the teachers and the learners.

Objectives are the means to achieve the aims. For example, if we want to learn a language it becomes our aim. To achieve this aim, we will follow these objectives:

(a) to listen with comprehension;
(b) to be able to speak;
(c) to read with comprehension; and
(d) to write correctly.

Completion of these objectives will take the learner towards the aims.

Objectives of Teaching English

According to the dictionary of Education, Objective is, "*the end towards which a school sponsored activity is directed*".

Effective tangible changes in pupils' behaviour at the end of schooling is known as objective.

Dr. B.S. Bloom has defined Educational Objectives as, "the designed goal or outcome at which instruction is aimed". The objectives of a topic in English help in realising some general aims of teaching English.

L.A.C. Strong once proclaimed, "For us who speak English, English is everything...., English is not a subject, English is our life".

But this is not true for English in India. In most Indian schools, English is being studied as second language. Its teaching and learning in schools is inspired by one aim – the utilitarian aim. This aim can be achieved by acquiring practical command of English.

Thompson and Wyatt rightly remarked that it is necessary that the Indian pupil should not only understand English when it is spoken or written, but also he should himself be able to speak and write it.

Yet clear-cut objectives should be stated so that right planning can be done and right type of methods and techniques of teaching can be adopted as pointed out by P. Gurrey, "The careful thinking out of a detailed and well–defined objective for the lessons will be more than almost anything else to improve a teacher's work and to make it effective".

The two main objectives of teaching English are:

(i) Language development; and
(ii) Literary development.

Characteristics of Good Objectives

The characteristics of good objectives are as under:

(i) It should be specific and precise.
(ii) It should be attainable.
(iii) It should be based on psychological principles.
(iv) It should be for the development of the students.
(v) It should be helpful in acquiring democratic aims.
(vi) It should be for changing or modifying students' behaviour.
(vii) It should be tangible in ordinary circumstances.
(viii) It should be useful.
(ix) It should be in terms of change expected in the pupils and not as duties of the teacher.
(x) Each statement should have one objective in it.

Objectives at Junior Level

(1) Make simple statements through English. He should be able to frame short, simple sentences to express himself through speech and writing.
(2) S/He should be able to speak well with proper stress and intonation.
(3) Write English legibly and coherently using proper punctuation and capitals where necessary and with correct spellings.
(4) Respond to short, conversational questions.
(5) Acquire reading ability.
(6) Acquire a genuine vocabulary.
(7) Understand English when spoken.
(8) Use English when she/he has to respond to calls, requests, greetings etc.

The ultimate aim of teaching English is to develop command over English. A.V.P. Elliott has also suggested, "The ability to speak and write English and the ability to read English should be regarded as of equal importance".

So it can be said that all the objectives should be regarded as paramount, and equal importance should be given to each.

☛Points to Remember

1. Correct listening is the basis for effective language learning.
2. Speaking with correct pronunciation and stress should be given at a due place.
3. Reader must learn to comprehend the meaning of written material.
4. Writing correct English is another important aspect of English language.
   All the above mentioned four aims are equally important.
5. Aims have wider scope whereas objectives have narrow scope. Aims are ultimate goals. Objectives are not ideals, they are behavioural and are the means to achieve the aims.

6

Stating Objectives in Behavioural Terms

How many of you have ever been asked to write objectives as a part of your planning and teaching? If you are teaching in some school, you probably have been called upon to state objectives specifying outcomes that your students can achieve. If you are a Principal or Supervisor, you probably have had the responsibility of stating objectives and helping teachers to state them.

Writing objectives has been viewed both positively and negatively. Some of you may consider it worthwhile other may find it useless.

Curriculum, syllabus, text-book, teaching methods, modes of evaluation, all these are based on certain theories of learning or teaching models. For the implementation of educational plans or improving the practice of teaching and learning, knowledge of various theories of learning and its outcomes are essential.

Evaluation is a process of ascertaining the nature and quantum of change and should necessarily be based on, or be directed towards such a goal. Goals and objectives are not synonymous. While goals are broad and relate to long-term vision, objectives are narrower and framed to meet the long-term goals in a phased manner. Objectives are the starting point of any educational process and their understanding is a basic requirement for all teachers to be successful in their mission of teaching and testing students.

For effecting teaching and learning, fixing the objective is essential. Dr. B.S. Bloom defines the educational objectives in the following words, "Educational objectives are not only the goals towards which the curriculum is shaped and towards which instruction is guided, but they are also the goals that provide the detailed specification for the construction and use of evaluative technique".

An educational objective is often limited to what is mentioned in the prescribed syllabus or to what the teacher does in the classroom. An educational objective may better be defined, "as a desired change in behaviour in a person that we try to bring about through education".— E.J. Frost. These changes have the basic characteristics of direction and nature (quality and extent). In other words, it may mean.

These objectives obviously have to serve as guide posts in learning. A platform of well-defined educational objectives provide the basis for systematisation, articulation, unity, balance and for determining priorities in an educational effort. The main purpose of stating objectives at the general level is to provide a basic platform for an educational system. They lay down fundamental guidelines for curriculum development but being broadly stated may be able to guide a specific educational activity only in a limited manner.

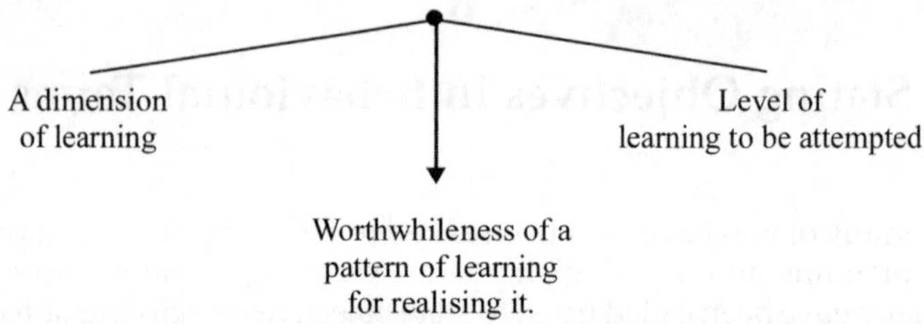

For your clarity, goals provide a broad guideline towards which one has to proceed, and objectives are specific and involve definite action to meet the goals. Behavioural objectives in education refer to the objectives that include all the three components of behaviours which are:

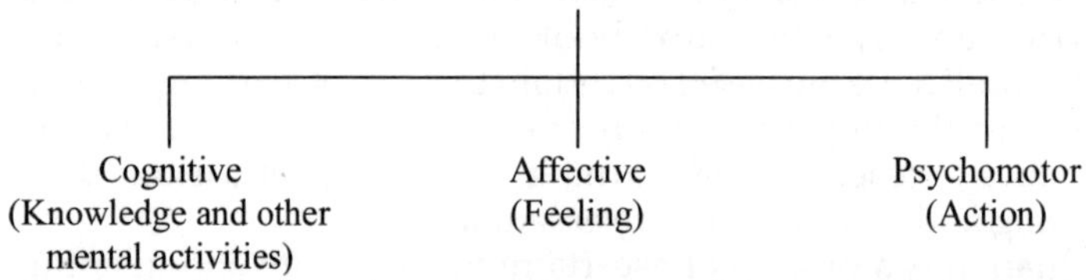

To ensure functionally, overall goals will have to be further broken down and made specific step by step to the level of actual learning experiences from goals to aims, from aims to objectives and from objectives to specifications. Hence, it will be desirable to apply the three-fold criteria to them:

- Worthwhileness from the standpoint of society's requirements.
- Practicability in the light of resources.
- Attainability in terms of pupil's readiness and capability.

Student's learning is influenced by instructional decisions taken by a teacher. Choice of material pacing and sequencing of activities, methods and techniques of teaching, and assessing from the basis of decisions. Different types of learning require different learning experiences and hence different types of objectives. Prof. Wilkins observes, "When objectives have been defined, the most important principle is to ensure that the linguistic and learning experience is planned. So to be completely representative of the objectives and of the different components of these objectives, once the behavioural objectives have been formulated, then comes the instructional objectives which prove helpful for the process of learning. This instructional process is helpful in the achievement of behavioural objectives. In short, behavioural objectives are complimentary to instructional objectives".

Teaching and learning are not separate entities. This process is better performed when instructional objectives provide goal clarity for teachers and learners.

An instructional objective describes the specific teaching outcome, the behaviour required to perform it and determines the means for meaning or evaluating it. Such evaluation is based on directional statements that identify the expected learner outcomes, establish purposes and stipulate levels of achievement.

Instructional objectives are specific behavioural and practical in nature. These are definite but differ subject-wise. These are mainly based on specific observable or measurable goals in pupils' learning. It provides the procedure for determining whether or not a certain level of attainment has occurred. These can be achieved in a short period. Instructional objectives state both what behaviour is intended to be developed (curricular aspect) and what actual behaviour is developed and tested (evaluation aspect).

The relationship between educational objectives and instructional objectives can be understood through the following model:

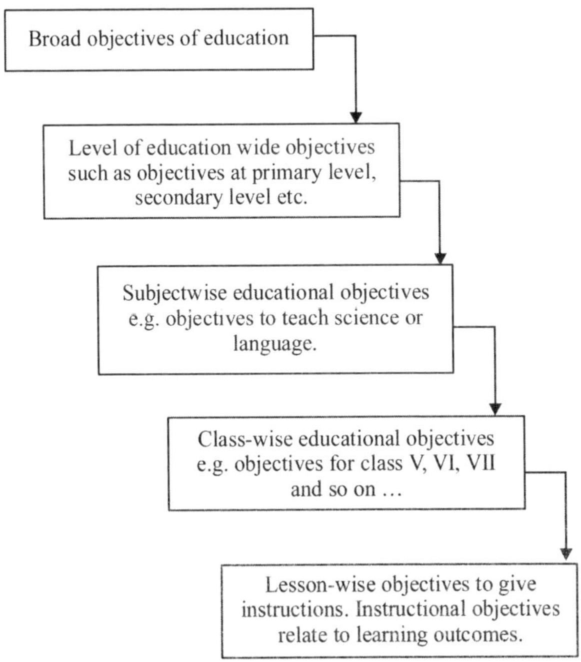

Relationship of educational goals and instructional objectives can be summarised as:

1. Instructional objectives specify learning outcomes more sharply than educational goals.
2. Source of educational objective is social philosophy whereas source of instructional objective is psychology.
3. Educational goals are usually normative, and do not account for the variability which can be achieved by instructional objectives. Hence, educational goals must be translated into

instructional objectives that are relevant to the specific situation and specific subject area.

4. Educational goals are changeable and instructional objectives are definite.
5. Educational goals are to be realised over an extended period of time whereas instructional objectives have an immediate intent.
6. Statement of educational objectives is often broad and global in nature. To make them amenable to evaluation, it is better to convert them into instructional objectives.

Characteristics of Behavioural Objectives

1. They are helpful in renovating and redesigning the educational structure.
2. Testing is also possible.
3. They also help in the selection of suitable teaching aids.
4. Feedback is also possible.
5. They also help in organisation of co-curricular activities.
6. Determination and delimitation of teaching activities become possible.

Procedure for Writing Behavioural Objectives

Writing of instructional objectives in behavioural terms provide direction to the teacher. The teacher should emphasise upon the right techniques and devices of teaching. There are various methods of writing objectives in behavioural terms.

Taxonomy of Educational Objectives

The word taxonomy comes from the Greek word 'taxis', which means arrangement or division. A taxonomy is a classification scheme followed originally in biological sciences wherein it is used to classify plants and animals. From biological field, the use of the concept is spread to other disciplines, and is also used to show a systematic arrangement.

Bloom's Taxonomy of Instructional Objectives

Professor B.S. Bloom (USA) in 1956, did a pioneer attempt. He organised instructional objectives in education in a systematic manner and this classification is known as Bloom's taxonomy of instructional objectives.

Bloom's Taxonomy Cognitive dimensions	Bloom, Maria Krath Wohl Affective dimensions 1964	Simpson and Harrow Psychomotor dimension 1964 and 1972

Advantages

(1) They are helpful in renovating and redesigning the educational structure.
(2) Testing is also possible.
(3) They also help in the selection of suitable teaching aids.

(4) Feedback is also possible.
(5) They also help in the organisation of co-curricular activities.
(6) Determination and delimitation of teaching activities become possible.

Taxonomy of Bloom, in regard to objectives, presents a system of classification of objectives. These objectives are related with the three aspects of an individual's behaviour:

(1) Cognitive (knowledge)
(2) Affective (feeling)
(3) Psychomotor (doing)

(1) Cognitive Domain (Knowing)

Cognitive domain deals with the recall of knowledge and the development of abilities and skills. Knowing includes activities, such as, remembering and recalling, knowledge, thinking, problem-solving and creating etc.

(2) Affective Domain (Feeling)

Affective means—which brings the change. Feeling includes the objectives which highlight the changes in aptitude, values, interests, development of appreciation and adequate adjustment.

(3) Psychomotor Domain (Doing)

This domain is concerned with how one does.

Dr. Bloom has given six categories of objectives in each domain mentioned above. These categories are as follows:

Cognitive Domain What (Head)	*Affective Domain Doing What* (Heart)	*Psychomotor Domain Doing How* (Hand)
Evaluation	Characterisation	Naturalisation
↓	↓	
Synthesis	Organisation	Articulation
↓	↓	
Analysis	Conceptualisation	Precision
↓	↓	
Application	Valuing	Manipulation
↓	↓	
Comprehension	Responding	Imitation
↓	↓	
Knowledge	Receiving	Impulsion

I. Cognitive Objectives

According to Bloom, Cognitive Domain of the taxonomy consists of six broad categories:

(1) *Knowledge*: It is concerned with the recognition and recalling of ideas, information, facts, objects and activities. It can be further divided into following parts:

(a) Knowledge of content: In a lesson of English, all ideas, narrations, events, descriptions, etc. are contents.

(b) Knowledge of ways and means of dealing with contents: It depends upon convention, sequence, classification, criteria and methodology.
- Contents and language are conventional because language is the product of society.
- Sequence is related to the order in which knowledge is imparted.
- Classification stands for selection and gradation of material.
- Methodology means devices and techniques to be used.

(c) Knowledge of universal and abstraction:
- Knowledge of principles and generalisation.
- Knowledge of theories and structures.

2. *Comprehension* (ability to grasp the meaning and material): It means the basic understanding of the facts, ideas, methods, procedures, principles or theories, etc.

3. *Application* (ability to use learned material in new and concrete situation): In this objective, the learner is required to acquire the ability to make use of the abstract and generalised ideas and principles in the particular and concrete situations. Application of objective has three levels:

(a) Generalisation of facts, laws, principles and theories.
(b) Diagnosis of pupils' weaknesses.
(c) Application of contents or terms and laws by the pupils.

4. *Analysis* (ability to breakdown material into its component parts for understanding different parts of words and sentences): It refers to an understanding of a higher level. It includes division of contents into its elements and these are mutually related. It has three levels:

(a) Analysis of elements.
(b) Analysis of relationship.
(c) Analysis of organised principles.

5. *Synthesis* (ability to put parts together to form the whole): The elements analysed in this step are assembled to give a complete picture and a new format is prepared. It has three subdivisions:

(a) Production of a unique communication.
(b) Production of a plan or a proposed set of operation.
(c) Derivations of a set of abstract relations.

6. *Evaluation* (ability to judge the value of the material for a given purpose): It aims to develop the ability to make proper value judgement

about what has been acquired by him in the knowledge, understanding, application, analysis and synthesis. It has two sub-divisions:

(a) Judgement in terms of internal evidence.
(b) Judgement in terms of external evidence.

II. Affective Objectives

Bloom, Krathwohl and Masia (1964) has divided the affective domain into five parts:

(a) *Receiving or attending*: It increases sensitivity towards human values and attitudes. It is essential that the learner should receive the desired events, objects or ideas. It includes:
  - Awareness
  - Willingness to receive
  - Control the attention

(b) *Responding* (active participation and reaction on the part of students): Once learner receives a particular idea or events, he must be made to respond to it as actively as possible. It has three levels:
  - Obedience for response
  - Preference for a value
  - Commitment of value

(c) *Organisation* (construction system of values): Here learners are supposed to internalise values and give some order to each value. It has three levels:
  - Organisation of values into a system
  - Determination of interrelation among them
  - Establishment of dominant value

(d) *Characterisation* (highest level): Here the learners are able to imbibe all the essential affective behaviour, i.e., attitudes, interests, values, value patterns and permanent set value structure. It has two levels:
  - Generalised set
  - Characterisation

(e) *Valuing*
Here learners are supposed to internalise values and give some order to each value. It has three levels:
  - Acceptance of Value
  - Preference of Value
  - Commitment of Value

III. Psychomotor Objectives

(i) Simpson Model

It is concerned with the training of the students' physical activities and the development of skills. The classification of psychomotor objectives was first produced by Simpson (1966), and later modified by Harrow (1972).

(a) *Perception*: Perception is primarily concerned with the activities related to senses. In simple words, assigning some objects or an event after looking at them is known as perception. It has the following levels:
- Descriptive level
- Prescriptive level

(b) *Set*: It seeks the cooperation of all the three aspects – mental, physical and emotional. The adjustment of all these sets gives birth to specific type of a set. It has three levels:
- Mental level
- Physical level
- Emotional level

(c) *Guided Response*: The abilities related to the complex skills are concerned with three guided responses. Under this activity the pupil is guided from outside and he shows his behaviour or responds under that guidance.

(d) *Mechanism*: The collection of possible responses is known as a mechanism but it includes correct responses.

(e) *Complex over response*: It is the highest level of psychomotor domain. At this stage the student acquires so much efficiency and skill that can accomplish most complex task with minimum energy and time. It includes:
- Perception (e.g., legible writing)
- Set (e.g., correct drawing)
- Guided response (e.g., type correctly with speed)
- Mechanism (e.g., to handle a machine properly)
- Complete over response (e.g., to construct a new thing or find out defects)

(ii) R.H. Dave's Model

It is concerned with the training of the students' physical activities and the development of skills. The classification of psychomotor objectives was first produced by Simpson (1966), then modified by Harrow. Dr. R.H. Dave (NCERT) 1971, proposed a taxonomy of educational objectives in this domain which can be summarised as below:

1. *Impulsion* – accounts for the lowest level of psychomotor behaviour. It starts as an inner push or impulse. It is represented by covert inner rehearsal of the muscular system.

2. *Imitation* – child copies action of others. Objectives of this category include assessing the action of the child in performance as learnt through imitation.

3. *Manipulation* – is the next higher level of psychomotor behaviour. It involves following directions selecting certain actions in preference to other and acting accordingly. It means the beginning of the fixation of operation and the end of initial fumbling in the manipulative actions.

4. *Precision* – is reached when reproduction of operation is carried

out with speed and refinement giving the learner the ability to control (increase, decrease or modify) his action in response to requirements.

5. *Articulation* – can be said to have been attained when the learner is able to handle a number of actions in unison, keeping in view their sequence and rhythm. It involves coordination in action i.e. right sequence in right proportion of time or at the right moment.

6. *Naturalisation* – when an action is learnt, in initial stages, mental energies and functions are involved. Gradually, it became a habit and action comes automatically. It is the highest level of proficiency in the development of skill to perform.

1. Cognitive (Knowledge)
2. Affective (Feeling)
3. Psychomotor (Doing)

(iii) Ragsdale's Model

He mentioned only three categories:

(a) Object motor activities;
Manipulation or acting with object.
(b) Language motor activities;
Movement of speech, sight handwriting.
(c) Feeling about activities;
Movements communicating feelings and attitudes.

(iv) Guilford Taxonomy (1958)

He mentioned seven categories:

(a) Power
(b) Pressure
(c) Speed
(d) Static precision
(e) Dynamic precision
(f) Coordination
(g) Flexibility

(v) Harroul's Taxonomy

Six categories:

(a) Reflex movements
(b) Basic fundamental movements
(c) Perceptual abilities
(d) Physical abilities
(e) Skilled movements
(f) Non-discursive communications

Interrelationship between Different Domains

The tripartite division of instructional objectives into domains is not watertight or an exclusive one. Firstly, the achievement in one domain is to a quite appreciable degree, dependent on the other domains of learner's behaviour. For instance, understanding (comprehension) may be a prerequisite for attaching proper value to an object or proper cognition necessary for arousing proper interest. Similarly, interest and attitudes affect the quality of performance in both cognitive and psychomotor domains. Comprehension is a natural component of the precision level in the psychomotor domain and similarly, interests can be traced an affective components of almost all the cognitive proficiencies. Lower levels of each domain draw relatively closer to each other e.g., knowing, receiving and imitating are very much interdependent among themselves. In the higher categories too, there is discernible parallelism. A particular category of one domain, may correspond to one or more categories of the other.

While planning the instruction for realising an objective, it may be considered as to how best the corresponding objectives of other domains can be exploited. Every learning experience does not result in the same quantum of growth, in all the three domains, thus when a learning experience is planned and provided, it emits currents of growth in different domains. It may also be mentioned that due to individual differences, the same learning experiences may result in different levels of growth in the three domains among different individuals.

Methods of Writing Objectives in Behavioural Terms

The commonly acclaimed and popular approaches of writing objectives in behavioural terms are following:

Instructional Objectives and Recent Changes

In 1963 and 1967, an examination reform was initiated, developed and sustained among professionals. Everywhere around the country, the committed evaluation experts were orienting teachers and other concerns to the concept and practices of evaluation. There were also American subject-cum-education experts who were suggesting the introduction of new lesson-plans having objectives in terms of Expected Behavioural Outcomes (EBOs), Learning Experiences (LE) and Evaluation in terms of Real Learning Outcomes (RLOs). The subject and pedagogy experts of NCERT skilfully observed both these exposition concepts viz. NCERT objective-based evaluation and the American objective-based instruction, and, developed the initial curriculum scheme. The vertical American presentation got changed into the horizontal lesson-plans as given below:

Understanding Education

Expected Behavioural Outcomes (EBOs)	Content	Learning Experience (LE)	Evaluation Real Learning Outcomes (RLOs)

Understanding Education

A lightly sophisticated approach to instruction and evaluation was realised. If education is being imparted for the total development of the child, why then should learning not be defined in terms of pupils' behaviour and why the methods, modes, teaching aids, evaluation items, not be selected which relate to the pupils' behaviour.

Bloom with his associates, on the invitation of the Government of India, visited India and conducted seminars/workshops, made commendable efforts to reform the structure of examination also.

The NCERT version of the Bloom system led to the horizontal approach to lesson-planning by the Regional College of Education, Mysore (RCEM). It was argued that to evaluate what is not developed is unjustified. A shift from produce to process was tried and an integrated lesson-plan was developed. In this lesson plan, Expected Behavioural Outcomes (EBOs) are to be realised through teaching Learning Experiences (LE) by a given content of the syllabus. This content is further to be evaluated simultaneously. This is termed as Real Learning Outcomes (RLOs). The team experts finally evolved the following 14 Expected Behavioural Outcomes (EBOs). They also arranged them for the first time in a specific hierarchical order, on an ad-hoc basis.

Knowledge	—	1. Recognition
		2. Recall
Understanding	—	3. Seeing relationships
		4. Citing
		5. Discrimination
		6. Classification
		7 Interpretation
		8. Verification
		9. Generalisation
Application	—	10. Reasoning
		11. Formulating hypothesis
		12. Establishing hypothesis
		13. Inference
		14. Prediction

Knowledge, understanding and application are broad instructional objectives.

Relevance of Taxonomy of Objective

Teaching is purposeful. Understanding and assimilating on the part of learners is must. A good teacher must facilitate it. A teacher always want to know how much learning is acquired by the learners. For this 'what and how much' purpose he/she ascertains some assessment devices. You can say objectives provide a direction towards which a teacher, in his/her instruction has to move along with learners. Methods of instructions can be planned by the teacher according to the objectives. The learning objectives help in laying down criteria for assessing the extent of learning that has taken place. On the basis of the objectives, learner's learning can be evaluated. This categorisation may help in identifying and grading teaching learning situation which can be an important source of selecting proper situations. Preparation and analysis of text-books based on well-defined objectives may prove a big improvement. Selection of techniques and tools of assessment will be easy. The classification through its well-defined criteria will provide a bridge for further communication among teachers, between teachers and evaluators, curriculum and research workers, psychologists and other behavioural scientists. The taxonomy has also opened new avenues for research in education.

Principles for the Statement of Instructional Objectives

1. An objective should be conceived and stated in terms of pupil's expected behavioural outcomes.
2. Objectives should be stated non-compositely so as to avoid confusion, repetition and contradiction.
3. Objectives should be framed keeping in view social acceptability.
4. Realistic objectives should be framed.
5. Avoid overlapping in framing objectives.
6. They should be developmental in nature.

Methods of Writing Objectives in Behavioural Terms

The commonly acclaimed and popular approaches of writing objectives in behavioural terms are following:

1. Robert Mager's Approach
2. Robert Miller's Approach
3. RCEM Approach
4. NCERT Approach

1. Robert Mager's Approach

Robert Mager is of the view that the objectives should be written like this:

(a) To identify the terminal behaviour and name it.
(b) Important conditions, under which the behaviour will be expected to occur, be described.
(c) Finalisation of the criteria with which the learner's behaviour will be compared.

Mager intends to seek the help of associated action verbs for the description of different objectives in a well-defined manner. Here below is the given list of action verbs.

Cognitive Objectives		*Associated Action Verb*
1.	Knowledge	Define, list, label, name, recall, measure, reproduce, state, write, underline
2.	Comprehension	Explain, change, illustrate, identify, judge, name, summarise, etc.
3.	Application	Discover, conduct, change, demonstrate
4.	Analysis	Analyse, associate, compare
5.	Synthesis	Argue, conclude, derive, discuss etc.
6.	Evaluation	Judge, criticise, choose, determine, appreciate, praise, recommend etc.

2. Robert Miller's Approach

Robert Miller has recommended an approach for writing psychomotor objectives in behavioural term. He has developed his approach on the basis of skill analysis, and recommended a list of associated action verbs for the psychomotor objectives. List is given below:

Psychomotor Objectives	*Associated Action Verb*
1. Reflex movements	Loosen, stop, lengthen, stretch, elasticity, relax etc.
2. Before fundamental movements	Catch, jump, hold, walk, run, etc.
3. Physical abilities	Begin, increase, decrease, start etc.
4. Perceptual abilities	Seeing, smelling, hearing, writing etc.
5. Skilled movements	Dancing, rafting, swimming, driving, knitting, playing
6. Non-discursive communication	Sit, smile, etc.

3. RCEM Approach

Mager's and Miller's approaches have remained unsuccessful in the task of writing all instructional objectives belonging to all three domains of behaviour. Mager's approach serves the purpose of cognitive and affective objectives. Miller's scheme is meant for psychomotor objectives. RCEM approach is modified form of the Bloom's taxonomy. Bloom has given six categories of objectives. But RCEM has given four categories, namely, knowledge, understanding, application and creativity.

Taxonomy of Educational Objectives in RCEM Approach

RCEM Taxonomy of Objectives	*Mental Processes of Abilities*
1. Knowledge	— Recall — Recognise
2. Understanding	— Seeing relationship — Cite examples — Discrimination — Classification — Interpret — Verify — Generalise
3. Application	— Reason out — Formulate hypothesis — Establish hypothesis — Infer — Predict
4 Creativity	— Analyse — Synthesise — Evaluate

Advantages of RCEM Approach

(1) This approach is highly applicable for cognitive, affective and psychomotor objectives.

(2) Easy and useful for Indian schools.
(3) This method explains human learning in terms of mental processes and abilities. Thus, there is shifting of emphasis from the product to the process.
(4) If the objectives are written in a correct manner, it is easy to make efforts in the right direction.
(5) It leaves no doubt in the preparation of criterion test items.

Limitations of RCEM Approach

(1) All the behavioural objectives can be written with the help of 17 mental processes or abilities only. Mental abilities are not only 17 but Guilford has mentioned 120 mental abilities.
(2) It is difficult to write objectives of subjects which lay emphasis on skills, attitudes, interest and appreciation.
(3) It is rather difficult to compare elements of contents with the mental processes.
(4) The number of mental abilities is to lessen the objectives like knowledge and creativity.
(5) In 'creative' objective there are three mental abilities whereas Torrence has given a list of five types of activities.

4. NCERT Approach

NCERT has condensed Bloom's approach into three categories of objectives, i.e., knowledge, understanding and application.

Objectives	*Abilities (The Child)*
1. Knowledge	- Recalls - Recognises
2. Understanding	- Translates - Cites examples - Identifies relationship - Detects errors - Compares - Classifies - Explains
3. Application	- Analysis - Hypothesis - Suggests methods and materials to test the hypothesis - Establishes relationships - Reasons - Generalises or draws conclusions - Predicts - Judges adequacy - Consistency and relevance

Writing Behavioural Objectives for Teaching English

Prose, Poetry and Composition

Prose

"Prose is words in their best form and poetry is the best words in their best form".

In case of teaching Prose, instructional objective in behavioural terms can be briefly described as follows:

I. Knowledge

(i) Students get knowledge of new phrases and words.
(ii) They can recognise and also recall those words.

II. Understanding

(i) The learners are able to understand the prose lesson.
(ii) They are able to use those language items.

III. Skills

The students are able to develop the different linguistic skills such as listening, speaking, reading and writing.

IV. Application

(i) The learners are able to make use of a few new words in their day-to-day life situations.
(ii) They are able to read the newspaper and other such reading material in a better way.

At the end of the lesson, the teacher is to see that all these instructional objectives have been achieved. Moreover, the learners have visible changes in their behaviour. Thus, the behavioural changes show that the behavioural objectives have been achieved through the process of teaching and learning English.

Poetry

Poetry is an important mode of expression in language. The main objective of teaching poetry is to develop the power of appreciation of beauty. The important objectives of teaching poetry are:

(i) To enable the students to appreciate the beauty, rhyme and style of the poem.
(ii) To enable them to enjoy music and rhythm of the poem.
(iii) To develop their imagination power.

Professor Billows opines, "To leave poetry out of language course is to renounce an extremely effective method absorbing useful language. It is also to abandon opportunities to humanise what otherwise may be a very dry and chilly traffic in words and information...."

Instructional objectives in behavioural terms can be as under:

Knowledge

(i) The students are able to recognise the ideas contained in the poem.
(ii) They are able to recall the thoughts given in the poem.

Understanding

The students get the understanding of the theme and contents of the poem.

Skills

The students are able to develop the different linguistic skills, i.e., listening, speaking, reading and writing.

Application

The students are able to apply the art of reciting a poem in their different life situations. They can entertain themselves and others through recitation.

Composition

The teaching of composition is a very significant aspect of teaching English.

As Professor Frisby remarks, "The facility for expression must grow out of the earliest mechanical activity of sentence-making and the use of words". The objectives of teaching composition are:

(i) To give the practice of four skills, i.e., listening, speaking, reading and writing to the students.
(ii) To develop their thinking process.
(iii) To develop their expression power.
(iv) To help them in organising the ideas in logical sequence.
(v) To develop their imagination power.

Instructional Objectives in behaviour terms can be briefly described as follows:

Knowledge

(i) The students get knowledge about the story/paragraph.
(ii) They are able to recall and recognise.

Understanding

(i) The students are able to understand how the need motivates someone to say something.
(ii) They are able to construct sentences related to the topic.

Skills

(i) The students get listening practice.
(ii) Pronunciation is improved.
(iii) Writing power is improved.

Application

(i) The students are able to apply moral of the story in their day-to-day life situations.

Thus, the objectives can be written in behavioural terms. Evaluation should also be done to ascertain whether the objectives have actually been reached or not.

☛Points to Remember

1. Behavioural objectives are complimentary to instructional objectives and help in redesigning the educational structure.
2. Writing of instructional objectives in behavioural terms provide direction to the teacher.
3. Taxonomy of Bloom presents following system of classification of objectives:

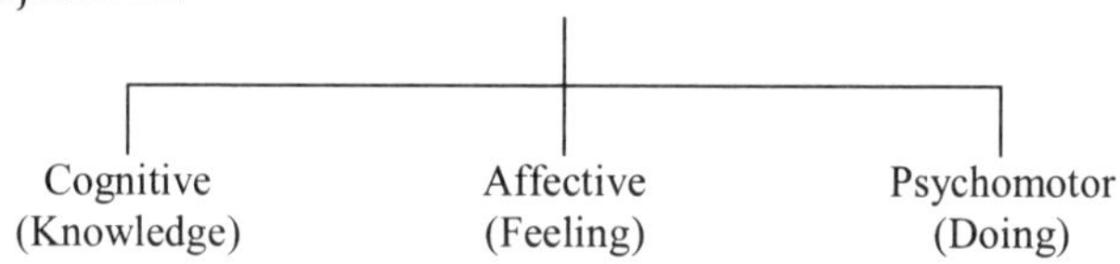

4. Common and popular approaches of writing objectives in behavioural terms are following:

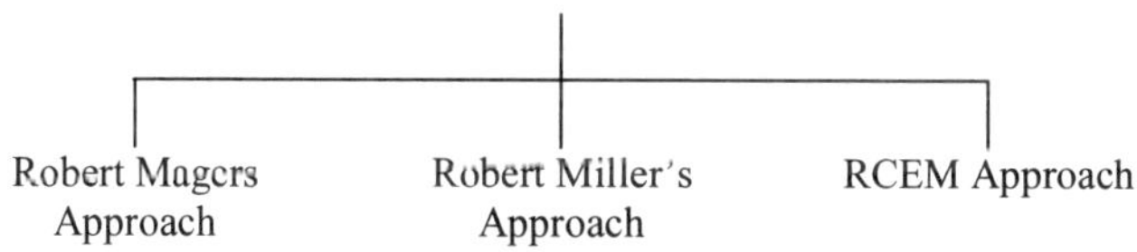

5. Behavioural objectives for teaching prose, poetry and composition, differ and should be written carefully. Evaluation is also must to see whether objectives have actually been reached or not.

7

Philosophical, Social and Psychological Bases of Language Learning

Learning a language is a natural and inevitable process which starts from childhood. In learning a first language, the environment and experiences which one encounters help a lot. The experiences acquired by an individual enriches the understanding of language.

Habit Pattern of first language creates obstacles' in learning a new language. One has to approach differently in learning a second language while grouping the things and relationship. The experiences and environment being the same, one has to deal with "What, why and how" of second language. Environment being the same, one makes comparison between the two languages, consciously or unconsciously. As second language often creates problem for learners.

The various factors which influence the nature of second language learning are discussed here under:

(a) Psychological Basis of Language Learning

- Age
- Motives
- Native skill
- Intelligence
- Memory span
- Readiness to learn
- Emotion

(i) *Age:* Penfield has given examples that the children have more capability of learning a language in comparison to adults. Further he says that adults focus more on content of the language while children on the form of language.

Researches also support that early start of the language has many merits:

- easy imitation;
- previous experiences interfere less;
- lack of hesitation;
- flexibility of speech;
- ease in training; and
- lack of finance

(ii) *Motives and Drives*: In learning a first language, the motives and drives are natural but in second language learning one has to make efforts as the good results depend on one's efforts. The learner has to set his/her mind in acquiring knowledge because the interest in L2 is scholarly rather than social. The learner has to set his/her mind to acquire new language skills. The levels of accomplishments expected, the leaner's urge to learn, the teaching techniques adopted, and the very purpose of learning they are all vitally connected with the second language.

The other factors like teaching methods, objectives of learning and one's will to learn also significantly contribute in learning a second language.

(iii) *Native Skill*: Learners capacity, willpower and efforts differ. We know that skill in learning a language is inherent. Regarding the linguistic skills, individuals show difference of command in grammar, vocabulary and pronunciations, while some others have a good grasp of grammar, others do not. It is also difficult to account for variety of talents found in individuals in learning different aspects of the language. Some are good speakers, others may be good in creative writing.

(iv) *Intelligence*: One has to apply his/her intelligence in learning a language. Imitating a language is easy and one does not need to apply much intelligence in it. But speaking skill is highly influenced by one's intelligence. For example, comprehension of language is a challenging task and requires intelligence. To grasp the meaning of contents a reader has to make use of reasoning and reflective thinking and below average children may not have that much intelligence.

(v) *Auditory Memory Span*: Listening to pure sounds and discrimination between correct and incorrect sounds is essential. Listening to good models form the basis of good speech. Good listening has a firm grip on the mind, a child proceeds to learn speaking the language well.

(vi) *Readiness to Learn*: If the language habits are formed at an early level, then it is commendable. Environmental opportunities also facilitate the learning. If a learner is told the usefulness of the material, it may also facilitate the learning. The influence of speaking the language will also provide readiness to a great extent. Teacher must understand that to learn a language, child must be ready.

(vii) *Emotions*: It is clear that some emotions are associated with a particular language for which the learner starts developing a special liking. Moreover, the past associations and experiences make the learner attracted towards learning the language.

The psychology of teachers as well as learners plays a significant role in learning a language. Knowledge of the psychological factors like personality, attitude and interest help in selecting the effective language teacher. Moreover, it points out how to form favourable attitudes towards other cultural group.

(b) Linguistic Basis of Language Learning

Osgood has explained how meaning is developed directly through classical learning principles or how meanings are "assigned" by "teachers" in our social environment. Osgood's concept of meaning has influenced the researchers and is of great significance in learning a language. It can be of great help to the language teachers as it offers a new style of instructions and methods of teaching. The comparison of teaching methods done in this way can be effective for language teachers.

The work of Staats and Staats indicates how favourable (or inadvertently unfavourable) emotional components of meaning can be assigned to foreign language vocabularies as they are being learned. The work of Lambert and Jakobovits show how meaning can be dissipated or satiated when continuous repetitions of words take place, as in vocabulary drill.

The other way suggested by psychologist is the "associative method" that is possibly done by verbal association. Verbal linkages of this sort are learned according to principles of law of association, in particular the laws of contiguity, similarity and frequency. This is a chain thinking; one idea gives rise to another.

If we talk about development of human skills, learning of a foreign language is most difficult. The viewpoints given by Carroll is significant. Where he talks about language aptitude, he makes it clear that component skills are important and must be taught by teachers and learnt by students.

While speaking about language aptitude Carroll says that phonetic coding is the first important task in learning a language. It is not only to make an echoic response to phonetic material, but the ability to 'code' or represent it somehow is imagery so that it can be recognized or reproduced. This ability can be tested by phonetic script tests, when the individual has to learn how a series of speech sounds are represented by alphabetic characters. The second important variable is language aptitude in dealing with grammar, its form and arrangement in natural utterances. The third variable is that of rote memorization in learning a foreign language and that too in a short time span. The fourth variable is the ability to infer linguistic forms, rules and patterns from new linguistic content with minimum supervision and guidance. Method of presenting the material is also important. Moreover as the situation changes one's skills are also influenced.

The learning of a foreign language is one of the most difficult of human skills to develop. Carroll turns his attention to the selection of those with great potential for languages, and in doing so, his study of the components of language aptitude reveal for us the component skills that must be taught by teachers and learned by students.

There arises a question – What are the components of language aptitude? Caroll's answer to this question is—one of the most important variables in learning a foreign language is phonetic coding, the ability to 'code' auditory phonetic material in such a way that this material can be recognized, identified and remembered over longer than a few seconds. Thus the ability is not the ability to make an echoic response to phonetic material, but the ability somehow to 'code' or represent it in imagery so that it can be recognized or reproduced after an intervening period filled with other activities. This ability, it would seem, is measured chiefly by the phonetic script test, in which the individual has to learn how a series of speech sounds are represented by alphabetic characters.

(i) A second important variable in language aptitude is the ability to handle 'grammar' i.e. the forms of language and their arrangement is natural utterances.

(ii) A third variable is that of rote memorization ability for foreign language materials. The ability has to do with the capacity to learn a large number of these associations in a relatively short time.

(iii) A fourth variable is the ability to infer linguistic forms, rules and pattern from new linguistic content itself with a minimum of supervision or guidance.

Carroll says that variables other than 'aptitude' like: 'presentation' of material, adequate opportunity to learn must be included which vary from situation to situation.

Carroll, therefore, views language aptitude as a relatively stable personal characteristic, one which is made up of various component skills or 'abilities'. It will be instructive to consider what is meant by 'abilities' since they play such a fundamental role in more complex aptitudes.

If learning is continued, little change in behaviour occurs. Speed of individuals differ to reach this point of behavioural stability. These individual differences, Ferguson argues can be attributed to some complex by product of biologically transmitted capacity, and, the type and amount of "learning which occurs at particular stages of life".

(c) Social Basis of Language Learning

It is essential that the language teacher has a command over the language. A descriptive acquaintance with the language of the target group is also essential.

Human beings live in a society. Relationship between them is important. Various aspects contribute in this relationship. With the help of language, Human beings interact in the society. Since one does not live in vacuum.

Linguists say that language is a means of communicating thoughts. These days it seems partially true, and sometimes misleading and illuminating. An apt definition of language these days is, "Language is a means of social control".

Secondly, thoughts are communicated through language. For example, when an instruction is given to students by the teacher, thoughts have first to be interpreted and then acted upon. The response is as automatic as the appearance of light when a switch is pressed. This is a simple example of a normally more complicated process, the use of language to co-ordinate activities. Any cooperative effort carried out by a number of people skilled in that operation depends entirely on its unity and success on language, though that language may not be communicating thought.

Communication between the groups is important. Suppose you are sitting in a group, one must talk on any issue, even if there is nothing to say.

This sociable use of language has been given the name phatic communication.

When there is an exchange of words in the group, a sort of union or relationship is created. The members in the group come close to one another. This kind of conversation is essential to get along with one another.

In such Phatic communication, words matters little but facial expression and intonation are probably more important.

Some formal Questions, when meeting a person:

How are you?

Where are you from?

How much money do you earn?

What is your name?

What do you know?

Expected Replies are purely formal.

Personality, manner of walking and the way you carry your clothes. How you dress up is also important, but it is your speaking skill which matters. Because the words you utter reveal your personality and your inner thoughts and ideas.

However, speech is often an astonishingly sure guide to one's personality which requires very remarkable delicacy of perception, of which most people seem to be capable.

Thirdly, your social habits are also important. Because within a language community social groups or classes are influenced by forms of speech.

Pronunciation influences speech behaviour in social groups. There is one misconception that French Word 'Tu' is used for intimacy or inferior person but it is not a sign of personal familiarity rather it is regularly used between social groups, political parties and so on.

The question arises: whether to use a slang or not? Slangs are fascinating to foreigners, and their acquisition seems to promise admission to the real intimacy of communication. Sometimes the use of a slang shows poor behaviour.

Human beings establish their relationship through language.

Language reflects the world and our thinking about it. Language is not a passive reflection rather an active practical approach to the world.

Language enables man to live in a society, but the kind of society in which he lives will profoundly affect his language. Semantic structure and social structure are intimately connected. Semantic structure does not merely reflect the psychological environment resulting from social structure. Due to the languages of the Indo-European and Semantic families, dependence of thought on languages has not been realized.

Language is not necessarily a written Language. A literary language is the language of Literature initially. It usually becomes the accepted norm for written communication for any purpose and exercises some degree of influence over the spoken language. For all uses of the language, it becomes a standard, and everyone has to adhere to it.

One is not supposed to paraphrase or translate into another language. Rhythm is an important phonetic feature. Sometimes phrases are misunderstood if carried in another language.

Language is the medium of literature, and its use in artistic creation is nearly always associated with "literary language", more or less different from the language is not necessarily a written language, neither is it a prerogative of civilized people. A literary language, however, is usually a written language, and usually derived from some particular dialect, to which chance have given prestige, of the spoken language of the people. A literary language, though primarily the language of literature usually becomes the accepted norm for written communication for any purpose, and exercises some degree of influence over the spoken language. Its standard of correctness becomes the standard for all uses of the spoken language. For all uses of language, it becomes a standard and everyone has to adhere to it

(d) Philosophical Bases of Language

Inter-lingual effect of languages is important to understand. When the learners get exposure to the target language, the order in which learners acquire features of their new language stays remarkably constant, even for learners with different native languages and regardless of whether they had the language instruction. Being one of the most important disciplines, linguistics deals with the investigation of language, and applied linguistics. In order to understand changing paradigm within the field of applied linguistic research, it is essential to keep in mind the philosophical background.

The birth of Second Language Acquisition (SLA) as an interdisciplinary fields took place in 1970s, with the conversant developments in linguistics, psychology and education. Born out of the studies on child language acquisition and fuelled by the need to teach English as a Second Language (ESL) to a growing number of SSL learners around the world, SLA research mainly focussed on the study of teaching and learning of second and foreign languages in educational settings.

In its early stages, SLA research focussed on contrastive analysis of languages on account of the fact that at that time field linguistics was mainly concerned with description classification and cataloguing at native Indian language and by the time they were asked to apply their findings on the teaching of some of these Indian languages because these languages were facing extinction and had to be taught. As a result, applied linguistics of that time found it the best to compare and contrast the data that they have obtained during the description and classification of their languages. In a similar vein, translation was also influenced by the works of these early linguists such as Nida. In 1960, he pointed out that translators go through stages at analysis, transfer and reconstruction. In short, the prevailing paradigms at those times was to describe language on the basis of their common structural patterns and learning of languages was thought to benefit from such studies (Rajagopalan, 2004). Then Contrastive Analysis (L1 and L2) was being followed (Lado, 1957). This approach did not last long on account of the fact that learners were not ready to imitate L2 structures and Contrastive Analysis was not easy.

Appearance of Chomsky on the stage downgraded the validity of Contrastive Analysis. Chomsky's theories were solely concerned with L1 acquisition. Sometime later, though, it was understood that universal Grammar did not have much to offer to language teaching. It led the scholars to discuss SLA.

The growing understanding in the 1980s, was that having theoretical linguistics' accounts do not ensure success in language learning in actual practice. Canale (1983) claimed that the term communicative competence was a buzzword stating that the distinction between communicative competence and actual communication remains poorly understood, and, somewhat, surprisingly, or marginal interest in second language acquisition.

The emerging view, as a result of the competence debate was that what the field needed was not to add to the existing theories to form new ones in order to shed light of language teaching and learning, but to come up with ground breaking ways of accounting for L2 learning that are independent of or unaffected by existing theories (Rajagopalan, 2004).

In regard to L1 or FL acquisition, the following questions are some of the fundamental Questions applied linguistic research attempts to answer:

- In case of linguistic variation and regional differences what are the rules which should be followed?
- To what extent the non-native speakers should imitate the native speakers?
- What stylistic differences do learners bring with them to the acquisition of another language?
- How does language in discourse both reflect and create social structures and political ideologies?
- What is the relation of social and cultural aspect in learning a

language?
- To what extent does institutional discourse defends what is taught and learned in schools, and, language classrooms in particular?

These questions seem to be highly relevant to the teaching and learning of language.

It comes to the forefront that there are various factors which are involved in learning a language like psychology of learners, learning theories and policy issues etc. Therefore, as a general conclusion, it is possible to say that AL is one of the disciplines which provides data for language teachers for some important issues. Now we seem to be at a juncture to decide whether to place ELT under auspices of applied linguistics or SLA research. This does not, however, come to mean that opting for one of them discards the other totally. Due to the interdisciplinary nature of L2 learning, language teaching practitioners or theoreticians are invariably bound to borrow from a wide range of disciplines.

Philosophy of language is concerned with four central problems—

1. The meaning
2. Language use
3. Language cognition
4. Relationship between language and reality

1. ***Meaning***: First and foremost philosophers of language prioritize their enquiry to explain what it means to 'mean' something. Such topics include the nature of synonymy, the origins of meaning, and how any meaning can ever really be known. Another project under this heading of special interest to analytic philosophers of language is the investigation into the manner in which sentences are composed into a meaningful whole out of their meaningful parts; and how the meanings of such complexes are derived from the meaning of parts.

2. ***Language Use***: Secondly, they seek to understand better what speakers and listeners do with language in communication, and how it is used socially. Specific interest may include the topics of language learning, language creation and speech acts.

3. ***Language Cognition***: Thirdly, they would like to know how language relates to the minds of both the speaker and the interpreter for successful translation of words into other words.

4. ***Relationship between Language and Reality***: Finally, philosophers of language investigate how language and meaning relate to truth and the world. They tend to be less concerned with which sentences are real, and more with what kinds of meanings can be true or false, or whether or not sentences can express propositions about things that do not exist.

8

Teaching of Prose

The pupils should be occupied with the text repeatedly in such a way that they do not lose sight of the meaning. —Jesperson
Prose is words in their best order. —Coleridge

Reading is a complex phenomenon that embraces a wide variety of mental processes, skills and strategies. Besides one's reading ability is also influenced by several factors, such as, reader's purpose, his/her interest in the reading material, and the difficulty level of material being read. Special kinds of instructional help is needed for developing reading comprehension strategies in our children.

The word reading implies reading with comprehension. When I say I have read this letter, it means that I know its contents. It is not only the words in the letter that I have read but I have also got the sense that these words are meant to convey. The pupils should be enabled to grasp the ideas the writer wants to communicate.

According to Jesperson, "The main point is for the pupils to be occupied with the text repeatedly in such a way that they do not lose sight of the meaning so that they may, thus become so familiar with it that at last they know it almost or entirely by heart, without having been directly required to commit it to memory".

Aims of Teaching Prose

Teaching prose means teaching reading with comprehension. Having taught the students how to read a language, the next logical step is to teach them reading with comprehension.

The main aims of teaching prose are—

1. To give listening practice to the students.
2. To enable the students to speak fluently and correctly.
3. To give practice of loud reading and silent reading.
4. To enable the students to write properly.
5. To help the learners to enhance their vocabulary.
6. To enable the students to understand English properly.
7. To develop the habit of reading for pleasure.
8. To give them practice of structures and sentence patterns.
9. To improve their pronunciation.

10. To develop a feeling of love among the students for English language.
11. To enable the students to read prose effectively and with a reasonable speed.

Specific Aims

These vary according to the subject-matter depending upon whether it is descriptive, a story, a biography, a play or an essay.

Descriptive

1. To acquaint pupils with the style of the writer.
2. To develop imaginative power of the students.
3. To develop among students a love for natural objects.

Story

1. To give knowledge of some facts through the story.
2. To teach some lesson through the story.
3. To train students' character.
4. To acquaint students with the style of story-writing.

Essay

1. To acquaint students with the style of essay-writing.
2. To make students curious.
3. To enable students to arrange ideas in a systematic way.

Biography

1. To get students acquainted with the lives and deeds of great men.
2. To have a feeling of respect for good character.
3. To inculcate among the students the desirable sentiments.

Play

1. To enhance their ability of self-expression.
2. To develop their conversational ability.
3. To make them able to play different roles.
4. To build their character.

What is Involved?

Reading comprehension involves the meaning of content, vocabulary, grammatical structures, concepts and relationship to ideas. These points are briefly discussed below:

1. *Vocabulary*: The new words occurring in a lesson are taught to the pupils at the practice stage of teaching structures. Reading reinforces the understanding of these words.
2. *Grammatical Structures*: The next step in reading comprehension is the understanding of grammatical structures.
   The difficulty is faced by pupils who do not have readers or text-books written in accordance with graded structures.

New structures should be presented in situations by showing a real object or picture drawing on the board, actions and gestures or creating verbal context.

3. *Concepts*: Third step in reading comprehension is the understanding of concepts. The subject matter should be according to the mental level of the students. Their social background should be kept in view.

Understanding a Paragraph

Students face difficulty in understanding the long and complicated sentences. Pupils should be helped to retain not the simple sentences in the mind but the ideas of a complete paragraph and they must be able to relate one idea to another.

Types of Reading Prose

1. Silent Reading
2. Loud Reading

1. Silent Reading

Silent reading means reading something without producing sounds, audible to others. In this type of reading, the learner of language reads everything quietly. He is not supposed to move his/her lips even.

This kind of reading is not meant for junior level but highly commended for senior level.

Handschin states, "Silent reading inculcates love for reading and is pleasurable and it gives the pupils a feeling of power and achievement".

2. Loud Reading

Loud reading means reading a book by producing sounds audible to others. This type of reading is useful for beginners. Possibility of committing errors is reduced. But it is not suitable for higher classes.

Pronunciation can be improved. But to quote Frisby is noticeable, "The danger of too much reading aloud as a method of teaching reading is that it may lead to the short circuiting of the meaning whereby the written word does not convey meaning but becomes merely a symbol for a collection of sounds, and is translated straight in sounds".

Moreover, reading aloud prevents the students from learning to understand the meaning of a sentence even when he may not know one word in the sentence. It prevents him from doing this because he is forced to struggle with the word in order to read the sentences aloud. On the other hand, silent reading encourages them to work for understanding rather than completing the passage.

Reading may be done (i) intensively, and (ii) extensively.

Sometimes it is also called reading for accuracy and reading for fluency respectively. The labels indicate a difference in classroom procedures as well as a difference in purpose.

(i) Intensive reading means a detailed study of the text-book. It involves the learners working through a relatively short passage under the guidance of the teacher and examining it closely and in detail. The aim is to arrive at a detailed and thorough understanding of the text. Material for intensive reading is chosen with a view to develop the students' power of judgment and discriminative reasoning of interpretation and appreciation. Student learn to scan for information, to read with careful attention and concentration, and to extract the major ideas and arguments. Attention is also paid to the logical development of ideas and style in writing.

(ii) Extensive reading means a non-detailed study of the book. It is different from intensive reading in the sense that it concentrates upon the subject-matter. The pupils should be led to understand, enjoy and appreciate from their reading, and in the process acquire wider vocabulary which will, in turn, improve their expression, both during and after their school life. According to Thompson and Wyatt, "The main purpose of extensive reading is the cultivation of taste for reading... and to make a form of visual instruction."

Students are encouraged to read widely on subjects which interest them personally and share what they have enjoyed with their fellow students.

Extensive reading should play an important part in the process of second language learning for several reasons. First, it is an activity that can be carried out by the students on their own, outside the classroom. It thus complements the learning that takes place in the classroom because it provides valuable reinforcement of language already presented in the classroom as well as gives students' useful practice in skills such as inferring meaning from the context when structures and vocabulary are not familiar. Besides class time is limited and the amount of reading needed to achieve fluency and efficiency is very high. So, extensive reading is necessary and material for extensive reading should be:

(a) easy, (b) short, (c) appealing and varied.

Using a Text

The most important thing about using a text for developing reading skills is to decide what you expect from the students. Do you want 'full' comprehension or do you want them just to have a general understanding? Do you want them to retrieve some specific information for a purpose or do you want to give further practice of a specific language item?

Need-based study is most efficient. The need is created naturally by circumstances. In the more artificial situation of the classroom, however, the teacher has to create specific needs for specific purposes.

How to Teach a Passage Intensively?

The teacher should proceed in the following manner:

1. *Introduction*: Suitable introduction is a must to arouse the curiosity of the students.
   A good introduction:
   (a) is usually short;
   (b) does not tell the students anything that they can find out for themselves by reading the text;
   (c) helps the students to relate the text to their own interests, experiences and aims; and
   (d) involves the students actively by means of questioning.
2. *Model reading by the teacher*: The teacher reads out the passage with the pupils keeping their books closed. He/she pays full attention to proper phrasing, pronunciation and intonation. The teacher reads at normal speed.
   The teacher reads out the passage again and this time students will keep their books open.
3. *Explanation*: At this stage new words, vocabulary, structures and other grammar position is explained. Students can be asked for drill repetition at junior level.
4. *Loud reading by the student individually*: This step is very important especially during the first three, four years. Pupils should be given practice in reading aloud. First, bright students should be asked to read aloud. Errors, if any, should be corrected on the spot. Then the other few students one by one can be asked to read aloud.
5. *Silent reading*: The words and phrases having been explained, the pupils now try to grasp their use in the context of the passage silently. They should be given sufficient time for understanding. Be careful that no lip movement should be there.
6. *Comprehension Questions*: For testing comprehension, some direct and simple questions from the text can be asked. Avoid answers which can be bodily lifted from the passage.

Extensive Reading

According to Otto Jesperson, "*The ultimate purpose of learning a foreign language is to have an access to the best thoughts and institutions of a foreign nation, its literature, culture—in short the spirit of the nation in the widest sense of the word*". By inculcating a habit and taste for 'extra reading' at the school level, one may help students to enrich and refine their minds so as to be able to use more worthily their native means of expression. The extra reading provides an extra coverage for linguistic and literary excellence.

Following are the aims of teaching extensive reading:

(a) *Intellectual aim*: It develops skills in scanning for the correct and target word groups.
(b) *Literary aim*: It encourages the readers to get into the spirit of the author, his mind, feelings and thoughts.

(c) *Linguistic aim*: It means extension of pupils' vocabulary.

How to Teach Extensive Reading?

(a) The teacher may give a very brief introduction about the lesson to be read.
(b) Difficult portion may be explained.
(c) Students are asked to comprehend the easy portion by silent reading.
(d) Then the comprehension questions are asked. Wrong responses are corrected.
(e) Full opportunity is given to them for participation.

The ultimate aim here is to develop pupil interest in independent reading, reading for pleasure and information.

☛Points to Remember

1. Teaching Prose means teaching reading with comprehension.
2. Reading comprehension involves the meaning of content, vocabulary grammatical structure, concepts and relationship to ideas.
3. Silent reading is suggested for senior students and loud reading for junior students.
4. Reading may be done intensively (means a detailed study of the book), and extensively (non-detailed which concentrates on the subject-matter)

9

Teaching of Poetry

"Poetry is made out of life, belongs to life and exists for life". — *Hudson*

Poetry increases the child's sensitiveness to beauty, especially beauty of language and thoughts, and, helps to develop imagination.

According to Ryburn, "Our aim should be to give pleasure and thus lay the foundation for an adequate appreciation of English poetry". Poetry aims at refining one's sensibility in contrast to understanding of the prose.

Some Thoughts on Poetry

(i) The basis for poetry is emotional and not intellectual although a lot of modern poetry appeals to the mind.
(ii) A poem involves the reader in a process of discovery, a familiar experience is placed in a new and unexpected light.
(iii) Reading a poem is an emotional and mental journey from what one already knows and feels to new ideas and feeling.
(iv) Poem makes the familiar strange whereas prose does its best to make the strange familiar.
(v) The reader of a poem has to hand himself/herself to the poem and let it take him/her to its destination.
(vi) Dissection, analysis and paraphrase can very often kill the spirit of a poem.
(vii) Poetry can help us to assimilate the typical rhythms of a language. It should, therefore, be read aloud to the class and then ask students to read aloud.

Should Poetry be a Classroom Teaching-Learning Subject?

Arguments in Favour

(i) Poetry has a great appeal for children. Exploit this appeal to the optimal level.
(ii) It educates our emotions and increases power of imagination.
(iii) Poetry imparts pleasure to the students in that spirit of poetic abundance "my heart leaps up when I behold".
(iv) It lays the foundation for appreciation of the language in all its refinement, nuances and expression.

(v) Poetry brings variety in the English course.
(vi) The rhythm of the poetry helps the learners acquire natural speech rhythms. So, finally, it does have a phonetic and phonological role to play. What is really needed is a band of dedicated teachers who themselves love poetry as well as teaching poetry.
(vii) Poetry is more memorable than prose because of its arrangement of rhyme and rhythm. It has been rightly defined as 'memorable speech'.
(viii) Poetry has the enabling function of raising the son of man to the position of the son of God.
(ix) It helps the learners in storing patterns of sentences through constant use.

Arguments Against

(i) Poetry does not serve any utilitarian purpose, i.e., it does not increase the students' mastery over the English language. It is because the language of poetry is very different from everyday speech. It is an unusual and special type of language.
(ii) Vocabulary of students is not enriched.
(iii) Metaphor and simile are beyond the understanding of the pupils.
(iv) Unfamiliar background to teach English poems is also a factor which goes against teaching poetry.
(v) Most of the teachers of English fail to appreciate and teach poetry.
(vi) Poetry follows a word order which is quite different from that of prose.

To conclude, arguments in favour of teaching poetry outweigh those against it. We are in full agreement with Billows when he says, "To leave poetry out of language course is to renounce an extremely effective and labour saving method of absorbing useful language". It is also to abandon opportunity to humanise and warn what otherwise may be a very dry and chilly traffic in words and information. It is to renounce the hope of delivering us from the pedestrian writing – if not platitudes of the textbook's writer. It is to neglect an important and powerful aid in establishing in the pupils' mind a favourable mental set. It is to stop short of what might be most rewarding in the pupils' experience of the language.

Difference between Prose and Poetry

The aims of teaching prose and poetry are different.

(i) According to Coleridge, prose is words in their best form and poetry is the best of the words in their best form.
(ii) Prose is a logical expression, and therefore, has an intellectual slant. Poetry appeals to the heart. It arouses your entire being.

(iii) Poetry is more powerful than prose.
(iv) Poetry is sounder than sight, whereas prose is more sight than sound.
The rhythm of the poetry outclasses the prose. Even from the utility point of view prose is more relevant. Nevertheless, poetry must be given its place of honour, though it can never supplant prose nor has it any such intentions.
(v) Poetry is for sheer delight, whereas prose is for information.
(vi) *Both differ in the aims of teaching*: Teaching of prose is primarily for development of linguistic skills; effective and appropriate communication develop interest for self-reading; use of English for the curriculum purpose etc. Prose is taught for enrichment and for correct use of grammar, phonetics and speech sounds whereas the aims of teaching poetry is to educate one's sensibility, sharpen and refine responses to the bounty of nature, for emotional enjoyment.
Prose and poetry are on different planes/domains of learning whereas prose belongs to the cognitive domain, poetry falls in the domain of feelings. Prose relates to intellect whereas poetry relates to emotions – the age-old dichotomy between understanding and sensibility. Hence, both are different to nature and have their own respective aims.
(vii) *Difference in teaching procedure*: While teaching prose one has to emphasise the vocabulary aspect as well as development of the linguistic skills, phonetics, grammar structures and usage. There are no such hassles in the teaching of poetry neither there are drills nor exercises. It is simply for the sake of reading, pleasure and enjoyment. As a matter of fact, even if one finds some problems with some of the word meanings or pronunciation of the words, briskly brush it aside and move on with the recitation of the poem. It should be recited with correct modulation, intonation, stress and pause, with enthusiasm and guests, with zeal and exuberance. Pupils should be encouraged to enjoy and appreciate beauty of the poem, emotions behind poetic outbursts.

How to Teach Poetry?

How to teach poetry? There can be no definite answer to this question. As Haddow says, "It is like making love, each must do in his own way".

Poetry cannot be taught. The teacher can only create conditions in which a poem may have its fullest effect for the pupils who read it. It is suggested that poetry reading should be used for enjoyment only and it should not be made a subject for examination. As far as possible the poem should be read as a whole but if the poem is too long, it must be divided in units in such a way, so that it may not lose its rhythm, music and emotional effect.

Steps in Poetry Lesson-Plan

(1) *Objectives*: Objectives of the poem are to be written in behavioural terms, the objective may vary from poem to poem depending upon the theme of the poem.

(2) *Teaching aids*: Selection of teaching aids should be appropriate, relevant and economical.

(3) *Previous knowledge assumed*: It is on the basis of previous knowledge that the lesson is introduced. It is also known as entering behaviour.

(4) *Introduction*: Gist of the poem can be given here, life sketch, and style of the poet can be given and some introductory questions can be put.

Presentation

(1) *Presenting thought content/gist of the poem*: To make the students familiar with the theme, teacher can present the main idea in few lines.

(2) *First model reading*: After the introduction and thought content, the teacher will make a first model reading with understanding and feeling. The pupils should not be allowed to open the book at this stage so that they can focus on listening and enjoying the poem.

The value of model reading cannot be overemphasised. "Poetry is an art of the ear not of the eye – in other words, poetry is sound not sight". Poetry is to be read for the charm of sound. The best way to teach a poem is to read it well. Good reading will never fail to render the thought crystal clear and make the poem vivid to the class.

(3) *Second model reading by the teacher*: It really matters how a poem is read. So, to make it more understandable, teacher should read the poem twice and this time the students can be asked to open the books.

(4) *Explanation of the poem*: The teacher should explain the poem, its difficult words, clear the references involved, figures of speech, thus making it understandable.

The teacher should guard against the tendency of explaining too much lest the poem lose its beauty.

(5) *Individual loud reading by the students*: The teacher can ask two or three students to read the poem loudly. He/she should help them to read with proper pronunciation, intonation, rise and fall of the tone. So that they can feel the beauty of the poem.

(6) (a) Comprehension Questions: Some simple questions can be asked just to know whether they have understood the meaning of the poem.

(b) Appreciation Questions: These questions can be asked to make clear the beauty, feeling and main idea of the poem.

(c) Choral Recitation: Students can be asked to recite the poem in a group (at junior stage).

(7) Home work/assignment.

☛Points to Remember

1. Poetry relates to emotions.
2. Poetry is to educate one's sensibility, sharpen and refine responses.
3. It should be recited with correct modulation, intonation, stress and pause.
4. Poetry cannot be taught, the teacher can create conditions which influence the readers to enjoy and understand it.
5. Poem should be read as a whole so that not to lose the emotional effect.
6. In case the poem is long, it can be divided into parts.

10

Teaching of Composition

"He who knows not how to limit himself knows not how to write."
—A French Proverb

The word 'composition' has been derived from the word 'compose' which means to put together. In simple words—Composition means the act of putting words together.

One of the aims of teaching English is to enable the students to express themselves correctly in the spoken and written forms. Writing is the most difficult of the linguistic skills as it aims at expressing thoughts through graphical form of language, i.e., students should be able to write correctly and legibly and should be able to describe events, to narrate incidents and to write reports, letters, etc. Habit of writing in simple and coherent manner is inculcated among students.

According to Frisby, "The facility for expression must grow out of the earliest mechanical activity of sentence making and the use of words." Composition is described by Chambers as "The act and art of composing an exercise in writing prose or verse".

Aims of Teaching Composition

Following are some of the aims of teaching composition:

1. It helps the students in listening, speaking, reading and writing.
2. It develops ability of better expression.
3. It enhances their vocabulary.
4. It develops the imagination power.
5. Communicative competence is also developed.

What is Required?

1. *Mastery of language*: The pupils should know the various vocabulary items and the structures that he has to use in writing a particular piece of composition, correct spellings and punctuation are also important to know. The pupils should also know paragraph construction, topical sentences and linking words, etc.
2. *Ideas*: Pupils need to have sufficient ideas for good expression.

Meeting people, visiting places and reading books can be helpful for gathering ideas.

3. *Organisation of ideas*: Organising ideas logically, coherently and sequentially, is also very challenging. Choosing the appropriate style and linking device is also very important.

Types of Composition

There are two types of composition:

1. Controlled/Guided Composition
2. Free Composition

1. Controlled/Guided Composition

In a controlled writing task, both the content and the expression are provided. A student is, therefore, neither at a loss for ideas or for the words, s/he needs to use. The chances of making too many errors are thus minimised and the students get to practice certain composition skills systematically and gradually. In this technique the students are provided with specific situations, ideas, structure and vocabulary, i.e., the Guided Composition is along some given lines, it is directed writing, it is close-ended because the students have to go in accordance with the teacher's direction. The control, however, is loose, because within the given ambit, the students have a choice of combination of word groups and composition of ideas.

2. Free Composition

As the name suggests, working freely and without restrictions. They are free to make use of any structure and vocabulary and ideas. They are on their own, though the teacher might help by giving suggestions. Students are expected to collect and digest a lot of information before putting it in a readable form. Being open-ended, the students are free to express their ideas in their own language. It will gradually help the pupils to acquire a style of writing. This is the ultimate aim of composition. But it should come at its own time, neither too early nor too late.

Dangers of Starting Free Composition at Early Stages

(a) The students are raw and have no idea about the use of words, word-groups, structures and ideas etc. If allowed free composition at early stage, their efforts will be full of mistakes which are likely to be permanent.
(b) The quantum of mistakes will discourage them.
(c) Heavy load of correction on teachers will affect their efficiency.
(d) Resorting to giving explanation, the teacher will further complicate the situation.
(e) The teacher may also be forced by the extent of remedial effort required.

(f) If started at early stage, the free composition will deprive the students of the practice of structures and vocabulary.

They will switch on to an easier path, damaging their own linguistic proficiency.

Stages for Teaching Composition

1. Pre-composition stage
2. Oral composition stage
3. Written composition stage
4. Correction work

Exercises in Controlled/Guided Composition

Composition is a difficult activity, especially when it is in a foreign language. A student, therefore, should be carefully guided by the process of graded exercises in composition. The following steps are suggested:

I. Skill Exercises

(a) *Dictation*: It is a useful exercise in guided composition. Dictation reinforces learnt words and structures improve spellings and structure, help students gain speed in writing. It also helps in note-taking. It also ensures good hand-writing. Moreover, it cultivates the habit of listening.

(b) *Transcription*: Transcription is the simplest kind of writing exercise and is very useful for improving hand-writing and for familiarising the pupils with common usage. It implies copying the given model sentences or words in note-books by the pupils.

II. Language Exercises

(i) Converting questions into statements:
Question: Is Mohan a good singer?
Statement: Mohan is a good singer.

(ii) Fill in the blanks:
He entered .... the room (in, into, none)
Deepak jumps .... the wall (over, on, upon)

(iii) Use of Either—Either you or your brother should do it.

(iv) Pairing the sentences:
Match the sentences given in the columns A and B

A	B
I saw a man	I cannot drink it.
You are tired	Who was very intelligent.
The coffee is too hot	You should have rest.

(v) Transformation of sentences:

I am writing a letter. Change this into negative sentence.

(vi) One sentence controlled next free force:
Have you read Shakespeare?
I have read Shakespeare. I have read Tempest, True Love, Macbeth and Hamlet.

(vii) A clue for the rest of the sentence:
If I were Prime Minister.....

III. Completion and Insertion

This is the house I live.................... There was .... bird in the cage.

IV. Substitution Table

Substitution tables are important language exercise in learning English.

<table>
<tr><td rowspan="2">This</td><td rowspan="4">is</td><td>a chair</td></tr>
<tr><td>a table</td></tr>
<tr><td rowspan="2">That</td><td>a book</td></tr>
<tr><td>a pen</td></tr>
</table>

V. Reproduction of Exercises

It is just an advancement upon substitution table. The teacher creates a situation in the class. They listen to him/her carefully. Later on, the teacher asks the students to reproduce those sentences in speech or writing. For example, teacher speaks following sentences:

Today I will teach you a lesson.
I will go to Bombay in the evening.
Change the first person into third person.

VI. Mime

Teacher will only make the gestures and the students will understand and act.

After guided composition, Free Composition is brought into practice.

EXERCISES IN FREE COMPOSITION

1. Paragraph Writing

Paragraphs form a part of any continuous piece of writing in essays, reports, letters etc. So, it is necessary to teach our pupils to write good paragraphs. Following are the characteristics of a well-written paragraph:

(a) It has unity and deals with a specific idea.
(b) A paragraph is well-organised and it has a definite plan. There are various types of paragraph organisation, e.g.,

exemplification of an idea narration, i.e., a time-sequenced organisation of events, comparison-contrast, etc.

(c) A paragraph has coherence – each sentence logically follows from the previous sentence, and anticipates the next sentence.

2. *Filling in Forms*

On several occasions we need to fill in forms for different purposes, e.g., application forms, forms for reservation on trains, money-order forms, cheques etc. Many people feel intimidated by forms and always require someone else's help to fill them in. Very often our forms are rejected if they are not filled in properly. This can be regarded as one of the most basic writing skills – where vocabulary is involved and accuracy is important.

3. *Dialogue Writing*

Of course, dialogue belongs to spoken English but are included as part of the composition syllabus because it is difficult to test spoken English. Beginners are advised to concentrate on simple dialogue, e.g., telephone conversation, conversation with a stranger at a railway station.

4. *Diary Writing*

A diary is a personal record. Hence, the way in which we write a diary differs from the way we write English normally. Here, thoughts and feelings are expressed in a disconnected manner, as they flash through the mind.

A diary entry reflects the writers' fears, joys, expectations, disappointments and hopes about what happened and what might happen. Everything is personal. But this is an excellent device to get the children in the habit of writing.

5. *Information Transfer*

It means transferring information from one form to another, e.g., writing a paragraph based on a graph, or drawing a table based on given data. Changing non-verb communication, i.e., from chart etc. to verbal communication, develops composition skills, the reverse process enables learners' to develop their comprehension skills. This is an important study-skill which would be useful to children in every subject.

Task: Read the Following Description of Vaibhav's School

I study in VSPK School. In front of my school there is a public library. R.G. Mall is behind my school. To the left of my school there is famous Bhagwati Hospital. To the right of my school Big Balaji Temple is situated.

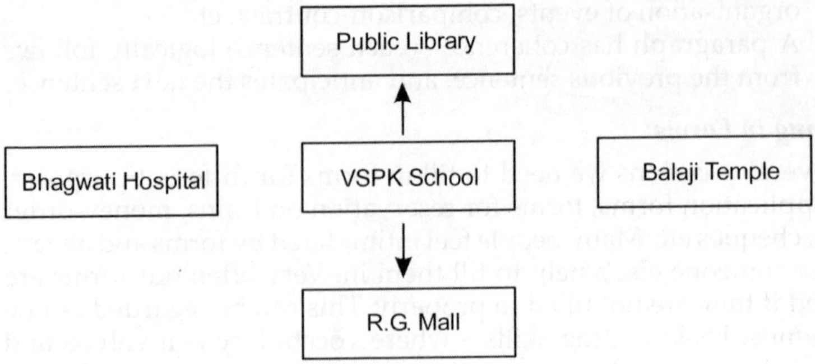

Now look at the Plan around Amit's house and write a paragraph.

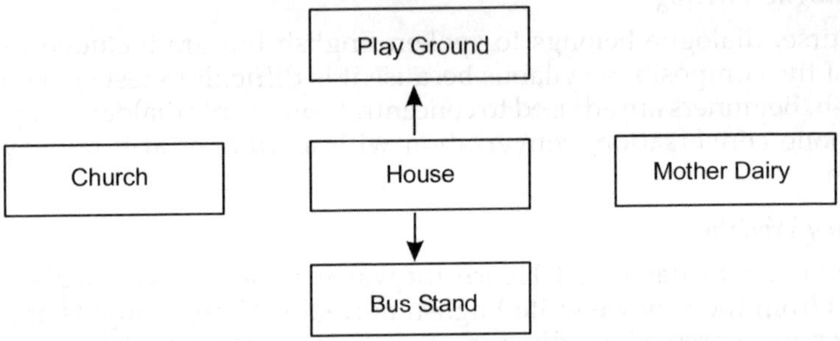

6. Picture Composition

Composition ranging from a short paragraph to a complete essay may be developed by showing appropriate pictures to the learners.

Pictures should be clear and big enough to be seen by the whole class. Pictures can stimulate and provide information which could be used in conversation, discussion and story-writing.

But an essay is only a series of some paragraphs which deal with the sub-titles of the main essay.

Instead of a single picture, a series of pictures must be shown.

7. Story-Writing

Children are interested in stories. This interest can be exploited to write simple stories. A story may be introduced by the teacher with the help of a set of pictures or by putting leading questions. After the story is complete, it may be reconstructed by the class. The teachers may give them an outline of the story along with key words written on the chalkboard.

8. Paraphrasing

Paraphrasing means explanation of a poem in a prose. It is a useful exercise.

9. Summarising and Note-Taking

Summarising and note-taking is a useful but difficult exercise which is suggested in higher classes. The pupils, therefore, are asked to summarise certain passages in their intensive and extensive readings. They may be asked to give summary of the whole lesson. Thus practice in summarising is provided in the language material already known to the pupil. The pupils should be told to read the passage till they are able to distinguish the important points from the unimportant ones. They should express the ideas in their own language within the prescribed limit of words.

This type of exercise helps the learner in expressing the ideas clearly and effectively. He learns how to choose the right words and express in a logical order.

10. Letter-Writing

Letter-writing is a more useful exercise, and is called half way destination between controlled composition and free composition.

All of us write letters for various reasons. Letter-writing enables us to communicate with people who are away from us. Some of the reasons for which we write letters are to inform, to invite, to enquire, to complain, to congratulate, to express sympathy etc. Every letter has a writer, a reader and a situation. Letters may be classified into two broad categories:

(a) Personal and

(b) Business letters.

The various parts of a letter are fixed. The pupils are supposed to adhere to them. Personal letters should be written in a conversational style and the pupils should be made to imagine the presence of the person to whom the letter is addressed.

Business letters should be of a formal nature. They should be to the point.

In the end, it can be said if free composition is to be made effective, the teacher must plan the various aspects of composition work. It is better if the composition is written under the supervision of the teacher. Correction of the written work of the pupils is essential as a necessary follow-up work.

Correction of Composition

It is seen that checking of the composition exercises pose a major problem because closer checking entails lot of time. Moreover, it is monotonous.

To begin with, only the more glaring errors in grammar and spelling may be brought to the notice of the students. Errors in idioms and usage can be taken later on. Over–correction should be avoided. Over-correction may inhibit fluency and freedom. Do not interfere with the pupil's exposition during corrections.

At higher level, students must be able to correct their own mistakes themselves. It may be done by using the conventional signs which indicate the nature of mistakes. It will save time and energy, and will involve the students in their remedial work. It is more effective and memorable.

Suitable correction symbols are:

(1) S — spellings
(2) O — omission
(3) A — article
(4) P — punctuation
(5) G — grammar
(6) W — wrong word
(7) T — tense
(8) E — English
(9) ? — truth of the statement questioned
(10) ; — exaggeration
(11) Z — irrelevant

In most cases even an indication of error is enough for correction. The teacher should note the general mistakes and discuss them with students using the chalkboard.

☛Points to Remember

1. Composition means the act of putting words together.
2. It develops the ability of better expression.
3. Mastery of language, sufficient ideas and their proper organization is must for composition.
4. There are two types of composition:
   - Guided/controlled composition is suggested at junior level
   - Free composition is suggested at higher level.
5. Following are the stages of teaching composition:
   - Pre-composition stage.
   - Oral composition stage.
   - Written composition stage.
   - Correction work.

11

Teaching of Grammar

"Who climbs the grammar tree, distinctly knows where noun, verb and participle grow."
—*Dryden*

What is Grammar? Is there only one grammar? Is it compulsory that we should teach grammar? If so, how should we go about it? What is the role of grammar in language teaching? These are some of the questions that worry every English teacher.

The ultimate aim of every language teacher is to acquire the ability to speak and write the language correctly. In order to do this, she/he requires knowledge of grammar in some form or the other. Hence, any course in language teaching assigns an important role to grammar. As teacher of English we need to know:

(a) What is Grammar?
(b) How should we teach Grammar?

What is Grammar?

The meaning of the term 'Grammar' has been given differently by different people. To some, it is something that helps in learning a language. To others, it is a body of rules and regulations of a language. It is also described as a descriptive science which describes the structure of sentences, function of words and their relation to one another. Every language has its own grammar and it is important because a language should be intelligible or otherwise it loses its sense. The acceptability of a usage depends upon notions and norms of grammar being followed by its users.

Some of the definitions of Grammar are—

According to Chapman, "Grammar is the study of language by specialists, made in order to establish the rules and principles which are followed more or less unconsciously or instinctively by the native speakers".

Professor Syce opined that, "Grammatical propriety is nothing more than the established usage of a particular body of speakers at a particular time in their history. It means that the correct usage is not fixed for all time".

Language is always in the process of evolution.

In the words of Dr. West, "Grammar is not a code of rules, it is like etiquettes and table manners".

Jaggar describes the function of grammar at school level as "Description of the main laws of the structure of current English couched in terms which are sufficiently precise".

The Longman Dictionary of Contemporary English defines grammar as "The study and practice of the rules by which words change their forms and are combined into sentences". There are two basic elements in this definition: the rules of grammar; and the study and practice of rules. Here grammar constitutes a subset of rules relating to word formation (morphology) and sentence formation (syntax).

According to modern linguistics, "Grammar is a device that specifies the infinite set of well-formed sentences and assigns to each of them one or more structural descriptions". In other words, grammar tells us what the possible sentences of a language are and provides a description of them.

1. All of us are able to speak our mother tongue correctly. We do not make any grammatical mistakes. If someone else speaks our mother tongue incorrectly, we are able to identify the mistakes and correct them. Even an illiterate native speaker is able to identify the mistakes, without knowing the rules of grammar. Grammar, in this sense refers to the total mechanism of the language, which enables its users to communicate with each other. Let us call this Grammar 1, or G1.

2. Consider the following sentence:

"He is going to school every day".

A native speaker can correct it as 'He is going to school every day' without telling the rule. But a native Grammarian can tell that it is wrong because the 'ing' form of the verb is used without the auxiliary 'be'. Such an ability to think intuitively is also referred as Grammar. We can refer it as Grammar 2 or G2.

3. Grammar also refers to the rules for correct use of language which may be prescribed for its users, for example, words beginning with a vowel sound are preceded by 'an' whereas words beginning with a consonant sound are preceded by 'a'. Let us call this third type Grammar 3 or G3.

4. According to modern linguistics there is a fourth meaning for the term 'Grammar'—'Grammar' is regarded as the innate capacity which all human beings possess, it allows them to acquire language. In this sense grammar is a property of the human brain, rather than type of any language. This may be termed Grammar 4 or G4.

Why Study Grammar?

Traditional teachers of English considered grammar as an integral part of the language curriculum. Hence students were taught all about articles, prepositions, conditional clauses etc. Moreover, development of language skills and structure of language can be taught scientifically and systematically.

But in the early years of the *Communicative Approach* it was felt that knowledge of grammar may not be necessary for one to communicate in a language even without knowing grammar. The other arguments they gave against the teaching of grammar were:

- Much input produces little output. What is learnt is not applied.
- It does not provide ideas, thoughts and feelings to the learners to express.
- Grammatical analysis breaks up the unity of thought by its focus on detail and fails to relate the detail to the whole.
- It hinders the spontaneous learning of a foreign language.

Types of Grammar

Broadly speaking, there are two types of Grammar.

(1) Prescriptive/Traditional/Formal Grammar

(2) Descriptive/Functional Grammar

(1) *Formal Grammar*: This is the old traditional grammar. It prescribes rules for the language. Here the main stress is on form. The main limitation here is that there is no scope for change whereas rules of grammar must change accordingly.

(2) *Functional Grammar*: It does not give rules rather describes the behaviour of language. No doubt there are certain prescribed rules in it but these are not as rigid as in the formal grammar. The main emphasis is on the functional aspect.

In recent years there has been a rethinking about Grammar teaching. While as a reaction to the structural approach, the learners in a communicative classroom were expected not to 'puzzle their heads with grammar', it is being increasingly accepted that "language learning is essentially learning how grammar functions in the achievement of meaning". — (*Widdowson*, 1990-97)

But instead of isolated sentences which were mostly used for drill and practice in the structural approach, the emphasis is now on providing suitable contexts to make the "learners realise the communicative value of grammar in the very achievement of meaning".

What should English teachers do then? Should they teach grammar or not? With the introduction of 'Direct Method', grammar is fast disappearing from school curriculum. In spite of it, grammar has an important place and should be taught for the following reasons:

- We encounter ambiguity, imprecision, unintelligible speech or writing. To deal with these problems, we need grammar to work out what went wrong.
- To develop scientific attitude about the language.
- To develop learners' mental abilities of reasoning and correct observation.
- To enable the students to assimilate the correct patterns of the language without rote memorisation.

Approach to Teaching Grammar

It is the context which determines the best approach to teach various approaches are:

(a) Formal explanation of grammatical rules
(b) Practice of common grammatical patterns
(c) Situational teaching
(d) Deductive method
(e) Inductive method

(a) Formal Explanation of Grammatical Rules

This is called traditional method. In this method a book containing the rules on grammar is used. There are several grammar books which present the rules of English grammar, e.g., Wren and Martin, Nesfield etc. These rules are prescriptive. But connotations of the words have been changed in the present scenario. Some of these rules are no longer valid.

The mastery of the rules of grammar will surely make our learners veterans in Grammar but find difficulty in communicating.

(b) Practice of Common Grammatical Patterns

In this approach emphasis is given on practice of usages.

Look at the substitution table given below. How many sentences can a learner generate from this table?

Boys		studying
Girls	are	writing
Ram and Shyam		playing

But there is danger that they may not know when to use these patterns.

(c) Situational Teaching

Here the learners are provided with the situations to speak which enhances their proficiency.

(d) Deductive Method

Here the teacher first tells the rules to the pupils and the students apply those rules in different situations of language learning. Formal grammar is generally taught with the help of deductive method. The deductive method has its own advantages. It saves time and makes the process easy.

(e) Inductive Method

In inductive method, the teacher should present certain examples before the students, and then frame the rules with their help with the help of examples, the students are able to induce rules. This method has its own advantages, it breaks the monotony, and teaching is made more interesting through situational teaching and performing actions in the classroom. This method lays emphasis on teaching of functional grammar. It stimulates their power of thinking and reasoning, assimilation and initiation.

Eclectic Approach

Celce Murcia and Hills suggested an Eclectic approach which consists of following four parts:

1. *Presentation*: The teacher selects a grammar structure relevant to students' need and introduces it.
2. *Focussed Practice*: In this stage, students get practice, teacher corrects their answers and remove errors.
3. *Communicative Approach*: At this stage learners are engaged in communicative practice. They are given feedback from peers.
4. *Teacher's Feedback*: Teachers point out the errors and give opportunities to remove their mistakes.

Suggestions for Successful Teaching of Grammar

1. Grammar lessons should begin with language. It must correlate with speech in which a sentence is a unitary whole with reading. After the students have listened to it, try to guide them to deduce the pattern that we want them to use.
2. Grammar should not be taught as an intellectual exercise of the pupils but the aim should be to make them skilful users of language.
3. Teach grammar for communication not grammar for its own sake. We are not interested in producing grammarians. We should help the learners to communicate effectively. We want our learners to acquire knowledge of language and not knowledge about language. It is not necessary for them to know what a noun or verb is; they can still communicate without such knowledge. Hence, let us not frighten our learners with excessive use of grammatical labels. An analogy might help you to understand this better. If you want to learn driving, it is not necessary for you to know everything about each part of the car. Teach grammar as discourse— not isolated sentences.

☛Points to Remember

1. Grammar refers to the rules for correct use of language which may be prescribed for its users.
2. There are two types of Grammar
   - *Formal Grammar*: It prescribes rules for the language.
   - *Functional Grammar*: It describes the behaviour of language.
3. *There are various approaches to teach Grammar like*: Formal explanation, situation teaching inductive-deductive method.
4. Teach Grammar for communication not Grammar for its own sake.

12

Pedagogical Analysis: Based on Unit Analysis

Long back teacher was known by the name Pedagogic. The terms 'pedagogue, pedagogy and pedagogical' are generally used. 'Pedant' is another name given to the teacher. A pedantic teacher is that teacher who lays too much stress on book learning, technical knowledge, rules and adherence to rules.

Let us talk about the word 'Pedagogy' which means science of teaching. Science is defined as a systematic study. So pedagogy can be defined as a science of teaching or systematic teaching or scientific way of teaching.

What is Analysis?

In a layman's language, analysis is opening a thing into parts and then studying these parts one by one in a progressive sequencing and then coming to a conclusion. To have a better understanding of a concept it is always recommended to study its constituent's parts. It means 'analysis' is bifurcating a topic into units and sub-units and other similar units, if possible. Therefore, the topic has to be opened up and studied accordingly.

Pedagogical Analysis is a combination of two words, i.e., pedagogy and analysis. Therefore, pedagogical analysis is a scientific and systematic study or teaching of a topic.

A good syllabus is that in which the different content items are put under different units. All those units are numbered in a sequence—from easier to difficult. This unit wise study is called Unit Approach.

What is a Unit?

According to Jaromilck, "Unit as a means of organising material for instructional purposes which utilises significant subject-matter and involves pupils in learning activities through active participation-: intellectually and physically, and modifies the pupils' behaviour to the extent that he is able to cope with new problems and situations more competently".

According to NCERT Report, "A unit of study may be understood as a block of closely related subject-matter which can conveniently be overviewed by the learners within a short span of time. The size of a unit could, of course, vary".

Meaning of Unit Approach (Morrison Approach)

This approach is associated with the name of Professor H.C. Morrison

(1871-1945) of the University of Chicago. It lays greater emphasis on the unit method for the planning of the teaching-learning activities, and that is why it is termed as unit approach. Mastery over the subject-matter is the main concern here. For this, division of subject-matter into small but meaningful unit is done. In each unit the different sub-units are interlinked, interrelated and interdependent. A teacher has to visualise and write down the possible objectives and specifications that are likely to be developed by teacher for a particular unit or sub-unit while planning his lesson. Again, the teacher has to be careful in selecting the teaching points and maxims of teaching, teaching aids and teaching activities. After teaching the unit, evaluation procedure and devices are to be considered carefully.

How to Plan Unit Method

Teaching of language becomes more effective if a teacher divides the full syllabus into units. Following points are to be considered:

(a) *Clear understanding of the objectives*: Curriculum framers must be clear about the knowledge and information they want to give through a particular unit; which abilities, skills, interests and attitudes they want to develop in the students.

(b) *Selection of content*: The selection of content material of each unit must be done keeping in view the objectives of the subject.

(c) *Clear description of students' activities*: After each unit individual/ group activities should be specified.

(d) *Teaching aids*: Audio-visual teaching aids needed for teaching should be identified.

Limitations of Unit Method

1. Expert and trained teachers are required for organisation of unit-wise content material.
2. It is difficult to categorize the content into strict and homogeneous units.

Fixing up Objectives for the Unit

It is always expected of a teacher to formulate instructional objectives in behavioural terms. It means the content that is to be taught should become the part of the behaviour of an individual for whom teaching is done. Knowledge of various approaches like: Bloom's taxonomy of teaching and learning, Robert Mager's Approach, Robert Miller's Approach and RCEM Approach helps the teacher to formulate instructional objectives in behavioural terms. A good knowledge of phases of teaching, domains of teaching, stages of teaching and levels of teaching help a teacher in formulating instructional objectives.

Instructional objectives are the 'learning outcome'. It is the end product or the result of instruction in the form of learning by Pupils. Learning is change in behaviour. The change in behaviour may be in any of the domains, *viz.*, cognitive, affective and psychomotor. The cognitive domain covers all the behaviours related to the thinking processes in the learner. For example, in a situation where the learner is to exhibit his knowledge or understanding about certain concepts, his behaviours, that operate, are mostly in cognitive domain. The effective domain covers attitudinal, emotional and valuing behaviours of the learner like his interests, attitudes etc., which are more dominated by feeling rather than thinking. Psychomotor domain cover activities like speaking, reading, writing and playing etc.

Learning Experiences

Learning experiences with the chosen methods are provided to the learners. For this activity method is used. Inductive approach is effective to bring the desired results. Questioning technique prove helpful in order to make the students active participants. Subject-matter is divided into smaller and simpler sub-units according to the teaching points identified earlier. Maxims of teaching are kept in view. The teacher should have understanding of the age level of the students in order to provide/transfer the learning experiences of the students. The content selected to be taught should be relevant to the objectives framed earlier. Logical continuity and psychological organisation of the content is very important.

Methods of Teaching

There are three methods of teaching:

(1) Translation method,
(2) Direct method,
(3) Bilingual method.

It depends on intelligence of the teacher which method is to be given preference. Because the four skills: listening, speaking, reading and writing can be developed through the proper selection of method, so a judicious use of method is to be made.

Teaching Aids

In the present era of technology, use of teaching aids make the lesson interesting and effective. Nature of knowledge given by the present teacher has also changed. He has to teach variety of subjects. His duty is not to provide spiritual knowledge only but a variety of knowledge making it a compulsion to use teaching aids. A judicious use of teaching aids is always recommended. They should be relevant and according to the mental level of the students and help in obtaining the objectives. For this, the proper selection and presentation of teaching aids is essential. All this is helpful in creating situations, and develops imagination skill. Lastly, it can be said that the use of teaching aids make maximum senses active and all gateways of knowledge are opened up.

Evaluation

The last step in the procedure of pedagogical analysis is that of evaluation. In the beginning of the teaching procedure the teacher formulates instructional objectives. And on the basis of these objectives he plans his teaching. He selects different methods, styles and techniques of presentation of the content. He divides the content into simpler and smaller units and puts them systematically in a progressive sequence and teaching aids are used. Then tries to know what has been learnt by the students. The testing of the students by the teacher at the end of the lesson is called evaluation in terms of pedagogical analysis. Evaluation is continuous assessment of a person. Here all-round development of a person, i.e., scholastic and non-scholastic achievement is taken into account.

Evaluation at the end of the lesson comprises of two aspects:

(i) Recapitulation
(ii) Home work

Every student is being tested every day and at all times in the class.

Weekly tests or bi-weekly tests may be held. For that purpose a few test items are given below:

Scholastic Achievement

(a) Fill in the blanks type test items

I. Fill in the blanks in the following:

1. Have you finished your work?
   Is your work....
2. Do you respect your parents?
   Are your parents....
3. He always speaks the truth
   .... by him always.

II. Fill in the blanks in the following:

1. He always .... the poor.
2. Honesty is the .... policy.
3. Cricket is .... by him daily.

III. Complete the blanks:

1. .... (Active)
   Letter is not written by me. (Passive)
2. A noise is not made by the children. (Passive)
   .... (Active)
3. Obedient students are always appreciated by all. (Passive)
   .... (Active)

Non-Scholastic Achievement

Personal and social qualities of the students can be: regularity, punctuality, cooperation, sense of responsibility and initiation, etc.

Design of a Question Paper of a Unit Test

Design of a question paper of unit test is broadly policy statement made by the examination authorities and passed on to paper setters for framing a question paper and to schools for preparing students on the lines suggested. Before preparing the design of a question-paper, decisions regarding the following should be taken:

(i) Weightage to objectives.
(ii) Weightage to content.
(iii) Weightage to form of questions.
(iv) Weightage to difficulty level.

Blue Print

A blue print is more or less a detailed document on which question paper is based. While different blue prints can be prepared from the same design, a number of question papers based on the same blue print will be more or less similar.

In preparing the question paper following steps should be considered:

(1) Preparation of the design.
(2) Preparation of the blue print.
(3) Construction of questions.
(4) Editing the paper.
(5) Preparation of scoring key.
(6) Question-wise analysis of the paper.

Model Pedagogical Lesson-Plan Tables

In order to be more systematic and organised to bring better achievement, we need a proper planning of the content to be taught and evaluated. A model plan is given below in the form of three tables:

(1) Yearly Plan

Yearly plan table provide the information about outline of the content of the course, the teaching objectives to be realised and the total period of teaching assigned to the score.

Yearly Plan: Teaching Grammar

Teaching Content	*Knowledge*	*Skill*	*Knowledge Application*	*Interest and Attitude*	*Total Period*
1. Noun	4	½	½	3	8
2. Pronoun	6	1	2	3	12
3. Verb	2	½	½	2	5
4. Adjective	2	—	½	1½	4
5. Adverb	5	1	1½	4½	12
6. Preposition	5	1	½	2½	9
Total	24	4	5½	16½	50

The yearly plan table indicates that the grammar course content is to be completed in total fifty periods. This table further reveals that the main emphasis has been given to knowledge objectives, as 24 periods are assigned to this objective. The second major objective is the interest and attitudes as 16½ periods are allotted to this objective. The knowledge application is the third and skill objective the fourth.

2. *Unit Plan Table*

Unit plan table provides the information about the unit of the content regarding the structure of the unit content and teaching objectives to be realised.

Unit (Teaching Grammar—Noun)

Teaching Content	*Knowledge*	*Skill*	*Knowledge Application*	*Interest and Attitude*	*Total Period*
1. Noun	1	¼	¼	½	2
2. Kinds of Noun	1½	—	¼	1	1
3. Material Noun	1	¼	¼	½	2
4. Collective Noun	1½	—	¼	¼	1
Total	3	½	1	1½	6

A unit plan reveals that the unit Noun in English is taught and completed within 6 periods of classroom teaching. It may also be noted from the table that 3 periods are assigned for knowledge objective, 1½ period for interest and attitude, 1 period for knowledge application and ½ period for skill objectives.

3. *Lesson-Plan Table*

A teacher has to plan a lesson to be taught within period of classroom teaching. She/he has to select a topic which is to be covered within a period of 45 minutes duration.

Topic Noun

Teaching Content	*Knowledge*	*Skill*	*Knowledge Application*	*Interest and Attitude*	*Total Period*
1. Noun	8	—	—	2	10
2. Kinds of Noun	10	—	—	2	12
3. Material Noun	5	—	2	3	10
4. Collective Noun	8	1	2	2	13
Total	31	1	4	9	45 mts.

The above table indicates that the topic Noun is taught within 45 minutes, 31 minutes for knowledge objectives, one minute for interest and attitude, 4 minutes for knowledge application and one minute for skill objective of teaching.

Thus, these tables are used for teaching as well as testing, and both can be made objective-centred.

☛Points to Remember

1. Pedagogical Analysis is a scientific and systematic study or teaching of a topic.
2. Teaching of language becomes more effective if a teacher divides the full syllabus into units.
3. Fixing-up objectives for the unit is essential.
4. Learning experiences, methods of teaching, teaching aids and evaluation are the various important steps in the procedure of pedagogical Analysis.

13

Microteaching Skills

"Microteaching is a real teaching reduced in time, number of students and range of activities."
—*B.M. Shore*

Do you consider it a healthy practice, if a pupil-teacher is sent in the class to teach after teaching the theory of any subject? I feel certainly not. It is like taking a person to river for swimming who has learnt theory of swimming.

In the teacher training institutions, efforts are done to acquaint the pupil-teachers with certain teaching skills to get the desired results. Let us first understand what is a teaching skill?

N.L. Gaze has defined the teaching skills as specific instructional activities and procedures that a teacher may use in the classroom. These are related to the various stages of teaching or in the continuous flow of the teacher performance.

Passi and Kulshresta (1986) pointed out that in order to make teacher education programme effective and to bring qualitative improvement, microteaching technique can be very useful.

Now let us discuss what is the innovative microteaching technique?

Meaning of Microteaching

This technique was propagated by Dwight Allen in 1963, at Stanford University, California. Later it was used in developed countries like USA and UK. But in India it was introduced in 1967, by D.D. Tiwari at Government Central Pedagogical Institute, Allahabad.

The technique has been refined over a long period of last few decades. This is used to shape the teacher's behaviour.

As the term itself indicates, microteaching is a scaled down teaching in which the teacher teaches a short lesson to a small group at a time. Thus, microteaching is a miniature form of teaching in which teaching is scaled down in terms of class size, complexity and activities which focus on developing a specific teaching skill.

Definitions of Microteaching

Some of the definitions are given below:

Passi and Lalita (1976),

"Microteaching is a training technique which requires student teachers to teach a single concept using specified teaching skills to a small number of pupils in a short duration of time".

Jangira and Singh,

"Microteaching is a training setting for the student teacher/teacher trainee where complexities of the normal classroom teaching are reduced".

(a) Practicing one component skill at a time.
(b) Limiting the content to a single concept.
(c) Reducing the size of students from 5 to 10 in a class.
(d) Reducing the duration of the lesson from 5 to 10 minutes.

R.N. Bush,

"Microteaching is a teaching technique which allows teachers to apply clearly defined teaching skills and carefully prepared lessons in a planned series of five to ten minutes encounters with a small group of real students".

Characteristics of Microteaching

On the basis of above definitions we can make out the following characteristics of microteaching:

1. It is a training technique.
2. Time, content and class size, all are taken in a minimised form.
3. One skill is practised at a time.
4. Students' participation is focussed.
5. Immediate feedback.
6. Maximum transfer.

Steps in Microteaching

1. *Defining the skill*: To provide knowledge and awareness, a particular skill is defined in terms of teaching behaviour.
2. *Demonstrating the skill*: Selected skill is demonstrated.
3. *Planning the lesson*: Pupil-teacher plans a short lesson under the guidance of supervisor.
4. *Teaching the lesson*: Pupil-teacher teaches the lesson to a small group of 5 to 10 pupils for 5 to 6 minutes.
5. *Discussion*: After teaching, discussion is done to give feedback. Such discussion will give reinforcement to the pupil-teacher.
6. *Re-planning*: Keeping in view the points of discussion the pupil-teacher re-plan the lesson for practice.
7. *Re-teaching*: This re-planned lesson is re-taught to another small group of students of same class for the same duration to practice the same skill.
8. *Re-discussion*: The teaching is now followed by discussion of suggestions and encouragement to the teaching performance. The feedback is again provided to the trainee.
9. *Repeating the cycle:* The cycle is repeated till the desired level of skill is achieved.

To gain perfection repetitions can be done.

Principles of Microteaching

1. *Principle of reinforcement*: Here the teacher encourages the pupil by using verbal praise, accepting their responses through non-verbal praise like smile. You must know that teachers' encouragement can do wonders.
2. *Principle of experiments*: Pupil-teacher and supervisor need the controlled conditions for experiments as the time, content, technique and many more factors can bring change.
3. *Principle of precise supervision*: Supervision has to be very alert as she/he has to fill an observation schedule and assess the performance on rating scale.
4. *Principle of continuity*: Microteaching requires continuity. The teacher learns and re-learns the teaching skills. Its unique feature, discussion—planning—teaching—feedback—re-planning and re-teaching, bring the proficiency.
5. *Principle of practice*: Repeated practice is surely a step towards mastery of a skill.
6. *Principle of evaluation*: Alertness on the part of supervisor in evaluating the skill is very effective. Self-evaluation can be done with the help of video tape recorder.

How many Skills?

Various researches have been conducted on micro skills. Some findings have given a list of 14 skills and others have given a list of 21 skills. Out of them four very important skills essential for teaching English are being described here under:

1. Questioning skill
2. Explaining skill
3. Illustration skill
4. Stimulus Variation skill

QUESTIONING SKILL

Questioning is an integral skill of a good lesson. The renowned philosopher, Socrates, was the first to give the idea. According to him, the teacher should present the subject-matter in such a way that the learner recognises the truth and he/she can identify himself/herself with it.

Questions are fundamental to the concept of learning. They arouse mental activity. A good question is key to all educative activity. Boredom and dullness created in lecture and explanation is eliminated through questioning. It is the most effective instrument in the tool kit of a teacher to make the teaching-learning activity meaningful and effective. Teacher should have the art of questioning their framing and relating the new one with the old one.

Raymont in this regard says, "The acquisition of a good style of questioning may be laid down definitely as one of the essential ambition of young teachers".

Questioning is an integral skill of a good lesson. In the process of questioning, the following considerations should be kept in view:

1. The question should be relevant and meaningful.
2. The question should be in simple form.
3. It should be pin-pointed.
4. Its language should be accurate and clear.
5. Its language should not be ambiguous.
6. It should be according to the age and mental level of the learners.
7. The questions should be objective-based.
8. They should not be too complex that the students find it difficult to answer.
9. Questions should be evenly distributed in the class.
10. The question should not be suggestive.

Purpose Behind Questioning

In every classroom situation, the questions are put keeping in view one purpose or the other. Usually the following component behaviours are involved:

1. Prompting
2. Seeking further information
3. Re-focussing
4. Re-direction
5. Increasing critical awareness

1. *Prompting*: The teacher put questions just to give them clues to react and speak. The learners start to think, and creativity in ideas enhance.
2. *Seeking further information*: Such questions are asked to have more information from the learners. They are supposed to add the information already given by them. For example:
   - Tell us something more about democracy.
   - What is your opinion in this regard?
3. *Re-focussing*: These types of questions are put in order to test the concept taught earlier. Understanding ability of the learners can be tested. Learners can help to focus their attention on the concept.
4. *Re-direction*: Here the purpose of putting the question is to redirect the attention of the learners so as to get the desired response. Suppose a student has given a wrong answer the teacher tries to take him on the right track and make him speak the right answer.
5. *Increasing critical awareness*: Another purpose of putting the questions to the students is to increase the critical thinking. Questions based on "how" and "why" are asked from the students. Here the interest of the students can be sustained. For example: Questions like—what is your viewpoint about effect of Media on children?

Aims of Questioning

1. To diagnose the weak points of the students.
2. To revise the lesson.
3. To stimulate the curiosity and keep the children mentally alert.
4. To promote initiative and originality.
5. To know whether the students are following the lesson or not.
6. To enable them to recall and recognise something.

Basic Principles

Following are the principles:

(i) Theory of unfoldment. All knowledge is within the learner, the teacher cannot teach any new knowledge to the students.

(2) The knowledge can be emitted by linking the questions with the answers.

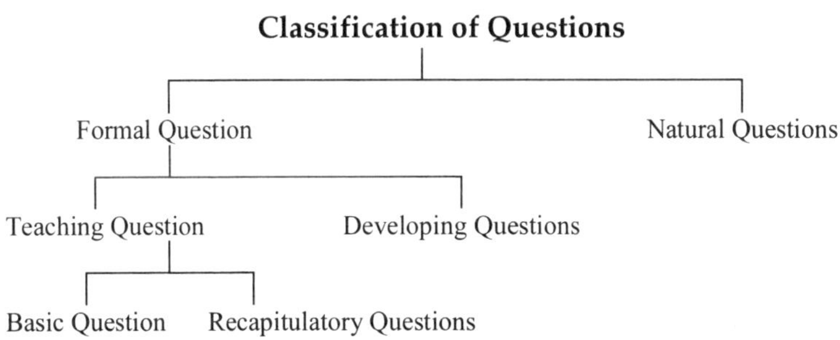

The teacher's attitude to pupil's Questioning:

1. The students should be encouraged to ask questions.
2. The teacher should encourage questions which indicate disagreement with the students.

Advantages

Following are the major advantages:

1. It is based on psychological principles of learning.
2. Learners remain active.
3. New knowledge can be linked with the previous one.
4. Verbal interaction is improved.
5. Self-confidence is created.

Limitations

It has the following disadvantages:

1. Arrangement of questions in psychological sequence.
2. Not applicable or useful in higher classes.
3. It appears mechanical and artificial in nature.
4. Only few sharp students participate, and the back-benchers and shy ones remain quiet.

EXPLAINING SKILL

Explaining means to expand, to elucidate, to clear the ambiguity and to develop understanding.

Explanation forms a bridge between telling and revealing knowledge to the learners.

To present the subject-mater in the simplified form before the pupils and making it acquirable is termed as skill of explanation. The use of skill of explanation is considered necessary in all the subjects. Presentation becomes effective through explaining skill. The main objective of explanation is to enable the children to take interest in all the proceedings of the class, to grasp the purpose of what is being done and to develop their understanding of how to do it. It is useful in skill and knowledge lessons. Here, the teacher explains the subject-matter with the help of easy statements, audio-visual aids and illustrations so that the students can understand it. While explaining, the teacher should use words, statements and examples according to the mental level of the students. It is essentially a verbal skill, useful in knowledge and skill lessons.

Some Considerations while Explaining

1. While explanation, specific aim should be kept in view.
2. There should be a logical sequence.
3. Language should be simple and straightforward.
4. Use of too many phrases should be avoided.
5. Proper interaction is essential, so students should be allowed to ask questions.
6. Controversial discussion should be avoided.
7. P.T. should focus his/her ideas on the main topic.
8. To ascertain whether the students have grasped the material, the teacher may ask some questions from the students at different stages of development.

Merits

1. Skill of explaining gives the teacher great confidence.
2. Skill of explaining enables the teacher to make lesson interesting and win over the hearts of the students.
3. It enhances the imagination power of the students.

Demerits

1. Sometimes while explaining the teacher goes ashtray from his/her topic, as great skill is required in explanation.
2. It is difficult to determine to what extent explanation must be done.
3. If it is not planned, results in drastic consequences.

ILLUSTRATION SKILL

To *illustrate* means to make a point or idea clear and intelligible. It means to explain or to elucidate or exemplify ideas with the help of verbal or non-verbal aids such as examples, figures, comparisons or some concrete material like maps, charts, and diagrams etc. in order to make the meanings clear, and help the children acquire proper knowledge, the teacher in his/her class uses illustrations. In this skill along with the use of pictures etc. various types of apparatus like chalkboard, scientific and geographical apparatus or models or diagrams and sketches can be used. In fact, illustration includes anything which makes an appeal to the senses and the imagination of the learners.

Importance of Illustration

1. Teacher can make the students attentive through illustrations by breaking the dullness of lecture.
2. Concrete description to the abstracts, ideas and thoughts is possible.
3. They are useful for the young children, as they do not indulge in abstract thinking.
4. Teachers make use of verbal and non-verbal illustrations to facilitate the learning of an important point. It can be done through comparisons, examples or analogies and non-verbal illustrations.
5. Teacher can emphasise any particular point in the lesson by using illustration.
6. Teacher can stimulate the imagination of the students by using illustrations.
7. It develops the retention power of the students.
8. This skill cultivates the power of observation and judgement.

Types of Illustrations

There are two types of illustrations:

(a) *Verbal illustrations*: These are illustrations which influence the mind through the medium of related ideas expressed in words. It can be further divided into three categories:
   (i) Stories, anecdotes and descriptions.
   (ii) Analogies and comparisons
   (iii) Similies and words.

(b) *Non-verbal or concrete illustrations*: These are illustrations which act directly through senses. They may be called non-verbal, natural, concrete, material or objective illustrations.

Advantages

1. Teaching through illustrations brings long-lasting effect on the students.
2. Difficult lesson becomes easy.
3. Situations can be created which is helpful in teaching-learning process.

Suggestions While Using Illustrations

1. Illustrations should be exact and accurate.
2. They should be easy and intelligible.
3. They should be properly handled and exhibited.
4. They should be self-explanatory, obvious and meaningful.
5. Use of too many illustrations should be avoided.
6. They should be interesting, stimulating and according to the mental level of the students.
7. Technical vocabulary and hyperboles should not be used.
8. Use of metaphors and conceits are also to be avoided.
9. There should be variety and novelty in the use of illustrations.
10. Students should be given sufficient time so that they can pay full attention to understand them.

Drawbacks

1. It is time consuming, if not planned in advance.
2. Sometime use of it becomes a costly affair.
3. Use of many illustrations do not allow the mind of the learners to think properly.

STIMULUS VARIATION SKILL

Stimulus means something that helps to develop better or more quickly. In other words, something that produces a reaction in human beings.

Teaching depends upon the stimulus provided by the teacher during teaching. A good teacher goes on varying the stimulus in order to bring in variety in his/her teaching. That way he/she is able to attract the attention of the students. Thus, the teachers are trained in movements, gestures, focussing, international style etc. The teacher can draw attention of the students through various activities and behaviour. Some of them are discussed below:

1. *Modulation*: Modulated voice with loud and slow pitch bring a greater effect in attracting attention of the students.
2. *Contrast*: For bringing more attention contrast stimulus are suggested.
3. *Movement*: Movement of the teacher in the class while teaching makes the presentation lively.
4. *Self-activity*: While explaining, the teacher should keep the class active by asking them to write side by side in their notebooks. This way attention can be sustained.
5. *Change*: For bringing greater effect the teacher can shift his/her position, use gestures.
6. *Teacher's Personal Behaviour*: Teacher's personality can break the dullness of the class. So, he/she should be stimulating and energetic.
7. *Audio-visual Aids*: Teacher can use various audio-visual aids to focus the attention of the students.

Components of Skill of Stimulus Variation

1. *Movement*: Movement of the teacher breaks the dullness. But it should be meaningful and related to the teacher.
2. *Gestures*: Gestures of hands, eyes, and face can be helpful in emphasising the points or emotions.
3. *Speech Pattern*: Changes in tone, volume or speed of verbal expression can bring emphasis on a particular aspect.
4. *Focussing*: Verbal communication or gestures help the teacher to have focus.
5. *Interactional Style*: Interaction between teacher-pupil and pupil-pupil is important stimulus.
6. *Pausing*: When the teacher goes on talking and putting questions continuously without giving time to think and respond to the students they become inattentive. Then the teacher should make use of certain pauses during teaching. This way attention of the students can be secured and they can have enough time to frame an answer.
7. *Change in the Sensory Focus*: There are different sensory focusses during a lesson like listening, speaking, doing, writing and demonstrating etc. When a teacher changes the sensory focus for imparting information to the pupils from listening to looking, from speaking to doing or from writing to demonstration etc. It is called changes in sensory focus. This way level of attention can be maintained.
8. *Students' Participation*: Students can be actively involved in various activities like reading, writing etc. In this way we can sustain their interest in the teaching-learning process.

Micro Lesson Plan on the skill of questioning.

MICRO LESSON PLAN—I

Roll No.: Skill: Questioning
Subject: English Duration: 5-6
Minutes
Topic: Determiners Class: IX

Criteria of the Skill

1. Structuring the language of the questions appropriately.
2. Asking more questions within specific time.
3. Encouraging the students to respond.
4. Maximum participation of students.
5. Improving the correctness of responses.
6. Developing critical awareness among the students.

Opening Statement

Dear students! Today, I shall put some questions to you about Grammar. If you know...

Pupil Teacher's Activities	*Students' Activities*	*Components*
P.T. will put the following questions ➢ There is little hope of his success. ➢ A little of the money has been stolen. ➢ The little boy whom you saw in my house is my nephew.	Students listen carefully	Specific
Q. What are these underlined words grammatically?	These words are determiners.	Grammatically correct
Q. What do you mean by the term 'Determiners'?	Determiner is the name of a word which is used before noun to show how they are being used.	Relevant
Q. Make the difference between little, a little and the little	Little means not much/hardly any. A little means some. The little means all of that.	Pin Pointed
Q. Can you make a sentence by using little and a little	Little—There is a little milk in the jug. A little—A little knowledge is a dangerous thing.	Distributed in the Class
Q. What is the difference between 'many' and 'much'	— Many denotes number — Much denotes quantity	
Q. Make sentence using the words many and much.	Many—Many students were absent yesterday. Much—I have much work to do.	Well-structured
Q. What is the difference between less and several?	Less is the opposite of much. Several means many.	

Well, students I hope you have understood the rules.

Observation Schedule Rating

Components	*Average*	*Good*	*Very Good*	*Excellent*
● Specific ● Grammatically correct ● Relevant ● Pin-pointed ● Distributed in the class ● Well-structured				

Signature of the Supervisor

MICRO LESSON PLAN—II

Roll No.:	Skill: Explaining
Subject: English	Duration: 5-6 Minutes
Topic: Use of articles	Class: IX

Criteria of the Skill

1. Introducing an idea or concept to the students.
2. Establishing structural relationship in language for flow of ideas.
3. Covering main ideas of the concept.
4. Keeping normal speed in explanation.
5. Attending completeness of idea.

Opening Statement

Dear students! Today, I shall explain the use of articles.

Pupil Teacher's Activities	*Students' Activities*	*Component*
The determiners 'a', 'an' and 'the' are called articles. 'A' and 'An' are called indefinite, whereas 'The' is called definite article. I will tell you about the use of 'An'.	Pupils are listening and noting down in their note books	Covering essential points
This is an inkpot.	Students are understanding	Use of explaining lines.
An is also used before words beginning with 'h' where it remains silent (writing on chalk board) e.g.		Covering the essential points
• Ram is an honest man • He is late by an hour		Use of relevant examples
There are also some words which begin with vowel but do not give the sound of vowel	Students are listening and understanding	
• He reads in a university • I have a European friend		Use of relevant examples
PT asks the students to fill the blanks	Students give responses	
1. He is ..... M.P.	1. He is an M.P.	Testing pupils' understanding
2. .... Ox is domestic animal.	2. An Ox is a domestic animal.	
3. I saw .... elephant in the zoo.	3. I saw an elephant in the zoo.	
PT will say, well students! Today, we have learnt about the articles 'A' and 'An'		Concluding statement

Observation Schedule

Components	Average	Good	Very Good	Excellent
1. Use of appropriate introducing statement 2. Use of closing statement 3. Use of explaining links (but, therefore, thus, why, and, because, since, so that) 4. Use of visual techniques 5. Defining technical words 6. Covering essential points 7. Testing Pupils' understanding				

Signature of the Supervisor

MICRO LESSON PLAN—III

Roll No.: Skill: Stimulus Variation

Subject: English Duration: 5-6 Minutes

Topic: Poem (Encroachment) Class: IX

Criteria of the Skill

1. Getting pupils' attention.
2. Clarification of the content.
3. Creating interest among the students.
4. Maximum involvement of the students.

Opening Statement

Dear students! Today, we shall recite, enjoy and understand the poem 'Encroachment'.

Pupil Teacher's Activities	*Students' Activities*	*Components*
One evening after work groping in the mailbox for messages, letters, from nowhere, My fingers encountered Sprigs, twigs and eggs A bird had nested right inside my mailbox. Annoyed I cleared it all except for the eggs.	Pupils are listening and enjoying	Pausing, change in voice
PT will tell the meaning of different words on chalk board 1. Groping = searching 2. Encountered = sudden meeting 3. Sprigs, twigs = dry grass 4. Annoyed = angry	Students note down	1. Movements 2. Visual Switching

(*Contd.*)

Pupil Teacher's Activities	*Students' Activities*	*Components*
PT will explain and then ask some questions from students. PT will ask Suman	Students are giving response	Physical involvement of the students
1. When did the poet grope in the mail box (PT smiles at the right answer)	In the evening	Change in voice gestures
PT ask from Amit		
2. What did she find in the mail box?	She found sprigs, twigs and eggs	Change in interaction style
PT asks from Ajay	Ajay gives incorrect answer	Change in interaction style
3. What did she leave in the mail box?	Nest of the bird	
4. PT again asks this question from Asha. What did she leave in the mail box?	Asha answers: Eggs of the birds	Focussing

PT concludes. Well students! You must have enjoyed and understood the poem.

Observation Schedule

Components	*Average*	*Good*	*Very Good*	*Excellent*
1. Movements				
2. Gestures				
3. Change in voice				
4. Focussing				
5. Change in interaction style				
6. Pause				
7. Audio-visual switching				
8. Physical involvement of the students				

Signature of the Supervisor

MICRO LESSON PLAN—IV

Roll No.:
Subject: English
Topic: Tenses

Skill: Illustration
Duration: 5-6 Minutes
Class: IX

Criteria of the Skill

1. Using different teaching aids for explaining the concepts.
2. Making illustrations effective and interesting.
3. Highlighting important features of the concept.
4. Highlighting the points of difference/similarities between the two ideas.

Opening Statement

Dear students! Today, we shall study about tenses.

Pupil Teacher's Activities	*Students' Activities*	*Components*
PT will show a chart with some rules written on it. PT will explain		
I Present tense in main clause may be followed by any tense in subordinate clause, e.g.— (a) Amit says that Sheela is his sister. (b) She says that Geeta was her friend.	Students are listening	Use of chart for clarity Formulating relevant examples
II. Past tense in main clause must be followed by past tense in subordinate clause, e.g.— (a) Anil said that he wanted to see the match (b) Sheela said that she wanted to become a lawyer	Students note down in their note books	Use of deductive approach
III. Past tense in main clause may be followed by present tense in subordinate clause in case of universal truths, e.g.—	Students are understanding	
(a) The teacher said that the earth moves round the earth. (b) She said that the sun rises in the East.	Students note down	Formulating relevant examples

PT will conclude. Well students, I hope you have understood the rules of tenses.

Observation Schedule

Components	Average	Good	Very Good	Excellent
1. Relevant examples 2. Use of media 3. Approach Deductive/Inductive 4. Students' involvement 5. Demonstration				

Signature of the Supervisors

☞Points to Remember

1. Microteaching is a miniature form of the teaching in which teaching is scaled down in terms of class size, complexity and activities, which focus on developing a specific teaching skill.
2. Various principles are to be considered in Microteaching like:
   - Principle of reinforcement
   - Principle of experiment
   - Principle of precise supervision
   - Principle of continuity
   - Principle of practice
   - Principle of evaluation
3. Questioning Skill
   (a) A good question is key to all educative activities.

(b) By this skill you can diagnose the weak points of the students and make them able to recall and recognize something.
(c) This skill is based on psychological principles and verbal interaction is possible.
(d) Sometimes it appears mechanical and shy students remain quiet.

4. Explaining Skill
   (a) It is a verbal skill useful in knowledge and skill lessons.
   (b) While explaining specific aim should be kept in view.
   (c) Controversial discussion should be avoided.
   (d) It gives the teacher a great confidence.
   (d) It increases the imagination power of the students.
5. Illustration Skill
   (a) It means to exemplify ideas with the help of verbal or non-verbal aids.
   (b) This skill is useful for children.
   (c) Teacher can stimulate the imagination of the students.
   (d) Illustrations should be exact and accurate.
   (e) They should be planned in advance.
6. Stimulus Variation Skill
   (a) You can make your students perform better by giving them stimulus.
   (b) You can use variety of stimulus like movements, gestures and focussing.
   (c) Students become active and teaching learning becomes effective

14

Major Methods of Teaching

The questions what should be taught and how should it be taught are intimately connected because if better methods of teaching are devised, it is possible to learn more. —*Bertrand Russell*

Selection of method depends on the aim. Aims take precedence over methodology, which, in fact, is concerned with how best to achieve specified aims of teaching a language.

Meaning of Method

Chamber's Dictionary describes method as "mode or rule of accomplishing an end: orderly procedure… manner of performance". So, method directly deals with a teacher's manner of performance and the mode he adopts in accomplishing his task and hence, is a means to an end. It assists in reaching out to pupils in a manner that satisfies their intellectual pursuit and hence, is an index of teacher-effectiveness. It also helps a teacher organise his lesson in an orderly manner for ease of communication. Therefore, method of teaching is equally important from the tri-polar nature of a teaching-learning process. It is a body of technique that a teacher adopts in classroom teaching-learning situations to put across the subject-matter in an effective and efficient manner.

It can be said that method is an overall plan of teaching language material based on some approach.

According to Anthony, "Method is an overall plan for the orderly presentation of language material as part of which contradicts and all of which is based upon the selected approach".

(A) TRANSLATION-CUM-GRAMMAR METHOD

"Interpreting is not everybody's art" —*Luther*

This method is the oldest one. It enjoys the widest popularity in the teaching of English especially where it is being taught as a second language, along with the mother tongue and/or a regional language, as in our country. This method was equally important and popular in teaching of other languages like Sanskrit, Persian, Arabic, Latin, Greek, French and German.

It envisages a two-pronged treatment of the language, namely, grammatical explanation and translation of a language pattern, regardless of the purpose for which a particular language pattern is to be taught to the pupils. Explanation is done in terms of rules. As its very title suggest, words, phrases, idioms and sentences are to be taught with the help of mother tongue. It is a word-to-word translation of a given passage in the language to be learnt into the mother tongue or vice versa. Hence, English should also be taught in the same manner because it is believed that the vocabulary and phraseology of a foreign language can be learnt through translation into mother tongue.

It lays emphasis on enrichment of vocabulary for word-to-word translation, "The unit of teaching therefore is 'word', not a 'sentence'." Grammar becomes integral to the teaching process, and is learnt in a deductive manner. The linguistic scope of English is restricted to reading and writing, not speech, not even loud reading. You may simply read and translate.

Objectives of Translation Method

The following are the objectives:

1. This method provides the students a perfect knowledge of the grammar of the language with all possible rules. It is also hoped that the students may be good in writing the language correctly by their existence in translating from the mother tongue into the language learnt.
2. Another objective is to impart the learner a sound knowledge of the vocabulary.
3. It develops the ability to understand and appreciate the literature of the language.

Principles of Translation Method

Following are the principles:

1. Translation interprets the words and phrases of the foreign language in the best possible manner.
2. The foreign phraseology is best assimilated in the process of interpretation.
3. The structure of the foreign language is best learnt when compared and contrasted with those of the mother tongue.

Characteristics of the Method

The main characteristics of the method are as follows:

1. Each word and phrase is translated with the help of mother tongue.
2. Unit of teaching is a word.
3. Rules of grammar are memorised.
4. Grammar is also taught with the help of mother tongue.
5. The text-book occupies an important place in this method.

Merits

Following are the merits of this method:

1. Foreign phraseology is quickly explained. This is the easiest way of explaining the words and phrases of the foreign language. Unit of teaching is a word.
2. It saves the time in understanding so it brings exactness and definiteness.
3. Here a quick memory bond is established between the foreign words and the mother tongue.
4. There is rapid expansion in the vocabulary of the students. Translation from foreign language into the mother tongue enables the pupils to develop their vocabulary rapidly.
5. Teacher's labour is saved. This method is liked by the teacher as he/she is not to put too much labour in making the students understand the exact meaning.
6. The working knowledge of the mother tongue also helps them to learn grammar of a foreign language based on the maxim of learning 'from known to unknown'.
7. It requires no teaching aids in explanation.
8. It is an economical approach as it saves the energy of the teacher.
9. This method can be used in any situation.
10. It can be used in crowded class also.
11. Abstract words and phrases can also be explained with the help of translation method.
12. It is a practical method as it is based on the maxims, from known to unknown, simple to complex, concrete to abstract.

Demerits

1. It is an unnatural method. The natural order of learning a language is listening, speaking, reading and writing. But here the sequence is disrupted and the process starts with teaching of reading.
2. Speech is neglected. Pupils are not provided any practice in oral work, more and more exposure is given in mother tongue and pupils fail to form the habit of speaking the foreign language fluently. Thus, they pay a very heavy price for following this method which has been described by linguists as wasteful.
3. Exact translation is not possible. Language is social by nature and expresses a particular culture shaped by its geographical situation, climate, ethnic background, its people, their nature, habits and modes of living. Every language has its own character best understood and appreciated by those for whom it was originally evolved. Hence, it is difficult to find equivalent words in any other language. Translation in this regard be only approximate.
4. Literal translation spoils the beauty of the language, e.g., the

question does not arise will be translated as:
Ye to sawal hi paida nahi hota, or
Mera dil baag baag ho gaya as My heart became garden garden are the funny examples.

5. The golden rule of translation is that it should neither change the context nor the spirit of the passage. Translation method, because of its inherent inadequacy, fails to capture the delicate expression of English.
6. It teaches English through rules. Translation method attempts to teach English through rules and not by use. As Dr. Ballard has very aptly pointed out, "To speak any language, whether native or foreign, entirely by rules is quite impossible". A language is a skill subject. It is learnt by practice and not by just memorising the rules. The idea will also come in the mind in Hindi and then the learner is supposed to translate it in English which takes time.
7. It is uninteresting. Translation method is dull and mechanical. The learner is a passive recipient of knowledge. He does not take part actively in the learning process.
8. It does not provide pattern practice. A person has learnt a language only when he has made its patterns as habits. But translation method does not provide any practice to the pupils to learn these patterns as habits. It is this lack of practice on the part of the pupils which is responsible for the failure of this method.

Though it is condemned yet it is being used in the schools for its easiness. Use of this method is the main cause of the poor attainment of the pupils in English. It prevents them from self-expression. Sooner the method is given, the better for the pupils.

(B) DIRECT METHOD

"Grammar is not regarded as an end in itself but as means to an end."

—*Champion*

It developed as a reaction to the translation and grammar method. Its main objective is to impart perfect command of foreign languages by making students think in that language. That is the crux of the problem. Make them think in English. As language is speech, children will pick it up in the same natural manner as with regard to their mother tongue.

The term 'Direct Method' was coined in 1901, and originated from France receiving official sanction in 1908. It was revised in 1909, and again in 1925.

Direct method aims at teaching the language directly. The main focus is to create a direct bond between the words and their meanings, thought and expression.

In this context Kirkman opines, "The principle is that a foreign word or word group should be associated with its meaning directly—in other words—without the habitual intervention of the native speech".

P. Gurey defines this method as, "The fullest appreciation of the method is the associating of a complete thought expressed in words with the real experience that would give the occasion an impulse for the thought".

Process

The process is directly associating the words with the things they stand for. For example, word 'Book' is to be taught, the teacher may take the book in hand and say this is my book. Same process may go on without using Hindi. The watch-word is DO NOT TEACH, SHOW.

Direct method, therefore, is activity-oriented. The teacher has to build up a situation to introduce new words and concepts, he may have to even dramatise to create the effect.

Essentials of Direct Method

According to H.E. Palmer, the following are the essential features of the Direct Method:

1. No translation.
2. Grammar, when taught is taught moderately.
3. Concepts (meanings) are taught by means of objects or by natural contexts.
4. Oral teaching takes precedence over reading and writing.
5. The use of disconnected sentences is replaced by the use of connected texts.
6. Pronunciation is taught on phonetic lines.

Aim of Direct Method

The direct method aims at establishing a direct bond between thought and expression, experience and language. The idea is that the learner should experience the new language in the same way in which he/she experienced his/her mother tongue. The learner need not think about mother tongue equivalents.

Principles

1. *Inhibition of the mother tongue*: The pupils are taught new words by actually showing them the objects for which they stand or performing the actions. This enables the pupils to think in English.
2. Sentence is the unit of speech.
3. *Oral training*: Direct method emphasises the value of oral training in learning a foreign language. The pupils are provided sufficient practice in listening to the language and then speaking it.
4. Proceeds from simple line situations to abstract concepts. Hence, proceeds from concrete to abstract.
5. Direct bond between thought and expression is established.

6. To memorise, we must articulate either audibly or mentally which is followed in this method. In this method, learning of grammar is not a pre-condition of learning a language.

Merits of Direct Method

1. *It is a natural method*: The language is taught through demonstration and conversation in context.
2. *Pupils acquire fluency of speech*: It facilitates the fluency of speech. Macnee believes that the direct method is the quickest way of learning and expanding vocabulary.
3. *Facilitates reading*: The reading of English becomes easy and pleasant. The learners remain alert and active. It aims at the practical command of English at the lower stage, but at the higher stage it promotes a habit of critical study.
4. *Aids written work*: The fluency of speech leads to ease in writing. As a matter of fact, the direct association of words and meanings facilitates reading and writing as well.
5. *It makes use of audio-visual aids*: Since language is taught through demonstration, direct method makes use of audio-visual aids. The use of these audio-visual aids facilitates learning and makes lesson interesting.
6. *For teaching idioms*: For teaching idioms, this method is more suitable.
7. *Psychologically sound*: It bridges the gap between the practice and the theory. As the unit of teaching is a sentence not a word, hence not the part but the whole.

Demerits

1. *It is not a complete method*: Direct method is not a complete method as it lays more stress on speech training and other aspects of language learning do not receive attention.
2. *Lack of skilled teachers*: Most of the teachers of English in the Indian schools themselves have poor command on English. How could they be expected to enable a child to have "full command of English" as stipulated in this method? Besides, the time allotted to English in the school programme is rather limited for this kind of a linguistic activity.
3. *Lack of proper atmosphere*: The success of this method depends on congenial atmosphere. For teaching English, a different kind of atmosphere has to be created in the classroom.
4. *Limited application*: This method aims at the active command of a language. This makes its learning more difficult and may be limited as "only the clever child can profit by the method".

   —*Dr. Brettan*
5. *Limited vocabulary*: As the method aims at directly associating words with meaning, it restricts the scope of vocabulary as all words cannot be directly associated with their meanings. For

example, the abstract words like 'honesty', 'truth', 'beautiful' and 'clever' cannot be directly associated with their meaning.

6. *Lack of facilities*: As grammar is to be taught inductively, we need well-equipped laboratories. But we do not have requisite audio-visual materials.
7. *Expensive method*: The cost of equipment and audio-visual material needed for this method is too high which is not possible for every school.

To conclude, in spite of the limitations of the direct method, it can be successfully applied in the lower and middle classes where less explanatory device in teaching English is required. The method is workable, as it provides more opportunities for speech.

(C) BILINGUAL METHOD

The Direct Method does not allow the use of mother tongue but it was felt that sometimes use of mother tongue becomes essential. So, it was recommended that a modified method should be used in which mother tongue may be used wherever necessary. Here, mother tongue is used to achieve the target language.

Bilingual Method is comparatively a recent method invented by Professor C.J. Dodson of Wales. He claims that this method is very effective in learning a foreign language because his experiments in pupils yielded desirable results. The bilingual method stands for the use of two languages, i.e., the mother tongue and the target language in teaching second language. Mother tongue is only used to make the meanings clear, i.e., in a restricted sense whereas in translation method, mother tongue is the basis of all teaching, in Bilingual Method it is used to make the meaning clear so that they may not remain vague to students, and the pattern practice becomes meaningful for them.

Principles of Bilingual Method

1. Teacher first explains the things in simple English, if s/he finds difficulty in making the students understand s/he can explain in mother tongue, thus there is no need to create the situations.
2. The time saved from creating situations for teaching sentences and words of a foreign language can be used for giving more pattern practice to the students.
3. Sentence is the unit of teaching.
4. Unlike the translation method, it is the teacher who uses the mother tongue. Pupils only make practice of patterns in English.

Merits of Bilingual Method

1. *Ensures accuracy*: Meanings become clearer to the student. For example, the word 'dew' when explained in mother tongue brings accuracy.
2. *Ensures fluency*: As the time saved in creating situation is utilised for patter practice, the students acquire fluency.

3. *Less costly:* As in Direct method lot of teaching aids are to be prepared. This involves a lot of expenditure. Bilingual method is less costly as teaching aids are not much required.
4. *It suits the majority of the teachers:* As there is dearth of such skilled teachers who can teach English in direct methods, this method suits majority of the teachers as they are not supposed to create situations and can make use of mother tongue for more clarity and ease.
5. *Judicious use of mother tongue*: Judicious use of mother tongue by the teacher does not spoil the atmosphere of teaching English.
6. *Proper training*: It helps in giving proper training for different skills, i.e., listening, speaking, reading and writing.

Demerits

1. It may create confusion among students due to the contrast between the feature of two languages, i.e., English and mother tongue.
2. It may degenerate into grammar-cum-translation method if the teacher fails to handle the bilingual method properly.
3. It is not useful for higher classes.
4. It spoils the continuity and fluency of the language.
5. It develops an undesirable habit of mixing up the languages.

We can conclude that bilingual method is worth relying but efficient and careful teachers are needed for its success.

(D) AUDIO LINGUAL METHOD OF ENGLISH

There are two basic or classical methods of teaching a language:

(1) Audio Lingual Method, and

(2) Cognitive Code Method.

(1) **Audio Lingual Method of English Language Teaching**: This method of language teaching involves two processes: (1) speaking and (2) listening. The speaking process implies content or ideas first and later on expressions. Listening is concerned with audio-aspect. These days due to globalization, the importance of communication competency is increasing. More emphasis is being given on verbal interaction, so Audio-Lingual method has gained importance. It highlights the purpose of developing language skills, speaking and listening as well.

(2) **Cognitive Code Method of Teaching English Language**: This method is used for developing the understanding of the thinking aspect of a language. It also involves two processes: (i) reading and (ii) writing. The writing process is similar to speaking that content or idea comes first to the mind of child or person, and expression comes afterward. In the reading process, the sequence of these operations are reversed. The expression comes first while reading a passage and content comes later on. This method is effectively used for developing thought process of language learning.

Language learning focusses on four skills—reading, writing, speaking and listening. So, both the methods are essential for teaching a language or to fulfill the aims of teaching all four skills. These methods are effectively used for teaching first language or mother tongue.

In our country, English is taught as first language but mainly as second language. The structural approach is most popular; teaching English as first language.

For oral presentation, memorization of dialogues and other such material are difficult in his/her own language which is even completely understood by the speaker. To enable our students to memorize larger segments at a time, and to deliver dialogue as a whole quickly and confidently with more understanding, we have to find out apt approach and techniques. For this purpose the approach suggested here seems to be fine and suitable.

Here the teacher has to be imaginative and imbibe the process of experimenting with new techniques, many new ways can be found to emphasis the audio aspect of the audio lingual approach.

The main principle has to be kept in mind 'teaching should be subordinate to learning'.

The other principles are—

(i) Language is primarily speech and not writing.
(ii) Language is a set of habits.
(ii) Teach the language and not about the language.
(iv) A language is what its native speakers say, and not what someone thinks they ought to say.
(v) Languages are different.

Main Features of the Audio-Lingual Method

1. The audio-lingual method says that all four skills: listening, speaking, reading and writing are important and independent
2. According to this method language is speech not writing, so it focusses more on listening and speaking.
3. The skills of reading and writing are not neglected.
4. This method lays more stress on dialogue delivery. In the dialogue delivery, one gets sufficient practices of pattern in the form of mimicry and memorizing.
5. Principles of Audio-Lingual method pattern drills are an essential part of this method and used as an important technique for language teaching/learning.
6. The language laboratory is introduced as an important teaching aid. It gives learners an opportunity to mimic a model and memorize language patterns.
7. The audio-lingual method avoids the use of the mother tongue.

Modern Audio-Lingual theory stresses a listening – speaking – reading – writing sequence in foreign-language instruction. The importance of ear training in developing speaking proficiency receives particular emphasis. There are strong arguments, both physiological and psychological for proceeding with speaking practice for training in listening comprehension.

For example:

- More emphasis on ear training facilitates speaking. How a learner speaks well, depends on his/her proficiency in listening skills. One has to be proficient in discriminating between sounds and later on memorization and internalization of proper auditory sound images.
- When there is concentration on one skill, learning becomes easy.
- After listening material is understood then speaking part must come. It increases the confidence of the learner.
- After listening, the individual should be able to discriminate between sounds and should try to retain correct sounds before proceeding to listening to other material.

It is not established that how much time should elapse between listening experiences and speaking practice. Most language programmes neglect listening comprehension. It is generally treated as incidental to speaking rather than as a foundation for it. Classroom exercises are mainly speaking exercises in which the student hears an audio-stimulus and then immediately imitates it or makes some other oral response. When students listen to and participate in exercises with partial sentences, backward build-up pattern-practice and pronunciation drills, they hear unnatural speech. As important as these exercises are for developing skill in speaking, the question may well be asked "When do the students hear the language as it is actually spoken?"

Texts, guides and courses of study frequently contain certain tests for evaluating progress in listening comprehension, but rarely do they contain specific learning materials designed for the systematic development of this skill. Until such materials become available, teachers who wish to do more with listening comprehension can adapt present materials for this purpose.

I. Present the dialogue as a story in the foreign language, but the language should be simple. New words can be explained with visual aids and synonyms etc. The idea should be conveyed, you are not supposed to teach all linguistic element.

II. For dialogue verbalism, role play and stick drawing can be used. Provide an English equivalent.

III. If possible, ask your students record dialogue, listen and practise. This way correct model of pronunciation can be achieved

IV. Have a 'programmed' (in the sense of programmed learning) true false activity based on the dialogue in order to insure comprehension. The teacher presents one or two lines of the dialogue, followed by a question or a statement. The students make a written yes or no response. The teacher checks the students' answers, by a show of hands and then immediately provides them with the correct response. Thus, the teacher receives a feedback regarding the students' comprehension. If number of students have difficulty with the item then teacher may wish to re-read the line of the dialogue that illustrates the correct response or take some other action to ensure comprehension.

V. Repeat entire dialogue, ask your students to close your eyes and listen only. This will help eliminating distraction and increases concentration.

VI. You, as a teacher, can organize role playing activity. Assign roles or leave them free to choose their favorite roles. This will save them from boredom.

VII. Any other kind of recorded material for teaching and correction of language elements can be used.

In the approach being suggested here, speaking practice would begin after items mentioned above. It is expected that students would be anxious and ready to speak at this point. Following the outlined listening comprehension activities, speaking practice might proceed according to this sequence:

(i) Pattern practice based on material taken from the dialogue.
(ii) Mimicry practice of the dialogue itself.
(iii) Memorization of the dialogue.
(iv) Performance of the dialogue in front of class and at seats with students changing roles and partners from time to time.
(v) Dialogue adoption.
(vi) Free (but guided) closely parallel conversation.
(vii) The situations in dialogues.

The Best Method?

Which method should be used has become challenging for a teacher. One cannot depend on any single method. The approach in this regard should be pragmatic, flexible and practical. It all depends on the efficiency and intelligence of a teacher as to which method should be given preference in a particular situation. Some features should be kept in focus by a teacher in selecting a method.

- ➢ Objectives of teaching English.
- ➢ Class in which English is initiated.
- ➢ Ability of the teacher.
- ➢ Age of the students.
- ➢ Availability of audio-visual aids.
- ➢ Social background of the school.

However, it can be said that bilingual method of teaching English is an improvement upon the translation method and direct method. Only one precaution has to be taken that teachers can take the help of mother tongue but do not allow the students to answer in mother tongue, otherwise the method will degenerate into translation method. Even the teacher has to make its use in a restricted sense.

☞Points to Remember

A method helps the teacher in teaching. It is a special tool in the hands of the teacher. A good selection of method is the key to success which helps the teacher till the goal is achieved.

(A) Translation Method

1. It lays emphasis on word to word translation.
2. Rules of Grammar are memorized.
3. This is the easiest way of explaining the words.
4. But speech is neglected.
5. Moreover literal translation is not possible.
6. Use of this method leads to poor attainment in English.

(B) Direct Method

1. Direct method aims at teaching the language directly. The main focus is to create direct bond between the words and their meanings, thoughts and expressions.
2. You are not to take the help of mother tongue.
3. Fluency of speech is achieved.
4. But you don't find appropriate environment and competent teacher to teach with this method.

(C) Bilingual Method

1. Mother tongue is used in a restricted sense, to make the things clear.
2. You need not create the situations.
3. First you can explain the things in simple English, if finds difficulty, in that case you can give clue in mother tongue.
4. It is liked by the teachers.

(D) Audio Lingual Method

1. The verbal interaction or communicative competency is developed by using audio-lingual method of teaching language.
2. This method focusses primarily on the skills of listening and speaking in accordance with the principle that the language is speech; not writing.

15

Approaches of Teaching English

"Approach is related to process and goals of Education."

—Anonymous

"With words alone you don't make the soup."

—*Romanian Proverb*

An approach of teaching indicates an overall plan or procedure to organize teaching-learning process. The main focus of approach is to realize the goals of Education effectively while the method is determined by the nature of content.

There are several approaches which are used in teaching-learning process. The main approaches are discussed below:

A. Structural Approach.
B. Situational approach.
C. Linguistic and Communicative Approach.
D. Project Approach.
E. Inductive-Deductive Approach
F. Whole Language Approach
G. Constructive Approach
H. Multilingual Approach

(A) STRUCTURAL APPROACH

Meaning of Structural Approach

It comprises of two words 'structures' and 'approach'. The word 'structure' relates to the structure whereas 'approach' stands for coming near. In this way the combined meaning of both the words is approaching English on the basis of structures.

In the words of *Menon and Patel,* "The structural approach is based on the belief that in the learning of a foreign language mastery of structures is more important than the acquisition of vocabulary". Hence, teaching English by helping the students to learn the pattern of English has been termed as structural approach.

You should be clear about the difference between Approach and Method. How languages are learnt (the approach) imply different ways of teaching language (the method) and different methods make use of different kinds of classroom activity techniques.

What is a Method?

Method deals with the 'how of teaching'. The methodology of language teaching indicates the sequence to be followed in a language task/ activity and the role of the learners and the 'teacher in it'. A method deals with form of things, i.e., selection, gradation, presentation and repetition.

What is an Approach?

An approach is concerned not only with how but also what to teach. It is a matter of principles derived from experience and is based on the psychological learning of the teaching-learning process. It selects and grades the teaching-learning material, whereas a method is concerned more with the presentation of this graded material in a logical and psychological sequence or manner.

What is a Technique?

It refers to the design and procedural component of a method. It may be described as an implementational sub-process of a method. It specifies the teaching-learning practices as well as the roles of the teachers and learners. According to *Anthony*, a technique is, "a particular trick used by the teacher in the classroom to accomplish an immediate objective. It must be consistent with a method and therefore in harmony with an approach as well".

Description of Structures

Structures are the tools of language. These tools of language are its sounds, stress, rhythm, intonation, its words and their structure. While using these tools, a teacher aims at developing the four-fold linguistic aims of English teaching-learning. We express ourselves in sentences in which the words acquire their meanings depending on their social context. As the context varies, so does the pattern of our sentences. Like any other language, English also has its own patterns.

Structures are not Sentences

Whereas a sentence is a grammatical order of words, the structures need not have any grammatical background. As structures are arranged meaningfully, they act as the tools of language. It is the arrangement of words that is more important than the mere words in isolation, e.g., in the sentence, "Good Morning". "Thank you". There is no grammatical background, yet the idea is communicated. Therefore, structures are not sentences.

The pattern of structure depends on the arrangement of words, e.g., Mohan is a good singer. Is Mohan a good singer? These two sentences convey different meanings due to different arrangement of words. These different arrangement of words or word patterns are called structures and the act of teaching through them is called structural approach.

According to Prof. C.S. Bhandari, "The structural approach to English is teaching the learner certain selected structures in a certain order".

In English there are following four types of structures:

1. *Sentence patterns*, have complete sentences, e.g., There are sixty boys. He plays cricket. I am reading a book.
2. *Phrase patterns*, emphasise phrases, e.g., "in the bag", "under the chair" etc., "with her pen".
3. *Idioms*, are groups of words that must be taught as a whole and not as separate words, e.g., She was born with a silver spoon. Life is not a bed of roses.
4. *Formulas*, are groups of words used regularly on certain occasions. Excuse me, well done.

A structural syllable concentrates on the handling of structural words. These words are:

1. *Prepositions*: such as, in, at, on, from.
2. *Pronouns*: such as, I, me, our.
3. *Helping Verbs*: such as, do, can, shall, could.
4. *Structural Adjectives*: such as, a, this, the.
5. *Structural Adverbs*: such as, ago, even, ever, again.

The structural words form the skelton of the language while the flesh and blood is provided by the content "words"—nouns, adjectives, verbs and adverbs. Structural words are very important for the construction of sentences. It has been found that 100 ordinary sentences in English have about 600 structural words—300 prepositions, 200 pronouns and 100 other structural words. Of the first 100 words in the frequency list, 95 are structural words. Although they occur so frequently, yet they are the most difficult words to teach.

Basic Principles of Structural Approach

Basic principles are listed below:

1. *The importance of speech*: The speech is given importance as the means of fixing firmly all groundwork. If you want to teach structures, importance of speech cannot be neglected.
2. *Formal language habits*: The importance of forming language habits particularly the habit of arranging words in English standard sentence patterns to replace the sentence patterns of the pupil's own language.
3. *Students' activity is essential*: You have to keep in view that students' activity is to be emphasised for teaching structures.

Objectives of Structural Approach

1. To provide a knowledge of about 275 to 300 structures up to 10th class.
2. To provide a vocabulary of around 2,500 words in active vocabulary and 500 words in passive vocabulary.
3. To correlate Grammar teaching with the lessons of English reader, i.e., with reading.
4. To teach listening, speaking, reading and writing.

Features/Characteristics of Structural Approach

1. *Speech is important:* You must know that speech is the necessary means of fixing all groundwork in English. Structures are presented orally and the students practice them through a number of oral drills, such as, repetition, substitution, question answer and chain drill. Reading and writing is taken later on.

2. *Mastery of structures*: In structural approach, emphasis is laid on the mastery of structures. One structure is taken up as the teaching point. It's listening, speaking, reading and writing practice is given to the learners step by step. Actually the effective language learning depends on aural-oral practice. The mastery of structures requires the sufficient practice of four skills.

3. *Formation of language habits*: As the language learning is a habit formation process, in it all the aspects are taken care of as all the four skills are practised. Thus, the structures are well fixed-up.

4. *Situational teaching*: Structural approach puts stress on creating situations with the help of objects, pictures, flashcards, actions and gestures. As this makes the teaching meaningful and effective.

5. *Pupils' activities*: Learning is meant for students. Therefore, the students are expected to be very active in the class for learning a language. Practice and drill is given which ensures effective learning.

6. *Proper selection and gradation later*: The approach involves selection and gradation of structures to be taught. This is done on the principle of frequency, simplicity and teach-ability. Mental level of the learners is also considered. Simple and those structures which have more teach-ability are taken first and the difficult, complex and less often used structures are taken at a later stage.

Multi-skill Approach

Structural approach is a multi-skill approach to teaching of English. Whereas translation method neglects listening and speaking, direct method ignores reading. Structural approach aims at achieving the four fold linguistic aims of teaching English with equal facility in each sphere.

Selection of Structures

It depends upon various factors like ability, age, mental condition, time given to the teaching of English, efficiency of the teacher and the availability of the material. Following are the important principles of selection of structures:

(i) *Simplicity*: The teacher should select those structures which are simple in comparison to difficult and complex structures. The simplicity of structure depends upon its form and meaning. For example, "This is a table" is an easy structure in comparison to, "The patient had died before the doctor reached the hospital".

(ii) *Utility*: It is vividly clear to you that our aim is to impart only working knowledge of English to the pupils, we should teach only those structures which occur more frequently than others.

(iii) *Productivity*: The structures which help in the production of other sentences should be selected first. "This is a table" has more productivity than "Do the needful".

(iv) *Teach-ability*: Teach-ability means that the structures should be such which can easily be demonstrated in the class in a realistic way, e.g., I am writing has more teach-ability than he is jumping.

Gradation of Structures

Grading of the structure means to put teaching material in an order. While grading structures, we should also ensure proper grouping and sequence. Grouping means what structure fits into what, and sequence indicates which structure follows which. Grading depends on the mental level of learners, their age, their educational and socio-cultural background and the aims with which we teach language.

F.G. French has suggested the following scale for grading the patterns of English during the first three years of learning English.

1. Simple two-part patterns:
   (i) He/went.
   (ii) Sita/danced.
   (iii) His brother/went away.
2. Simple three-part patterns:
   (i) That/is/a table.
   (ii) I/bought/a pen.
   (iii) She/was/singing.
3. Simple four-part patterns:
   (i) Hari/told/me/a story.
   (ii) I/gave/her/a gift.
   (iii) The teacher/asked/him/to write.
4. The negative form of patterns:
   (i) She did not write.
   (ii) They were not reading.
   (iii) Mother did not cry.
5. The interrogative forms:
   (i) Where do you live?
   (ii) How are you?
   (iii) Did you purchase a car?
6. Commands or request:
   (i) Stop here.
   (ii) Please give me your book.
   (iii) Go away.
7. Patterns with there:
   (i) There are thirty students in the class.

Advantages of Structural Approach

Following are the advantages of structural approach:

(i) *Carefully selected and graded language items*: As the structures are carefully selected and graded, and their repetition help the learner to make it their habit.

(ii) *Speech is emphasised*: It is said that language is speech and not writing. According to it much importance is given to speech.

(iii) *Habit formation is stressed*: As you know that language learning is a habit formation process. To cultivate habit, intensive drills are given.

(iv) *Language is taught in situations*: Items of vocabulary and structures are taught in appropriate situations.

(v) *Pupils become active*: Pupils who are asked to do drill work are very active participants in the teaching-learning process. They have opportunities to speak and practise structures.

Limitations

(i) *Uninteresting reading material*: You must know that rigid sequencing results in uninteresting reading material. There is need for some flexibility.

(ii) *Writing and vocabulary expansion*: Speech is overemphasised.

(iii) *Pupils' knowledge of mother tongue is not exploited*: There is no place for mother tongue. But pupils find it difficult to understand everything in English.

(iv) *Mechanical drilling*: Over-emphasis is given on drill work and that too does not ensure habit formation.

(v) *Not suited for senior classes*: This approach is fine for early classes but not for senior classes. Because senior level students must be given free hand.

Evaluation of the Structural Approach

Most of the allegations against structural approach are because of mixing it up as a method. Structural approach is not a method. It is a viewpoint, a matter of principles involved in the teaching of a language. Approach, therefore, is more pragmatic in its outlook and may go with any method.

(B) SITUATIONAL APPROACH

Language is always used in situations. A child learns his mother tongue easily and quickly, without much effort because every language item is presented before him (her) in its corresponding situation. In the beginning, he hears all the people around him speaking the language. Later on, he tries to speak the language to get his needs fulfilled. No body explains to him the meaning of words, even then he learns automatically e.g., His mother gives him water and says *Gilas se pani piyo*. He automatically establishes the relationship between the word and the thing for which it has been used. In this way she/he unconsciously develops a link between the meaning of the word and the situation in which it is used. Situational Approach is based on the belief that the second language should be learnt in the same manner in which the child has learnt his mother tongue. It tries to establish close relationship between the meaning and the situations. The situation may be real or contrived. Once a language item is presented in a particular situation, it leaves lasting effect on the minds of students. The child would use the expression whenever he would come across the same situation. Thus, the expression would become part of automatic habit.

Principles

This approach is based on the following principles—

(a) Mother tongue is always learnt in situations. Therefore, the second language should also be learnt in the same manner.

(b) The situations may be real or contrived. Once the bond is established between the expression and the situation, it becomes a habit.

(c) Situations make the teaching-learning process effective and interesting.

Procedure

Unlike the traditional method, the teacher here presents the situations, may be through actions (dramatization, mimicry etc.), or pictures (films, charts, models, figures, sketches etc.)

The teacher may speak some sentences like—
My name is Sanjay.
I get up early at 5 o'clock.
I like to play cricket.
I also participate in literary activities.
I am fond of travelling.

Teacher may ask some questions that on the basis of this pattern you introduce yourself.

Like:

What is your name?
When do you get up?
Which game do you play?
Do you participate in literary activities?
Are you fond of travelling? etc.
Situations may be created through pictures.
e.g., you want to illustrate a story, Lion and the Mouse.

Various pictures can be used like:

(a) Lion sleeping under a shady tree.
(b) Mouse jumping on its body.
(c) Lion caught the mouse in its paw.
(d) Mouse begged for mercy.
(e) Lion let it go.

(f) Lion caught in a net and crying.
(h) Mouse heard it and cut it.

On the basis of the same pictures, teacher can put questions, what do you see in picture nos. (a) to (h).

In this way imaginative power of the students will be developed, and procedure will become interesting also. But thorough planning is must. Situations must be appropriate. Sufficient practice should be given to make it their habit.

Merits

(a) This approach makes the learning easy.
(b) Learners remain active.
(c) Rote memorization is reduced and lasting memory takes place.
(d) Grammar is taught inductively.
(e) Imagination power is developed.
(f) This approach is psychologically sound. As the words are taught in situations not in isolation.

Demerits

(a) It is not complete in itself. All the aspects of language can't be taught through this approach.
(b) Reading and writing skills are being ignored.
(c) Grammar is not given due place.
(d) Printed text has its own importance. But it is also neglected here.
(e) We need active and trained teachers to use this approach. But we don't have.

(C) LINGUISTIC AND COMMUNICATIVE APPROACH

"Communication is the sharing of ideas and feeling in a mood of mutuality."
—Edgar Dale

'Communicative Competence'—A New Thinking

From the mid-seventies, 'communicative competence' (Hymes, 1972) became an over–riding concern of language pedagogy. It was felt by many that learners who were taught the structural approach were "structurally competent but communicatively deficient". Linguists pointed out that whereas the native speakers had an intuitive grasp of the linguistic, cognitive, affective and socio-cultural meanings expressed by language forms, a second language learner was unable to interpret the socio-linguistic conventions.

Developed and practised in the Far East, particularly China and Japan, the communicative approach to English teaching means "communicative competence" which includes linguistic competence plus an ability to use the language appropriately. Today, China and Japan have perhaps the largest number of people engaged in learning of English. It is due to American influence on both of them which has paid them rich and handsome dividend over the years.

Theoretical Assumptions

Underlying Rationale

The emphasis is on learning by 'use'. Chinese instructions followed the same strategy who forced the students to open their mouth and speak. Law of use is a very significant principle of learning and this approach fully exploits it. For them 'use' rightly means 'communication'. It lays emphasis on the social aspect of the language.

For example, a student might say, "shut the door, will you?" to a classmate. But to a stranger it would be more appropriate to say "Excuse me, would you mind closing the door?" The use of the formal version with a classmate or the informal version with a stranger would be equally likely to cause offence. While a native speaker knows how to choose the suitable thing to say in a given situation, a second language learner may unintentionally send out signals or formality and social distance of increasing familiarity and informality in wrong situations.

Language is always used in a context in a real-life situation, in a conversation one constantly has to interpret what is being said. To exemplify this point about interaction with context let us take an example: a straightforward sentence such as, 'why don't you close the door'? To quote Littlewood, "From a structural viewpoint, the sentence is unambiguously an interrogative. From a functional viewpoint, however, it is ambiguous". In some circumstances, it may function as a question—for example, the speaker may genuinely wish to know why his companion never closes a certain door. In others, it may function as a command—this would probably be the case if a teacher addressed it to a pupil who had left the classroom door open. In yet, another situation it could be interpreted as a plea, a suggestion or a complaint. In other words, whereas the sentence's structure is stable and straightforward, its communicative function is variable and depends on specific situational and social factors. A second language learner may not be able to interpret or judge the intention of a speaker, underlying assumptions/rationale.

(i) How one reacts verbally, depends on mental set-up. If you want your students to communicate effectively then create real-life situations.
(ii) Freedom on part of the speaker is essential, as it gives them a chance to manage the things themselves.
(iii) Exploit the thematic immediacy. Create situations which are real and which have thematic immediacy. If one is teaching English to troop soldiers, their thematic immediacy and real-life experiences must become the nexus of the linguistic enterprise. In the classroom, it should develop on the thematic immediacy

of the pupils, their interests and objectives. Create the need as the need compels a child to invent a language.

(iv) According to communicative approach, use of language has to be achieved through use itself.

(v) Content is important than the form. Not artificiality but the real life contact with the language helps the students to learn the language in its authenticity.

(vi) Adequate exposure of the target language is really helpful in communicating.

(vii) In this approach, objective of teaching English is the development of communicative competence where all the four skills when learnt help in effective communication.

(viii) Language learning is an active development process, and demands a higher degree of initiative from the learners. Communicative approach does not advocate for habit forming, as the communicative competence is something that involves functioning of the mind, giving sufficient credit to the learners' intelligence. Learning is viewed as a developmental process which must necessarily go beyond quantitative increase to qualitative change.

Unlike the traditional teaching, the communicative approach to learning English considers competence development as central role of learning a target language. It is the logical corollary of their educational philosophy which considers education as developmental.

Role of the Learners and Role of the Teacher

The communicative approach demands a high degree of initiative from learners and assumes that learners take a central role in learning. The learners learn to communicate not only by interacting with the teacher but through interaction with peers in organised small groups or pair-work. By making an effort to use whatever language is available to them, the learners not only use their linguistic knowledge and skills but also become aware of their own language needs in different kinds of communicative situations. Arranged in pairs or small groups, the learners not only learn from each other but also get to understand that successful communication is a joint responsibility and neither the listener nor the speaker individually can be held responsible for any breakdown in communication. This kind of cooperative learning thus makes the classroom learner–centred instead of teacher-centred and teacher–directed.

The teachers' role is one of a facilitator and organiser. With the learners as active agents in the process of learning, the teacher has to adopt a policy of 'non-intervention' especially when an activity is in progress. The teacher, according to Richard and Rodgers, has to suppress 'the inclination to supply gaps in lexis, grammar and strategy'. However, as an assessor the teacher needs to be aware of what is going on, and at the end of an activity provide feedback on the activity, suggest alternatives and assist the groups in self-correction. The teacher, thus not only organises the setting up of interactive tasks and activities and facilities by offering help if needed but also monitors and counsels whenever required.

Pre-requisites of Linguistic Communicative Approach

1. *Linguistic competence*: Linguistic competence is essential for learning a language. This way a learner can make use of language according to his needs and requirements.

2. *Learning of different forms of linguistics*: Linguistic is the science of language. It deals with different aspects of language. If a learner has an understanding of linguistics only then he can make use of language.

3. *Appropriate skills and strategies*: The language learner should develop all the four skills. Moreover, he/she should have the ability to select the strategy helpful for using language in different situations.

4. *Social setting*: For speaking the language effectively, social setting plays a very important role. The speaker should use the language suitable to the requirements of the audience. You should not forget that language is a social activity rather than as a means of individual self-expression.

You can communicate one thing in different ways:

(i) Please give me your book.
(ii) Could you please give me your book?
(iii) Would you mind giving me your book?
(iv) Could I trouble you to give me your book?

All the above said four ways are linguistic forms where different structures have been used. The user of the language should keep some strategy in mind and then he succeeds in communicating properly.

In the communicative function of the language, how do we say is also important along with what we say. It is because by a shift of stress from one syllable to another its meanings are changed. You can notice the sentence given below where the change in stress changes the meaning of utterances e.g. Mr. Gupta is my English teacher—can be spoken in different ways by shifting the stress.

(a) **Mr. Gupta** is my English teacher (Mr. Gupta only, not someone else).
(b) Mr. Gupta is my English **teacher** (why do you deny it?).
(c) Mr. Gupta is **my** English teacher (mine, not yours).
(d) Mr. Gupta is my **English** teacher (teacher of English not of Geography)

While communicating through spoken language, pause, wrong use of pause, and lack of pause make big differences in meanings.

Post Communicative Era: Changing Trends

The old traditional classroom practices and problems have been looked upon by linguists and experts in a different way.

You might have noticed that sometimes students are structurally competent but communicatively incompetent as they have not learnt to formulate expressions in communicative situations. Increased attention to the teaching of lexis (vocabulary) and a vast range of conventional expressions is one of the most important development of the post communicative era.

Instead of isolated sentences which were mostly used for drill and practice in the structural approach, the emphasis is now on providing suitable contexts. Now, the aim of learning language is not to discover grammar but to understand its meaning and functions in situations.

Advantages of Communicative Approach

1. You might have noticed your confidence when you communicate effectively. It gives you a sense of satisfaction.
2. Communicative approach is practical in use.
3. This approach is situational, meaningful, motivating others and is self-rewarding.
4. It lays stress on the functional value of the language.
5. It develops the speech ability.

Conclusion

Communicative Approach is the latest application of teaching language. A systematic theory of this application should be developed and the teachers of English language should be trained in this application. So that they may use it whenever it is required.

(D) PROJECT APPROACH

The Project Approach aims at bringing harmony in the curriculum, content of studies and the school. What is more important in Project Approach is that the child is the centre of all school activities. It does not 'impose on a child. It rather offers opportunities of freedom—freedom of thinking, freedom of doing and freedom of learning to a child.

Let us see how Project Method can be of utmost benefit in the learning process of English.

At Junior Level

The teacher's task at this level is to provide them with actual situation. The teacher will bear in mind the aims and objectives of teaching English and also the methods by which the pupils can pick up the linguistic habits. Emphasis on oral work is required.

Teacher can take them to the garden, observe everything and then write about his/her observation. The teacher may take them to the post-office and leave them free to know and arrange their information in a psychological order.

It is better and always safe to provide such situations to the children in which their energies find a free outlet instead of dictating essays. Projects like these may be selected even before reading and writing begin.

At Senior Level

By this time children grow in age and experience and they also get accustomed to such projects. By now they also know though unconsciously to organize projects themselves in their classrooms. Projects offer them a change. Here too, the teacher may simply initiate by way of suggesting them.

We are fast moving towards industrialization. It would be advisable if we take our students to these industries and leave them with those people, at least for a day, to learn the setup of such industries, the working of the machinery, its organization and all about their language. They will get a good direct experience. Cultural shows, debates, dramas, one act plays etc. are nothing but working on the principles of project. Excursions, visit to historical places, the Parliament or visits to holy places etc., all are ways wherein the process of project method is at full display and an experience in itself.

It is especially beneficial at this stage as the pupils need to expand their vocabulary along with their experience. This will be possible by offering them opportunities for expanding their observation and knowledge and for grasp of life situations, take them to the actual work place like hospital, industry, post-office, etc. No single printed essay, lecture or teaching aids can give them a comprehensive idea of real place that they are taken to and learn themselves through first-hand experience.

(E) INDUCTIVE-DEDUCTIVE APPROACH

A deductive and an inductive approach basically differentiate in lesson procedures, learner roles and usage of metalanguage in the teaching process.

In deductive approach first we teach grammatical rules, then give examples. Here we proceed from whole to parts. First, the teacher give examples after the rules then the students are asked to frame their own examples. Whereas in inductive approach language is taught from parts to the whole.

Deductive approach makes the learner passive whereas inductive approach makes the learner active as they explore the rules themselves. In deductive approach, learners understand the language easily in written as well as in spoken form.

The role of the teacher is deductive, approach is supreme. The authority lies in the hands of teacher. On the other hand, in inductive approach, the teacher is democratic. In other words it can be said that deductive approach is teacher-centered and inductive approach is students-centered.

That is to say, while the process of learning is experimental in inductive approach it is more traditional and descriptive in deductive approach. According to Thorubury (1999), the class where students are involved in the lesson actively is quite reasonable since it provides more comfortable and motivating environment for them. In inductive approach students discover the rules themselves, it gives them profound knowledge of language. Students remain active. They feel more democratic and this autonomy makes them good learners.

For example, when learners read a text with present continuous tense, it is remarked that it is unnecessary to apply inductive approach if the grammatical rules are quite simple, but complex grammatical items should be taught inductively in order to demonstrate usage of the rules in sentences clearly.

While grammar is learnt consciously in deductive approach, it is learnt subconsciously in inductive approach. So it can be said that inductive approach is more natural.

We have to keep in mind that the needs, age, background and level of the learners are different so they learn in different manners. The teachers have to adopt different strategies. If our target group is adult learner, we use deductive approach preferably but for young learners we choose inductive approach. As young learners explore grammatical structures from the examples rather than learning than deductively since they are more likely to learn by doing because grammatical rules are complex and abstract for them.

It can be concluded that inductive approach is natural. Moreover, we should keep in mind that students possess individual differences which are to be taken care of.

(Γ) WHOLE LANGUAGE APPROACH LEARNING BY IMITATION AND WHOLE METHOD

Most of the activities a child learns by imitation in life. The same is the case in language learning. Imitation is natural with a child. A child imitates what she/he sees or hears. Learning a language is not an intellectual activity.

Every language is a complex collection of sounds which seem to be confusing initially. But slowly, as the child listens to it more and more, these complex sounds begin to acquire a meaning. Listening comes first in learning a language. Understanding and Comprehension involves hearing of distinct sounds that go to make up a language. The next step is the reproduction of these sounds at first incoherently, and then correctly. Initially a child reproduces only words. It has its own peculiar vocabulary for its favourite things– 'it's bottle', 'it's mother, father', 'it's toy etc. Gradually he/she picks up meaningful words. By the age of two or three years, the child begins to speak two or more words together, so that meaningful words give rise to meaningful phrases and sentences, so that child learns to communicate, and expresses his/her basic urge.

The child imitates by trial and error. A bond of association is established between a situation and its right response. Learning experiences of the child enables him/her to attach various meanings to words and phrases.

Acquiring a new language becomes a pleasant activity involving a satisfying sense of achievement when it is attempted as one intelligible whole, and not analysed into its various components of words and their relevant meaning. Here the example of Gestalt psychology is advantageous that all knowledge should be presented as a whole. In this way the learner will get an idea of the language. The old traditional translation method and formal grammar teaching have become outdated. These days more emphasis is given on imitation of the dialogue. In the manner students are asked to repeat the sentences again and again to reach the right structure pattern. This mimicry memorization is accepted very well. But in this technique shy and introvert students do not participate. They hesitate to interact individually but in a group it works.

For beginners drill work in group repetitions is good. The student is less inhibited, in a group response, he/she recites more readily and everyone has a chance to practise every sentence. In the end, it can be said that teaching and learning process must be lively so that there is no monotony.

(G) CONSTRUCTIVIST APPROACH TO LEARNING

The advocates of constructive approach to learning emphasise the active role of the learner. It is concerned with how individuals build up certain elements of their cognitive or emotional apparatus. One's self concept, beliefs, identity and individual knowledge are taken care of in it.

Vygotsky's social constructivism emphasizes on that social interaction. Cultural tools and activity shape individual development and learning. By participating in a broad range of activities with other learners internalize the outcomes produced by working together. They acquire new strategies and knowledge of the world and culture. Although Vygotsky's theory is interested in understanding developments within an individual, it relies heavily on social interactions and cultural contexts to explain learning. He is, thus, both an individual and social constructivist. For example, in his concept of the zone of proximal development—the area where a child can solve a problem is where culture and cognition create each other. Culture creates cognition when the adult uses tools and practises from the culture (language, maps, music, stories) to steer the child towards goals and the cultural values (reading, writing, dancing, singing). The term constructivism is also used to talk about how knowledge is created in disciplines like Science, Math, Economics, and History etc. Even though there is no single constructivist theory, man constructivist approaches are recommended:

- Complex challenging learning environments and authentic

tasks.

- Social negotiation and shared responsibility as a part of learning.
- Multiple representations of content.
- Understanding that knowledge is constructed.
- Student-centered instruction.

According to constructivists, students learn more when they come across the complex problems where they have to do something.

Constructivism is a meta concept. According to this theory it can be said that each listener or reader will understand and use the content in his/her own way. This will be influenced by the information and experiences which already exist in the learner's mind.

History of Constructivism

The psychological roots of constructivism began with the developmental work of Jean Piaget (1896-1980), the development of the mind was highlighted, but unfamiliar experiences which do not accommodate into the mind, change its organization. Piaget proposed four stages in human development:

- The sensory motor stage
- Pre-operational stage
- Concrete operational stage
- Formal operational stage

For Piaget, the development of human intellect proceeds through adaptation and organization. Adaptation is a process of assimilation and accommodation, where external events are assimilated into existing understanding but unfamiliar events which don't fit with existing knowledge, are accommodated into the mind, thereby changing its organization.

John Dewey was of the viewpoint that education depends on knowledge and it depends on the situation asks what kind of experiences learners' draw out. He opines that each learner constructs his/her knowledge.

Vygotsky and Piaget's theories are often contrasted with each other in terms of individual cognitive constructivism (Piaget) and social constructivism (Vygotsky).

Principles of Constructivist Learning

1. By the use of sensory outputs, learners try to comprehend meaning.
2. Physical activity influences the learning.
3. Vygotsky gave the examples how language and learning are interrelated.
4. Learning is a social activity.
5. It is the context which provide meaning to learning.
6. As we gain more knowledge, we learn more so learning is influenced by knowledge.
7. Learning is not spontaneous. By practice we learn more, so it

takes time.

8. Motivation is a necessary component because it causes the learner's sensory apparatus to be activated. Relevance, curiosity, fun, accomplishment achievement and other motivators facilitate learning.

Nature and Role of Learners

The learners in constructive class-rooms always remain busy in constructing their own knowledge. The nature of learners is always inquisitive and always willing to learn.

Following are the points pertaining to the nature and role of the learners:

(i) The learner is active.
(ii) The learner is willing to learn.
(iii) The learner is willing to assimilate the knowledge and facts.
(iv) The learner believes in experimenting and discovering.
(v) The learner is ready to apply knowledge acquired in practical fields.

(H) MULTILINGUAL APPROACH TO LANGUAGE TEACHING

Multilingual approach means using two or more languages.

India is a land of diversity. Different people speak different languages. A person of Tamil Nadu does not speak Hindi. So, s/he can't understand Hindi of a person from North India. However, s/he can understand English.

With the help of the English language we communicate with each other. It has been called a link language. All development in trade, commerce, medicine and literature is available in English. In the era of globalisation, if we do not learn English, we will lack behind. It is an international language. It is also used in courts and offices. It has become essential for national integration in India.

The multilingual approach has evolved from a partnership between the Flinders University of South Australia, School of Education and the Department for Education and Child Development (DECD), Teaching and Learning Services (TLS). The key aim of this joint work is to foster student language learning in the primary years through a due language literacy approach that scaffolds literacy development within and across languages. It seeks to answer the question: What is it that we can achieve as a result of connecting literacy and languages education in the primary school?

Through this approach students learn to transfer their skill from one language to another. It also influences the areas of oral—comprehension, vocabulary need, phonemic awareness, recognition, knowledge, spelling, translation, grammatical conventions, writing and reading comprehension.

If the proper conditions are given a child can learn two or more languages easily.

The advantages that multilingual teaching exhibits over monolinguals are not restricted to linguistic knowledge only but extend outside the area of language. These are the various factors:

1. Cognitive
2. Social
3. Personal
4. Academic
5. Professional

Merits of Teaching-Learning in a Multilingual Classroom

1. This approach enhances awareness and sharpens language.
2. One learns more rapidly the native language and display improved performance in other language skills.
3. One becomes efficient communicator in L1.
4. Students become capable to understand mother tongue.
5. Vocabulary is increased.
6. Listening skill is improved.
7. Students become efficient readers.
8. Their thinking and problem-solving skills are also improved.
9. A person with multilingual approach has a broader vision.

Multilingual have broad vision. It leads to better understanding. Multilingual can expand their personal horizons and – being simultaneously insiders and outsiders – see their own culture from a new perspective, not available to monoglots enabling the comparison, contrast and understanding of cultural concepts.

With the multilingual approach any kind of problems can be solved easily. Critical thinking is improved which leads to better understanding and appreciation of people of other countries. It teaches a person to respect all races with their languages. It increases the job avenues of youngsters. This way they can be comfortable in any country.

Thus, just like Latin, once used to be taught as an academic exercise, mental gymnastics with the aim of cognitive training, it has been demonstrated that people who know usually think more flexibly than monolinguals.

Principles of Multilingualism in the Classroom

This way we can teach students to become better citizens of the world. Moreover, multilingualism teach students to appreciate, accept and honour different groups of people. Teachers can use multilingual approach to teach students in all subject areas including social studies, language, art, and music etc.

By using multilingual approach we can teach about diverse cultural groups. We can set an example in our school and community by studying and respecting all languages, paying equal status to them. This way we can teach our students to respect all languages and cultures of all groups. By adopting multilingual approach we can teach our students the lesson of equality between cultures, race and gender. Leave your students free to express their ideas in their first language.

Teacher's Role

Teacher is the role model for students. The teacher's personality sets the tone and standard for classroom participation and interaction. In a multilingual environment, the teacher must be aware of the background of students.

Teacher should encourage students to interact and participate in classroom discussion and dialogue but recognize that the cultural background of some students may make them hesitant to be vocal in the classroom. A multicultural classroom provides the opportunity for students to enrich themselves by bringing their multiple perspectives and background to a discussion of various issues.

The teacher can form small groups as it encourages them for interactive approach to learning. By multilingual approach s/he can teach students the cultural background of all languages. Students can take interest in learning and respecting languages of others. Initiating discussion on some topics can motivate students to participate and express their views openly in their own language without hesitation.

☞Points to Remember

A. Structural Approach

1. Method deals with the 'how of teaching'. But Approach deals with 'what to teach' whereas Technique refers to the design and procedural component of a method.
2. Structural Approach to English is teaching the learner certain selected structures in a certain order.
3. It should be clear to you that here speech is emphasised, pupils become active, language is taught in situations and habit formation is stressed.
4. It is to be noted that over-emphasis on drill makes the process dull and does not ensure habit formation.

B. Situational Approach

1. Situations make the teaching-learning process effective and interesting.
2. Grammar is taught inductively.
3. Imagination power is developed.
4. Rote memorization is reduced.
5. It should be clear to you that all the aspects of language can't be taught through this approach.

C. Linguistic and Communicative Approach

1. Here the objective of Teaching English is the development of communicative competence.
2. Linguistic competence, different forms of linguistics, appropriate skills and strategies, Social settings are pre-requisites of communicative approach.
3. This skill gives you confidence.
4. The basic idea behind this approach is to convey the message or thought.

D. Project Method Approach

1. Child is the centre of all school activities.
2. Teacher can provide situations so that students can pick up the linguistic habits.
3. Students can expand their vocabulary and knowledge by their own experiences in real-life situations.

E. Inductive-Deductive Approach

1. In Inductive approach examples are given first then the rules, but in deductive approach rules comes first then the examples.
2. Inductive approach is student centred, whereas the deductive approach is teacher centred.
3. In inductive approach Grammar is learnt subconsciously, but in deductive approach Grammar is learnt consciously.

F. Whole Language Approach

1. All knowledge should be presented in an organized whole manner.
2. Language learning becomes pleasant when it is attempted as a whole, and not analyzing into various components of words and their meanings.

G. Constructive Approach

1. The learners in constructive class-rooms always remain busy in constructing their own knowledge.
2. Here the learners are willing to assimilate the knowledge and facts.

H. Multilingual Approach

1. One learns more rapidly the native language and display improved performance in other language skills also.
2. By using multilingualism approach we can teach about diverse cultural groups. We can set an example in our schools and community by studying and respecting all languages.
3. This way we can teach students to become better citizens of the world.

16

Development of Linguistic Skills

Language involves four basic skills, i.e., listening, speaking, reading and writing. Learning to speak a language is always the first step in learning, reading and writing. Listening and speaking are intimately related to each other. Though listening is a recognition skill and speaking is the production skill, both the skills are interdependent.

Language exists first in its spoken form. It can be learnt primarily through speech. The ability to understand spoken English is needed in ordinary conversation, listening to lectures, speech, talks, running commentaries and news bulletins etc.

Development of Linguistic Skills

"Language is the flesh and blood of our culture."

—*Anonymous*

Learning of a language is a skill subject. Every skill requires a lot of practice. In the teaching learning of English the main four skills are: listening, speaking reading and writing. None of the skill is acquired automatically. One needs to practice. It should be clear to you that language learning is a habit formation process. One has to acquire new habits. For this correct models have to be imitated. Language learning is just like other skills as swimming, dancing and cooking. For all these you need constant-practice.

All the four skills are equally important.

Followings are the four Skills

Listening | Speaking | Reading | Writing

Listening is the basis of language learning, other skills are equally important. Knowing the meaning and rules of language is not enough. You should have command over all the four skills, for which you need to develop habit. A teacher must create a natural environment for learning all these skills.

Before we discuss how to develop the listening skill, let us discuss some conditions which are essential for listening skill. They are:

(a) Pupils should be able to understand the meaning of words

conveyed through sounds.
(b) Sounds must have meaning and sense.
(c) Their interest and attention is must.

Aims of listening skill must be clear to you. Following are the important ones:
(a) To lay the foundation of learning of a language.
(b) To develop understanding of concepts, ideas and facts.
(c) To provide verbal interaction between persons.
(d) To provide basis for education process.

If you want to teach listening skill, you have to take care of these principles:
(a) Sound should be clear, audible with correct pronunciation.
(b) Teachers and learners both have to be ready.
(c) Repetition is must for retention.
(d) Different activities have to be prepared at different stages of listening skill.
(e) Lastly, it depends on the efficiency of the teacher how she/he exploits the situation and which kind of listening material he/she selects for what particular levels.

Let us be clear about the three kinds of material—
- Authentic listening material,
- Recorded listening material, and
- Live listening material.

A. DEVELOPMENT OF LINGUISTIC SKILL OF LISTENING

"Listening skill is the basis of good learning of the language."

—*Proverb*

Exposure to variety of structures and sound is the first step to develop listening.

Oral work is the basis of good learning of the language. In fact, it strengthens the foundation of language learning. If a teacher develops the oral habit in students, reading and writing practice will come automatically and easily to the students. Following are the different ways of conducting oral work.

(1) *Reproduction exercises*: The teacher produces a sound, word and sentence and asks the students to reproduce the same first sound in group then individually.

(2) *Asking questions*: Teacher asks the question and students answer. This way their listening and speaking skill is developed.

(3) *Role play*: The teacher may ask some students to play the role of somebody, e.g., a painter, a doctor, an officer, a clerk and a businessman. This can be done through dialogue delivery, face expression and deportment.

(4) *By performing actions*. The teacher performs actions and speaks, and students are asked to observe and speak and perform accordingly.

(5) *Showing a film or chart*: The students are shown a film or chart and then they are asked to speak few sentences on it. They get opportunity of listening and speaking.

(6) *By giving an outline of a story*: The teacher gives an outline of a story and the students are asked to think and then speak a few sentences about it. This gives the whole class a lot of listening and speaking practice.

(7) *Through oral composition*: Oral composition develops the skill in speaking for a few minutes. Any topic is taken up and the students are asked to speak on it. The teacher may provide some guidance wherever needed. This exercise gives a lot of listening and speaking practice.

(8) In every class some time must be reserved for giving listening and speaking practice to the students. It paves the way to good learning of the language. While teaching anything of English, may be grammar, poetry, prose composition, approach should be made the basis of teaching. It will lead to effective teaching of English.

Listening as Stimulus

The listening material can be used as a stimulus to set the learner thinking along particular lines or put them in a particular mood.

Characteristics of an effective Oral Skills Lesson

Some of the important aspects to keep in view while planning and working on oral skill lessons are:

(i) *The simplicity of the task*: The task should be interesting for the learner as it gives purpose and direction. If the teacher needs to intervene to spell out or explain the task, then the purpose is defeated.

(ii) Integrating listening with speaking, reading and writing.

As in real life, we listen and respond either through speaking, reading or writing.

Listening as Input

(1) *As a Model*: Listening material can be used as a model for giving directions. Suppose one is given direction on telephone conversation how to reach a particular spot. Similarly listening to sports commentary can be used in writing a report or after listening to instruction one reads brochures and other tourist information. This way listening can be integrated with speaking repeatedly then learners would be wasting much of the discussion time in just listening reading or writing skills. Listening to instructions can be used in interesting role-play.

(2) *Preparation*: The task should be easy to prepare. It is difficult for teacher to hold oral skills if preparatory work is lengthy.

(3) *Tangible result*: A task must generate thought and its end result must be in the form of a tangible output. The learners may be required to write down the result, give a short talk, make a presentation or report and so on.

(4) *Language practice*: Sufficient language practice should be given through the task. Efficient task is that when given sufficient speech practice.

(5) *Interaction*: Task should be open-ended which gives the learners the opportunities to use their own ideas in an imaginative and creative way.

(6) *Interest level*: The task must be interesting but not too easy as to create boredom. So it should be challenging so as to generate activities.

(7) *Organisation*: Students tend to learn more in groups provided it is organised properly.

Advantages of Oral Work

1. Oral work improves the comprehension ability of the students.
2. Skill of speaking is also developed.
3. It gives a lot of pleasure.
4. It removes hesitation of the speaker and makes a good speaker.
5. It enables the learners to make all the links and associations in his mind required to fix the words.
6. A good speaker usually possesses a good personality.
7. It encourages the students for active participation in teaching-learning process.
8. The students learn to form new patterns and structures.

Suggestions for Good Oral Work

1. The class should be divided into small groups. A group should be of 8 to 10 students. Individual attention should be given to each student.
2. Teacher should come well-prepared.
3. Good teachers should be recruited.
4. One or two periods per section per week may be allotted for oral work exclusively.
5. When oral work is given to an individual, no interruption should be there. That would affect fluency and it would discourage the learner.

Importance of Drill in Listening and Speaking Practice

Drill is a device for fixing the subject matter in the minds of the students. It can be given in chorus/groups and then individually. Usually drill in chorus is given in junior classes. At this stage, base can be made strong because the language learning is a skill and it requires a lot of drill work. Thompson and Wyatt have rightly said, "The power of expression in language is a matter of skill rather than of knowledge, it is power that grows by exercise not merely by knowing meaning or rules". The drills can be used in order to form correct speech habits. This way pronunciation can be taught.

Types of Drills

Different types of drills are popular in the teaching-learning of English. Some of these drills are used commonly in the classroom situations. The different types of drills are:

1. ***Repetition Drill***: In this type of drill, the teacher speaks a word/ phrase/sentence and the students repeat after him. It is very important that the teacher's pronunciation should be correct as the students imitate him. For example,

Teacher	*Students*
This is a table.	This is a table.
Is it a new pen?	Is it a new pen?
This is not your book.	This is not your book.
Those are beautiful flowers.	Those are beautiful flowers.

2. ***Substitution Drill***: Substitution drill means the replacement of words. Here the learners have to substitute words provided by the teacher in the pattern already supplied. For example.

(a) *Single substitution drill*. In this drill work, the teacher gives a single word and asks the students to substitute word for that.

Teacher	*Students*
Sita is a good singer.	Sita is a good singer.
Sheela	Sheela is a good singer.

(b) *Double substitution drill*. When two words are substituted in a sentence, it is called double substitution drill. For example,

Teacher	*Students*
(i) Geeta is my friend.	Geeta is my friend.
(ii) Lata	Lata is my friend (single substitution)
(iii) Sister	Lata is my sister (double substitution)

(c) *Multiple substitution Drill*: Here more than two words are substituted by the learners. for example:

Teacher	*Students*
(i) That boy is my brother	That boy is my brother
(ii) This	This boy is my brother
(iii) Hari	Hari is my brother
(iv) Your	That girl is your friend
(v) Sister	This girl is your sister.

The learners have to be very careful while using this drill. The teacher also has to plan things before he comes to the class. He should not take any or every word that comes to his mind in the class for drill. He must come well prepared in the class.

(d) *Substitutional Agreement*. The teacher helps the students in understanding one or two patterns. Then he gives the students 'a word' and asks the students to substitute the word to produce the required pattern. For example:

Teacher	*Students*
This is a pen.	This is a pen.
These are balls.	These are balls.
Duster	These are dusters.
Chalk	This is a chalk.
Board	This is a board.

3. ***Conversion Drill or Transformation Drill*:** The students are asked to convert a pattern of sentence into another. For example, the teacher wants to give drill of negative sentences of continuous tense, he will explain by giving examples. Then drill will be given as below:

Teacher	*Students*
Mohan is singing a song.	Mohan is not singing a song.
They are playing.	They are not playing.

Thus, using this drill, any type of conversion of sentence can be taught to the students.

4. ***Completion Drill*:** In this drill, the teacher gives some model sentences and then he provides them with incomplete sentences. The students are required to complete them:

Teacher	*Students*
He is going to Bombay.	He is going to Bombay.
I Russia.	I am going to Russia.
She Canada.	She is going to Canada.

This drill is further divided into two types:

(a) *Additional drill.* Here a sentence pattern is given. Then some words are supplied one by one and the students add these words in the sentence already taken up. Addition may be internal or it may be at the end.

(i) *Internal Addition*

Teacher	*Students*
I purchased a pen.	I purchased a pen.
I purchased two pens.	I purchased two pens.
I purchase imported pen.	I purchased imported pen.

(ii) *Addition at the end*

Teacher	*Students*
He went to Delhi yesterday to attend a meeting.	He went to Delhi.
	He went to Delhi yesterday.
	He ment to Bombay yesterday to attend a meeting.

(b) *Synthetic Drill:* In this drill, two parts of a sentence are taken in wrong format, and the students are asked to re-arrange them in correct format. For example:

Teacher	*Students*
If I was going to Delhi, he asked me.	He asked me if I was going to Delhi.

Yesterday to attend a meeting. He went to Delhi yesterday to attend a meeting.

5. ***Chain Drill:*** In this the drill is given to the students and they work on chain system. The teacher will explain its working system in mother tongue to the students to make them understand what they have to do. In this chain reaction first student gives drill to the second, second to the third and so on. Suppose the teacher asks the first student, showing a picture of lion to him, about its name. He will simply reply 'lion'. Then the teacher will ask him to put the same question to the next student, in this way chain drill works.

	Teacher	*First student*	*Second student*
1.	What is this? Showing a picture of lion.	This is a lion (looking at the picture) What is this?	Looks at the object and answers. This is a pen. What is this?

Further, this drill can be practised for applying passive transformation, changing of narration, changing of the form of sentence etc.

(B) DEVELOPMENT OF LINGUISTIC SKILL OF SPEAKING

"The speech is the language" —*C.C. Fries*

"An important element of communicative approach is a students' ability to use and understand the spoken language". —*Leech and Svartik*

Language derives its vitality, sustenance and dynamism from speech. Learning to speak a language is always the shortest road to read and write it. Due emphasis must be given on listening and speaking. Speech skills have two major components:

(a) *Motor perception skill.* Wherein the learner of a foreign language is exposed to sounds and structures of the target language, which the learner perceives, recalls and articulates in the correct order. The learners practice the sounds of the language (phonology), vocabulary (lexis) and grammar (syntax) without the basis of content and situation. It serves purpose at elementary level. But does not make them fluent speakers.

(b) *Interaction skill.* The second major component of speaking skill is interaction skill. As the learner progresses through various listening-speaking contexts, she/he begins to reach a level where the foreign language is merged as if it were the situation and the learner begins to think in the language.

Objectives of Teaching Speaking Skills

1. Teaching of sounds of the language as well as stress, rhythm and intonation.
2. Stringing together features of pronunciation (sound, stress, rhythm and intonation) in grammatical and meaningful sequences.
3. Teaching the speech sequence in appropriate social situations to enhance social acceptability.

4. Teaching the learners to identify and select points relevant to the purpose and situation as per social acceptability.
5. Teaching the sequencing of ideas into a coherent whole in extended talk.
6. Helping individual learners to develop fluency, pleasant conversation and ease of speech.

Learners' Activities

It should be clear to you that most of the learners are not able to speak well due to various causes like not much emphasis on this skill, lack of exposure, non-availability of good teachers, dearth of good books and poor speech habits, etc. Let us talk about some important language functions and activities that the learners need to perform at secondary level, as it is assumed that by now she/he would have acquired skill of conversation and extended talk.

- greeting friends, superiors, strangers.
- introducing self and others.
- making telephone-calls and answering them.
- asking for or giving information.
- asking for things in shops, counters and restaurants.
- asking questions for clarifications, advice or help.
- expressing opinion or reactions to programmes, plays, books or films.
- participating in discussion and debates.
- describing things, persons or places.
- narrating anecdotes, stories and discussing them.
- giving a report of an event.

Role of the Teacher in a Speaking Class

Oral skills can be organised to improve speaking (they have been discussed in detail in listening skills). But reading aloud does not help much in learning speaking. Because of the following reasons:

- Reading aloud stops the imaginative thinking.
- It slows down the speed of reading.
- Sometimes it is purposeless.
- Sometimes creates embarrassing experience when errors are committed.
- Pupil's practice is random than specific.

But teacher can help the learner to read aloud for improving expression, voice modulation stress and intonation.

Well planned activities can be organised. Teacher has to see that each member of the group gets the chance to speak. Feedback session can be held wherein language errors are discussed and the correct forms are given to the learners. The teacher may even give a remedial exercise to help correct the errors that come to light during the activity.

Those activities can be like this:

1. Narrating stories

2. Participating in a discussion
3. Class debate
4. Role play
5. Radio show

It should be clear to you that effectiveness of speaking skill depends on the correct pronunciation of words. Before we proceed how to teach, let us discuss why our students make errors:

(1) Interference of mother tongue speech habits.
(2) Lack of exposure.
(3) Lack of teachers.
(4) Lack of good models.
(5) Lack of attention to English pronunciation.
(6) Lack of knowledge of intonation and stress.

What is R.P.?

R.P. means Received Pronunciation which is a standard model used for teaching pronunciation. It is a variety of spoken English which is prevalent in southern England. There is a need of standard model so that there may be a common pattern of pronunciation through out the world. By keeping different models in front, there will be chaos in spoken English because people coming from different countries of the world will not be able to understand one another properly. In order to overcome any such problem, R.P. is considered to be model pronunciation to be followed by one and through out the world.

Phonetics

Phonetics is a science of the sounds of a language. It is concerned with the mechanism by which speech sounds are formed, the manner of combining sounds so as to make syllables, words and sentences. This science grew out of the research of many specialists: linguists, anatomists, psychologists, physicians and teachers.

According to E.H. Sturtevent, "The science of phonetics treats the production, transmission and reception of speech. It includes a description of the physiological mechanism of the lungs, throat mouth, and nose and also of the ear".

Methods of Teaching English Pronunciation

1. Imitation Method

Good models should be presented before the learners as they imitate and learn. It is a natural way to learn. Your English teacher is also not the native speaker of English language. So she/he should take the help of English tapes and cassettes.

2. Phonetic Method

Imitation is not enough. Herein rules of phonetics are explained that there are 44 vowels and consonant sounds produced of 26 English letters. Speech organs and their functioning is also explained. Sometimes it becomes difficult and boring for learners. So we need trained teachers to learn through this method.

3. Subsidiary Method

Many other methods fall in this category like Recitation method, Song method, Language game, Loud reading, Dramatisation and Debates, Discussion etc.

Teaching Pronunciation

You might ask, Why do we need to teach pronunciation? We all know that English language has gained importance at international level. Clear articulation is must so that one's speech is intelligible and acceptable to native and non-native speakers of English.

Let us understand some features of pronunciation, of which we teachers need to be aware and which our learners also must be exposed to. These features are generally overlooked in the teaching of English, because we tend to concentrate on the written form of the language. *Ballard* points out, "Speech training should have precedence over learning to read, in point of time as well as in point of importance".

Speech Organs

"Pronunciation is the use of a sound system, stress rhythm, intonation, fluency and pause in speaking".

The understanding of pronunciation becomes easier if we know about various speech organs. They are divided into three groups:

(a) The respiratory system
(b) The phonetary system
(c) The articulatory system

The speech organs are:

(1) Lungs
(2) Trachea or windpipe
(3) Larynx
(4) Vocal cords
(5) Pharynx
(6) Palate
(7) Uvula
(8) Oral passage
(9) Nasal cavity
(10) Tongue
(11) Teeth
(12) Lips
(13) Nose

English Sound System

We follow British English called R.P. English. There are 26 letters and 44 sounds. There is an alphabet or symbol for each. These symbols are given by 'International Phonetic Association'. English sounds can be divided into (a) Vowel Sounds and (b) Consonant Sounds.

(a) Vowel Sounds

Vowels have been defined by P. Christoiherson as "Vowels then may be defined as voiced sounds in the production of which there is no obstruction, partial or complete of the air passage". It means when there is no closure of air passage by various speech organs, partial or complete, the result will be a vowel sound.

Although there are 5 vowels, viz., *a, e, i, o, u* but there are 20 vowel sounds which have been classified as

(i) Pure vowel sounds or Vocoids

(ii) Dipthongs or Contoids

Pure Vowels (12)

Sl. No.	Phonetic Symbol	Word	Transcription
1.	/i:/	See	si:
2.	/ı/	Sit, bit, it	sit, bit, it
3.	/e/	Get	get
4.	/œ/	Can	cœn
5.	/a:/	Ask	a:sk
6.	/⊃/	Was, what	W⊃Z, t/, W⊃t
7.	/⊃:/	All	⊃:1
8.	/∪/	Put, good	put, g∪d
9.	/u:/	Food, boot	f∪:d, b∪:t
10.	/^/	But	b^t
11.	/∂:/	Work, heard	w∂:k, h∂:d
12.	/∂/	Ago, about	∂'go∪, ∂'baut

Dipthongs (8)

It is a combination of two vowel sounds pronounced as a single syllable. It is a glide from one vowel to another. Diphthongs are also called impure vowel sounds because they do not have the purity of one sound only.

Sl. No.	Phonetic symbol	Word	Transcription
1.	eı	cake, came	keik, Keim
2.	∂ ∪∪	hope, no	houp, nou
3.	aı	high, cry	hai, krai
4.	a∪	house, cow	haus, ka∪
5.	⊃i	toy, voice	t⊃I, v⊃is
6.	/∂	here, clear	Hi⊃kli∂
7.	Σ∂	There, case	⊃Σ∂, KΣ∂
8.	∪∂	tour, poor	t∪∂, Þ∪∂

Consonant Sounds

English has 24 consonants sounds in all.

Sl. No.	Phonetic symbol	Word	Transcription
1.	/p/	put, pen	put, pen
2.	/b/	but, boy	bʌt, bɔi
3.	/t/	tea	ti:
4.	/d/	day	dei
5.	/k/	come	kʌm
6.	/g/	go	gou
7.	/f/	foot	fut
8.	/v/	voice	vɔis
9.	/θ/	thin	θin
10.	/ɤ/	Then	ɤen
11.	/s/	sit	sit
12.	/z/	Zeal	zi:l
13.	/ʃ/	Shut, Ship	ʃʌt, ʃip
14.	ʒ	measure, Pleasure	meʒə, pleʒə
15.	/tʃ/	choose, match	tʃu:z, matʃ
16.	/dʒ/	jug, jump	dʒʌg, dʒʌmp
17.	/m/	make	meik
18.	/n/	no, nut	nou, nʌt
19.	/ŋ/	Sing, King	Siŋ, Kiŋ
20.	/l/	last, lake	la:st, leik
21.	/r/	red, rate	red, reit
22.	/h/	hen	hen
23.	/w/	wine	wain
24.	/j/	yard	ja:d

Suggestions for Good Pronunciation

- Opportunities should be given so that learners can speak and can get feedback.
- Audio-visual aids can be useful.
- Environment must be congenial.
- Maxims of teaching should be considered.
- Individual drill and chorus drill both should be given.
- Native speakers are the best models to be provided. Learners can be encouraged to watch TV shows, plays and dramas and BBC News Channels.
- English should not be taught with the help of mother tongue.
- Learners should be helped to know the functioning of speech organs in correct pronunciation and how to follow them.
- Correct speech habits should be encouraged.

Lastly for the development of the skill of speaking English in his/her students it is desirable for an English teacher to speak English correctly and motivate the students also.

There are of two types of sounds:

Voiced and Voiceless Sounds

Most ordinary speech seconds contain either breath or voice. Which contain voice are called voiced sounds e.g. /v/, /z/, /b/ etc., which contain breath are called voiceless sounds e.g. /f/, /s/, etc.

In case of voiced sounds, there are no vibrations in the vocal cords.
Voiced sounds—/d/, /g/, /j/, /z/.
Voiceless sounds—/p//t//k//s//q/

Basic Components of Speech

1. Phoneme

A phoneme is a minimum unit of sound of a particular language which human beings are able to produce e.g. p, g, r, s, k, q, t, etc. are the phonemes of English language. In English we have 44 phonemes.

2. Syllable

A syllable is the next higher unit of speech. In a language separate phonemes like h, p, h are not spoken. We use these phonemes in a group, in the manner they occur in a word. A word is made up of syllables and syllables, are made up of phonemes. The basic rule of dividing a word into syllables is based on the number of vowel sounds which occur in a word.

3. Stress

The prominence of syllables in words in speech is called stress. The stressed syllable in English is a little longer and louder than others. So here the voice is the heaviest in a word or a sentence. It is shown by a vertical stroke placed above the stressed syllable. In a word, for example, 'conduct con'duct 'object (Noun) ob'ject (Verb) In *a sentence*—
He 'gave them' something to 'eat
The 'train stopped at a 'number of' stations.

In a sentence some words are stressed known as strong form and the other not stressed are known as weak form.

4. Rhythm

Generally rhythm can never be talked about without referring to stress. It is simply the flow or the regularity of the stress in a sentence. It is in fact, very significant characteristic of English speech. English language has stress timed rhythm. That means an equal amount of time elapses between one stressed syllable and the next, no matter how many or how few unstressed syllables may come in between. For example, let us take up the common necessary rhyme.

ˈJack and Jill', went ˈup, theˈ hill,
To ˈfetch aˈ pail of ˈwater.

5. Intonation

The rise and fall of pitch in voice is intonation. In other words, intonation is the variation in pitch. It is one by, slacking or tightening our vocal-cords and the sound. In pronunciation, intonation is very important. Just a change of pitch can change the meaning. A.W. Frisby points out "Much of the meaning of the spoken language is conveyed by the tune to which it is said."

Types of Intonation

(i) Falling Intonation: Here we start speaking with a loud pitch of voice and then the voice goes down. The pitch of the voice falls on the most important syllable. This type of intonation is definite and conclusive one. The symbolic line to be used for this type of intonation is—

Examples are as follows:

- Asha is a beautiful↘ girl
- Sit↘ down
- What are you↘ doing?
- What a↘ nice idea!

(ii) Rising Intonation: Here we start with a low pitch of voice and then the voice goes up. The pitch of the voice rise on the most important syllable. The symbolic way to represent this type of intonation is—

- Are you↗ coming?
- Do me a↗ favour please.
- You have↗ returned back (Surprise).

6. Fluency

Fluency means, saying word groups with no gaps or hesitation in the middle. It means words should be spoken without stumbling over the sounds and sequences of sounds.

7. Pause

Pause means to stop for a while. In English language, speaker should give a pause after a comma or full stop etc. The pause can change the entire meaning of a sentence, e.g. Girls read nicely—

Girls, read nicely.

Thus, for proper pronunciation a good knowledge of sound systems, stress, rhythm, intonation, fluency and pause are is needed. Following are the suggestion for good pronunciation.

Teacher must have good pronunciation and motivate the students for the same. Teacher must tell them how in our communication by giving stress on any syllable, can make the things clear and by giving intonation (rise and fall in the tone) in speech can make the meaning clear to the listeners.

Pattern Practice

Need for Pattern Practice

What is needed is practice that gradually enforces the student's attention away from the linguistic problem to the use of examples that contain the problem. This will engage the habit formation and more quickly establish the new habits.

Pattern practice is rapid oral drill on problem patterns with attention to something other than the problem itself.

Rapid Drill

In pattern practice, the student produces a sentence after each cue at normal conversational speed. A class may produce 20 to 30 different sentences by following as many cues supplied per minute by the teacher. This represents 1000 to 1500 recitations in a fifty-minute class. If you compare it with grammar translation method, you will come to know that one student takes one minute for his/her turn. This gives only 50 recitations compared with 1000. If learning increases with the number of recitation when the same utterance is not rèpeated more than three times, pattern practice must be far superior to group recitation. In pattern practice, the number of student responses in a class of 10 students would be 10 times—1000 or 10000. It shows why pattern practice is more suitable.

Teaching Grammatical Patterns

Mimicry memorization method is an improvement upon translation method and further pattern practice is a better step over mimicry memorization. Pattern practice is a much liked and used approach as it facilitates learning.

Pattern –Practice Approach

The mimicry – memorization exercise tends to give the same amount of practice to easy as well as difficult problems. It also concentrates unduly on the memorization of specific sentences, and not enough on the manipulation of the patterns of sentences in a variety of content situations. For those patterns that are functionally parallel to the native language, very little work need to be done, and very little or no explanation is necessary. On the other hand, for those patterns that are not parallel in the two languages, more specific understanding for the grammatical structure points at issue is needed while the sentences are learned and not before or after. Practice with pattern is necessary. It has been proved that this approach produced better results have been gained when teacher used it.

Basic Sentences: The memorization of sample sentences that contain the grammatical problems to be mastered is common to both pattern practice and mimicry memorization. For this practice there is ample justification in linguistics and in psychology. The utterances have to be readily available if students are to use them in the rapid sequence of conversation. Leonard Bloomfield says that this stage for the mimicry – memorization approach, the command of a language is not a matter of knowledge; the speakers are unable to describe the habits which make up their language.

It is an established fact that it is with the practice only that you can get command over a language. The knowledge of language is of no use, if it is not practised continuously.

To understand the forms is only the first step. Copy the forms, read them out loud, get them by heart, and then practise them over and over again day after day, until they become entirely familiar and natural.

Teaching the Patterns

A learner has to get mastery over the use of patterns and not only memorizing the sentences. Learning of pattern should be rather an unconscious habit.

By practice, many complete sentences can become automatic reactions of the learners. But it is to be noted that besides specific formulas, there are many "patterns" which should be included in the productive expression of the learners without being conscious. After reaching this stage their range of vocabulary will also increase.

The steps in teaching problem patterns are—

1. Make the class attentive.
2. The teacher should give examples.
3. Their repetition by the class should be done.
4. Students should give their own examples.
5. Comments or generalization elicited inductively from the students and confirmed by the teacher is made.
6. Practice is done with attention on the problem being taught.

These steps are intended to clarify the crucial point of contrast at the time when sentences are being learned. They should take only a small portion of the class time not more than 15 percent.

(C) DEVELOPMENT OF LINGUISTIC SKILL OF READING

"Our main purpose in developing the ability to read among our children is that we wish to put them in possession of the power gaining pleasure and profit from the printed pages." —C.C. Fries

Reasons for Reading

People generally do not read unless they have a reason for reading, i.e., they have a need of some kind that can be satisfied through reading. So we read because:

(a) We want information for some purpose.
(b) We need instructions in order to perform some task.
(c) We want to keep in touch with friends through letters, or understand official correspondence.
(d) We want to know what is happening (newspapers, magazines, reports).
(e) We seek enjoyment (novels, poems, etc.)
(f) Reading is a good source of self-education.
(g) According to Lord Bacon, "Reading maketh a full man".
(h) Professor Gandhi and Trivedi remark, "In fact education of a child is the ability to read, to decipher, to interpret and to

> understand properly the contents of a reading material. The intellectual advancement of the child is strictly limited, if he is unable to read".

The term 'reading' thus embraces a wide variety of tasks, activities, skills and mental process.

A.W. Frisby says, "Reading for those who have been guided to appreciate it, is one of the most important activities of life to bring to us not only a pleasant way of spending the time, but a way of entering into the life of the world and helping us to contemplate spiritual matters. Many of those who do not approach reading in this life have probably not received in their youth the right encouragement.

Meaning of Reading

The learners of English must know reading English because reading opens the gates of knowledge. Moreover, reading is a perennial source of joy and amusement.

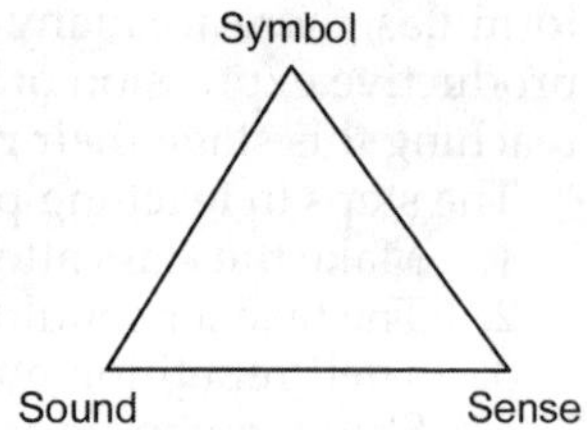

Reading is a process of looking at a written or printed symbol and translating it into appropriate sound. This spoken symbol is further associated with an object for which it stands.

Reading, in fact, is the ability which enables the pupils sooner or later to record with purpose of extracting from the printed page the thoughts, facts and information that it has to give him.

Mechanics of Reading

When a person reads, he does not try to recognise letters separately. Instead his eyes go on moving alongwith the printed or written symbols across the page. But this moving is not slow and steady moving across the page in one even movement, it is a series of short little jumps over phrases and group of words. In other words, "the number of words read in one complete movement is the eye span of a reader. The eyes of a good reader move quickly taking longer jumps in comparison to the poor readers who move slowly taking shorter jumps".

Therefore, the teacher should try to enlarge the eye span of the students while reading.

Characteristics of Reading

In the very early stage of reading instruction, teachers are generally concerned, with developing the mechanical reading skills. But as soon as they come to know that their students have these basic skills, they should move on as quickly as possible to develop in students the cognitive skills associated with different types of reading activity. If this kind of work is begun at the elementary stage, the students are more likely to become efficient readers early in their life. Following are the characteristics of efficient reading:

1. *Reading is purposeful.* When you read, it has a reason. Even if you read a novel during travelling your purpose is to pass time.

2. *Reading is selective.* The way you read differs according to the purpose. You quickly scan a page in the telephone directory to locate a name/number but you have to pay careful attention to every word in a legal document. But we skim, attempting to extract the gist of a text or we read intensively with the aim of decoding the whole of the writer's message.

3. *Reading speed varies.* Content and purpose has its effect on speed. You read a story book faster than the text book.

4. *Reading is silent.* Reading aloud is a specialised skill used, for example, by actors and newspapers but seldom by the general reader.

5. *Reading is text-based.* It is always the context which provides meaning to reading, it is not the mere decoding of individual sentences isolated from context.

6. *Reading involves complex cognitive skills.* Readers do not merely decode the message. They make predictions and inferences. They anticipate based on what they read.

7. *Reading is based on comprehension.* That is, understanding the meaning is integral to reading rather than the result of it. The more we comprehend, the more we can, and tend to read.

How do we Read?

The main ways of reading are as follows:

- *Skimming:* Quickly running one's eyes over a text to get the gist of it.
- *Scanning:* Quickly going through a text to find a particular piece of information.
- *Intensive Reading:* Reading shorter texts, to extract specific information. This is a more an accurate activity involving reading for detail.
- *Extensive Reading:* Reading longer texts usually for one's own pleasure. This is a fluent activity, mainly involving global understanding.

Skimming: We mean to get a central idea or gist from contents rapidly. It is done with purpose to find out whether the area of study in a newspaper, magazine or book is of our use or not. We read the content in detail, if we find it useful and we learn it otherwise we leave it after a glance.

Scanning: We mean to look for a text when we want to search for a specific item or piece of information that we wish to discover. This skill also involves the ability to reject or pass over irrelevant information. It is the kind of reading we do when, for example, we read through a biographical account to find out the date on which a certain event happened, or when we go through the table of contents in a book to see whether a certain aspect of a problem has been dealt with in the book, or when we glance through the telephone directory to look for a person's telephone number.

Intensive Reading: It is done for detailed understanding, to develop the power of judgment, discrimination, interpretation and appreciation. Students learn to scan for information, to read, with careful attention and concentration, and to extract the major idea and arguments. Attention is also paid to the logical development of ideas and style of its presentation.

Extensive Reading: Here the reading is done without bothering for every detail, word or structure. The main focus is on the fluency of reading with the guidance of a teacher.

Students are encouraged to read widely on subjects which interest them personally (artistic, political, social, scientific) and share what they have enjoyed with their fellow students. Along with the content, the teacher has to see its implications. Reading now has become a technique and not an end in itself, and language becomes a vehicle, a tool. The material that students are encouraged to read should be more easily and readily accessible in language and content than that which is studied intensively. How about reading in a second language?

How can we help our students to read extensively in English?

Extensive reading is a helpful exercise in learning a second language, as it is carried out without the help of another person. It provides valuable reinforcement. it gives students useful practice in skills such as inferring meaning from the context when structures and vocabulary are not familiar. As there is limited time in the classroom, extensive reading is much needed to complete the course. In extensive reading, learners read for pleasure. Learners get motivated to read. Their attitude towards target language is modified. Speed is also improved. But students must be guided how to read in an organized manner.

We should keep in mind that the purpose of reading always varies. Therefore, questions and activities based on the reading material must be planned accordingly.

Reading Aloud

Reading aloud is a skill to be cultivated in early stages. It trains the pupils to link the spoken word with the printed symbol. It helps them to develop speech with correct pronunciation. stress and intonation. Morris says "The pupils" only inclination is to concentrate on the single word; oral reading is first demonstrated by the teacher, and then practised in the class. It will help him to inculcate the correct habit of reading in groups."

Objectives of Reading Aloud

1) Reading with correct pronunciation.
2) Reading with comprehension.
3) Reading with expression
4) Reading for the practice of speaking.
5) To develop in the student a desire and preparation for silent reading.

Procedure of Reading Aloud

The teacher reads a passage with correct pronunciation, stress, rhythm and pauses, till the objectives of reading are followed by students.

The teacher does model reading aloud, students follow him/her individually then in a group. The teacher has to be vigilant so that each and every mistake done by students is corrected.

Advantage of Reading Aloud

1. Students learn by imitating the teacher which is the natural method of learning.
2. Students learn the proper method of reading because they follow the model reading done by the teacher.
3. It develops the skills of speech.
4 Mistakes are corrected by the teacher.
5 Sensory organs are trained.

Limitations

1. It does not give pleasure.
2. It does not help in getting the meaning.
3. It hinders in becoming an extensive reader.

However it is recommended for students at junior level.

Silent Reading

Silent Reading is reading without producing sounds audible to others. This is suggested at higher level. In the words of Handschin, "Silent reading inculcates a love for reading and is pleasurable and it gives the pupil a feeling of power and achievement".

Ryburn says, " The aim of silent reading is pleasure and profit, to read for interest and to get information".

Objectives

1. To enable students to read without making even lip movement.
2. To read with speed, ease and fluency.
3. To read with comprehension.
4. To expand students vocabulary.

Procedure

The teacher must make clear the aims and objective of silent reading to the students. S/he asks the students not to make even lip movement or finger reading as it lessens eye movement.

Having given time for reading, teacher can put up a few questions assuring their comprehension.

Advantages

1. It saves time
2. It saves energy

3. It develops students' interest for reading.
4. It proves of immense value in later life because it is used in higher classes.

Limitations

1. It is not suitable for small children.
2. It does not teach correct pronunciation.
3. It is uninteresting (sometimes).
4. The mistakes of students cannot be corrected.

It is important to understand what Ryburn says in this connection, "the teacher should test what the pupils have gained from, what they have read by questions on the subject matter. Another way of testing is to get pupils to give the substance of a paragraph they have read."

Different Ways of Reading

Meaning of any reading material operates at four levels:

1. *Literal*: Here the reader is concerned with the understanding of the information. That information may be facts and details, sequence of events, main ideas and generalizations, cause and effects. The key elements in comprehension at this level is that the information is present in 'black and white' in the text. Reader is not required to go in depth. This is an important stage. It requires a thorough understanding of paragraphs, sentences and word meanings.

2. Interpretive or Inferential: To read at this level is to read 'between the lines, to recognize ideas and information not directly stated. In doing so, the reader must make inferences. One may have to infer time relationships, cause and effect relationship, feelings and familiar relationships of characters, main ideas and generalizations. If these are not stated explicitly in the text, the reader must study the facts given in the text and put two and two together in making inferences. Writers do not always state facts directly. It is concerned with emotions and attitudes of the reader. For instance, an author may not state directly that a particular character is bad, but the words used to describe that person and the situation may convey the his/her attitude towards the character. A perceptive reader should be able to recognize this attitude.

Interpretative reading also involves understanding meaning expressed through idiomatic expressions and figures of speech.

So interpretive reading is when there is no literal meaning of words like he had no heart, one has to understand that particular person is cruel hearted. The reader must bring to bear his/her previous experience with language literature and life in constructing meaning.

3. Critical Reading: It means making judgment about the facts and handling of characters by the author. It requires some changes in the story or dialogue delivered and so on. In other words the readers need not accept the words on a page as given, but should have a range of interpretations legitimately provided in the text. L_2 readers especially may bring different kind of cultural assumptions to bear on a text, making it more challenging than the mainstream reading.

4. *Creative Reading*: It means the use of imagination, inventions or predictions and proposing an alternative conclusion. The questions, the answers to which one goes beyond the given text, putting oneself in place of a particular character and interpreting the text from his/her point of view.

Different Stages in Reading

Following are the different stages in teaching reading:

I. Preparatory Reading

It means the preparation of ground work on which teaching, reading flourish. Following steps can be useful:

1. *Letter recognition*. Interesting way should be followed for better recognition.
2. *Teaching through known objects*. The teacher can teach about word by showing actually, e.g.:
   This is a table.
   This is a fan.
   This is a bag, etc.
3. *Use of chalkboard*. If the teaching aid is not available, a teacher can make use of chalkboard by drawing and sketching.
4. *Through action*. The teacher can perform any action in the class and ask the students to write and read the sentence from the chalkboard.
5. *Use of pictures and flash cards*. The pupils can learn to read words orally through pictures. Flash cards can also be used for teaching words and sentences. Picture of cat, rat, etc. can be pasted on flash cards and students can be asked to read from it.
6. *Through word building cards*. The pupils can be guided to make new words and read through cards. For example:

First word	*Second word*	*New word*
Farm	er	Farmer
Play	ing	Playing
Write	er	Writer

7. *Teaching through games*. Some interesting games can be arranged for teaching reading. For example, instructions may be written on different slips.
   Open the notebooks
   Act like a leader
   Copy your teacher etc.

The teacher can ask the students to pick up the slip one by one and do what is required in the instructions.

II. Second Stage

Productive Reading: At this stage, the student's response to the set of shapes and visual patterns take the shape of automatic habits. During this stage, good reading habits are developed. The most important aspects of English language, i.e., pronunciation, stress and intonation are taught to the students during this stage.

III. Third Stage: Vivid Imagination Realisation

At this stage students can enhance their reading material with the help of their imaginative power. They can use reading and finding interest in it.

Keeping in view these stages, let us discuss methods of Teaching-Reading.

Methods of Teaching-Reading

The methods differ from country to country, state to state and even some time teacher to teacher. The methods of teaching reading can be divided into two categories:

1. *Letter /Analytic Method*: Alphabetic and Phonic Method
2. *Non-letter/Synthetic Method*, i.e. word, phrase, sentence and story method.

***Alphabetic Method*:** It is an old method of teaching reading. In this method the students are taught the alphabets, i.e., A, B, C,.... of the language. Here the unit of teaching is a letter. Later the students learn words by combining the alphabets. It is economical and helps the learners in learning spellings but on the other hand it is dull and boring.

***Phonic Method*:** In this method, the word is broken up into basic speech sounds. Therefore, the students are helped to learn the sounds of the alphabets and then they are helped to recognise and understand the symbols.

It is a very common method used in U.K. But it requires expert teachers. T.K.N. Menon and M.S. Patel opines, "The phonic method was adopted when realised that the sounds of letters, not their names, when uttered rapidly produce the word. It was also assumed that once these sounds had been learned, they should be combined into syllables and words and then into larger language units. The method is most effective for languages in which the forms of letter invariably correspond with their sounds".

If we get trained teachers, this method will definitely prove beneficial.

***Look and Say Method*:** It is also called word method, because the unit of teaching is a word learners are shown the actual objects, pictures and charts, they say what they see.

As it is interesting and psychologically sound and a very popular one. But it is impossible to teach everything through picture. Moreover, it will be a costly affair to teach like this in an Indian atmosphere.

***Phrase Method*:** In this method unit of teaching is a phrase.

According to Menon and Patel, "The phrase method is based on the assumption that phrases are not more interesting than words and place emphasis on meaning. It is believed that since good readers recognise group of words at each fixation of the eyes, the phrase method should foster rapid growth in efficient reading".

Here the students are taught like—on the table, under the chair, etc. All types of students cannot be taught like this.

The Sentence Method: In this method the unit of teaching is a sentence. Therefore, the students are to first learn a sentence and after that phrases, words and alphabets are learnt.

For example:

This is a table.
This is a pen.

With the help of these sentences the learners learn *a, c, t, h, l, k,* etc. letters. The repetition of these sentences helps the students in recognising the letters of alphabet.

Regarding this method *Anderson Dearborn* opines, "Sentence method helps to prevent word by word reading. This method lays foundation of all the attitudes and skills, required for good reading".

As it is a natural method. It lays the foundation of attitude and skills necessary for good reading. But it is difficult to understand a complete sentence without the knowledge of words and alphabets. Moreover, the process becomes time consuming.

The Ideal Method: Now the question arises which is the best method of teaching reading?

Each method has its merits and demerits and none is perfect in every respect and thus it becomes difficult to say which method is the best. Selection of a method depends upon the classroom situation and the background of the students.

Reading Problems

You must have noticed in your day-to-day interaction with students in the classroom, that they have reading habits that are faulty and which need gentle correction, the more serious problems, such as, Alexia need a special intervention programme. Let's look at some of these problems and how to rectify them.

1. Faulty Reading Habits

(i) *Sub-vocalisation*. Our eyes move faster than our tongue. If one reads aloud he/she tends to read word by word instead of sense groups, which slows one down. So efficient readers do not sub–vocalise.

(ii) *Finger pointing*. When children read with finger pointing, they fix their concentration on the word they are deciphering. In this case too the child reads word by word and not in sense groups.

(iii) *Regression*. This refers to regressive eye movements, i.e., the eye moves backward to check previous words instead of moving steadily forward. Sometimes, even a skilled reader may have to return to earlier parts of a text and reinterpret them in the light of what has followed. However, children should be trained to eliminate pointless and frequent regression.

2. *Neurological Problems*

Some children have learning problems arising from neurological dysfunction rather than from low IQ or poor motivation. The term Alexia is used to refer to a reading disability that may be related to the impairment of the central nervous system.

3. *Vision Loss*

Sometimes a child holds a book near the eye for reading, squints at the board, rubs the eyes or thrusts the body forward to see.

4. *Decoding Errors*

Through one to one oral reading child may commit mistakes of eye to eye decoding error, e.g., He sat on the sofa after dinner, reads the same sentence.
He sat on the soap after dinner. But it distorts the meaning.

5. *Unfamiliarity of Sounds*

English language has its own set of sounds, for example, in English V and W are two sounds but in Hindi there is one sound.

6. *Irregularity in English Spellings*

Silent words like K. in knife and known creates confusion, moreover F sound is denoted sometimes by (ough) enough and sometimes by ph. (photograph).

7. *Psychological Difficulties*

Some students are shy and introvert. They hesitate to answer a question but not in singing a song.

Suggestions for Improvement

1. *Proper guidance*: Teacher should guide the students that no sub-vocalisation, no finger pointing and proper eye movement will lead to proper reading habits.
2. *Regarding the irregularity of the spellings*: Teacher can guide them not to find the logic behind the language and try to understand the system lying behind a particular language.
3. The students who have vision problem should be attended sympathetically and referred to the Doctor.
4. Teacher should cultivate the habit of self-reading among the students. For this a survey of reading interest can be done so that they start going to library for consultation.
5. *Reading difficulties should be properly diagnosed*: This skill is needed both in reading 'aloud' and 'silent reading'.
6. *Oral work should be given proper place*: The learners must have an

oral command of the language material he is going to read in print. Sufficient oral practice is essential before a textbook is given in the hands of the students.

(D) DEVELOPMENT OF THE LINGUISTIC SKILL OF WRITING

"The Palest ink is better than the most retentive memory."

—Chinese proverb

What is Writing?

Learning to read and write is a process of experiencing language. Children learn to talk in a language of participating in communicative interactions. Once a child has begun to communicate orally in a language, writing can be introduced.

Writing is the physical expression of what you think. The close relationship between writing and thinking makes writing valuable. Thus, writing is closely related to the inner processes within a child's mind, i.e., the internal manipulation of external experiences. In addition to this, writing reinforces the grammatical structures, idioms and vocabulary that we have been teaching our children, writing skill makes the language items learnt firmly fixed in the minds of the learners.

According to Bacon, "Reading makes a full man, conference a ready man and writing an exact man". What he means is that writing is a useful means of organising thought and giving it precision.

According to Harold Rosen, "The writer is a lonely figure... He writes with one hand tied behind his back, being robbed of gestures. He is robbed too of the tone of his voice.. He is condemned to monologue, there is no one to help out, to fill the silences, put words in his mouth, or make encouraging noises".

In the words of Bell, "Writing is a tool used to enable us to express what is in our mind and for some people is almost as important as speech".

Mahatma Gandhi has also emphasised the importance of writing by saying, "Fair and legible hand writing is a tool used to enable us to express, what is in our mind and for some people is almost as important as speech".

S.S.M. Gaudar says, "Writing has an instrumental value in schools". He further says, "It is a means of preserving the knowledge which the pupil has gained or the judgement he has formed. It serves as a check on his forgetting useful items of knowledge and ideas. The habit of making notes of what is read and of summarising helps the recollection of what has been studied.

Aspects of Writing Skill

1. Syntax (sentence structure and choices, etc.)
2. Content (Relevance, clarity, originality, logic, etc.)
3. Grammar (Rules for verbs, agreement, articles, adjectives etc.)
4. The writing process (Getting ideas, getting started, writing drafts, revising)

5. Mechanics (Handwriting, spellings, punctuation, etc.)
6. Audience (The readers)
7. Organisation
8. Word choice (vocabulary, idioms, tone)
9. Purpose (The reason for writing)

Mechanics of Writing

It includes the following:

1. Make letters of the right shape and size.
2. Giving proper spacing between letters, words and lines.
3. Using capital letters and other punctuation marks.
4. Controlling the small muscles of the fingers and wrist to have fluent movement in writing.

Teaching writing mechanics has three stages as follows:

(i) Preparation for writing.
(ii) Learning to write.
(iii) Mastering a mature style of handwriting.

Characteristics of Good Handwriting

Some of the qualities of good handwriting are as follows:

1. *Legibility*: Handwriting should be legible and easy to read. Illegible handwriting creates a very bad impression on the readers. Bell says: "Illegible handwriting in a young man or woman is a sign of untidy and careless mind".

Headings should be written in a bold but simple manner. Extra strokes and curves should be avoided. Teacher can help the students in letter formation, spacing, alignment, regularity of slant and quality of line or stroke.

2. *Distinctiveness*: It means each letter should have a characteristic form of its own. It should be clearly and carefully written. The letters should not be distorted or overlapped. The beginners should not be encouraged to write code words like & (and) they should write each letter distinctively. This adds beauty to handwriting.

3. *Spacing*: Spacing in writing is an important feature. The letters in a word, the words in a line and the lines in a page should not be crowded too closely together. A harmonious spacing of letters, words and lines is necessary.

4. *Simplicity*: Letters should be simple, bold and free from all extravagant strokes and flourishes. A simple handwriting in which letters have no unnecessary parts, tails or loops is always easy to read.

5. *Size*: The size of words should be proper and moderate. It should be neither too big nor too small. The letters should have due proportion to one another.

6. *Letter style*: There can be three different styles of letters.

(a) Slanting towards the left (\\\\)
(b) Vertical (||||)
(c) Slanting towards the right (////)

It is generally noted that the boys adopt the third style whereas girls adopt the first style and the second style is common among both. Teachers can guide the students not to mix the two styles as it will give a shabby look to the writing so, vertical style is preferable.

7. *Uniformity*: There should be uniformity in handwriting. One may select any style of writing but it should be uniform in size, spacing and alignment.

8. *Speed*: Good handwriting also requires a genuine and reasonable speed. While writing, one should not feel laboured or burdened. Regarding speed A.W. Frisby opines "The writing should not be laboured but done at a reasonable speed". In the beginning, the students may write slowly, but gradually they should develop the habit of writing at a reasonable speed. At the beginning stage teacher can play an important role in helping the students to acquire a proper habit of writing. Because it is very difficult to change the habit of writing acquired earlier.

9. *Adjustment between writing and thinking*. It implies that there should be no omission of words or phrases due to quick thinking in fast writing.

Writing is a difficult art which needs practice and great attention. Therefore F.G. French has suggested that training in writing should begin with training in muscular control through fairly large movement using fingers in tray of sand or chalk or brown paper. The movement should include drawing of lines of various length and direction, half circles, strokes, etc.

Choice of Script

English letters have their origin in Roman script. There are three kinds of scripts (a) Print script, (b) Cursive script, (c) Rounded curve script.

(a) *Print Script*: Print script is the type of writing which pupils come across in their textbooks. The letters in this script are not joined together and is thus easier to learn. The common practice is to start with script and turn to cursive writing after a year or two. The advantages of print script are:

(i) The pupils concentrate more and more on the shapes of letters which they meet in the reader or in other printed material. Thus, at the early stage they are saved from the botheration of learning two different forms for each letter.

(ii) The unnecessary strokes required in the running hand to join the successive letters are dispensed with.

(iii) This makes the appearance of the script, clean, simple and inductive enough to copy. Letters in print script have simpler forms than in cursive hand.

(iv) Children can compare their letters with printed ones. Thus they can find their errors.

(v) Eye and physical strain is less in the reading of print script.

(vi) Print script is suited to the muscular and mental development of young children.

Disadvantages of Print Script

(i) Some pupils find it difficult to change to cursive hand later on.

(ii) Sometime children experience difficulty and confusion when they switch over to cursive hand. Some of them carry the habit of writing the print script throughout life.

(b) *Cursive Script*: Cursive writing is the running type of writing in which the letter in a word are joined together with strokes or loops. It is better to help the students to write in cursive manner, because sometimes they find it difficult to switch over to cursive writing. We want our students to write at a good speed. That will be obtained effectively in cursive writing.

General Considerations to be Kept in Mind while Teaching Writing

(a) *Choice of Script*: The choice of script is the first important consideration to be kept in mind while teaching writing to the beginners. Teacher must decide print script or cursive script to be introduced at which stage. For the beginners print script is suggested and later on to facilitate the speed cursive writing can be useful.

(b) *Choice of Style*: The styles of writing, *viz.*, vertical, forward and backward slant vary from individual to individual. But the letters should have uniform style. All styles are good even then students should be encouraged to write in vertical style.

(c) *Writing Material*: In the beginning the choice of material given to the pupils is very important. That material is to be provided which makes for the desired movement of the muscles involved in writing.

The movement of the arm should be regulated first. This can be achieved if broader surfaces are provided to the children to start their initial writings which consists of free lines, strokes, curves, circles, dots, etc. It may be well mentioned here that in the playschool for this purpose, children write with their fingers on sand. Equally valuable is the alternative use of the chalkboard and coloured chalksticks of good quality.

This will facilitate in acquiring easy hand movements and develop hand and eye coordination. Gradually, they can learn to write on paper. But it should not be glazed, and pencil should be medium in softness, pencil can be followed by ink pen.

(d) *Posture*: While writing, posture should be correct. When at their desks, they should sit comfortably in their seats in an erect position. Their both feet should rest on the ground. The body should lean slightly forward from the hips but should not touch the desk. The head should be so held so that his eyes are about a 13 inches away from the paper. The chest should be clear of the edge of the desk. Both forearms should be within two or three inches of the elbows and should rest highly on the desk.

Some other techniques helpful in the teaching-writing at the early stage:

1. *By overwriting*: The teacher writes something with a pencil on the notebooks of the students. The students are asked to overwrite it. English writing notebooks in which letters, words or sentences are written can be suggested. It will facilitate the students to have overwriting practice.
2. *Use of chalkboard*: Students are asked to copy down the material written on the chalkboard.
3. *Use of flashcards*: Some words are written on flashcards and distributed among the students, on seeing them, they will write the same word.
4. Copying the line written by teacher in the notebook. Teacher will write one line in their notebooks and students will write the whole page this way.
5. *By using substitution table*: Students' are asked to write more sentences with the help of substitution table.

All the above techniques will definitely help the students to improve the handwriting.

How is Writing Different from Speech?

Why is it that to a large number of students in India, writing in English seems to pose great problems?

Rosen points Out

- Writing is detached from the wide range of possibilities in speech.
- A writer is unable to exploit all the devices available to a speaker: gesture, body movement, facial expression, pitch and tone of voice, stress and hesitations.
- A speaker can backtrack, or clarify and revise ideas as listeners question or disagree.

A writer has to compensate for all of those disadvantages.

- Compared with speech, effective writing requires a number of things:
  - (a) a high degree of organisation in the development of ideas and information.
  - (b) a high degree of accuracy so that there is no ambiguity of meaning.
  - (c) the use of complex grammatical devices for focus and emphasis.
  - (d) and a careful choice of vocabulary grammatical patterns and sentence structures to create a style which is appropriate to the subject matter and the eventual readers.

It is these demands which present particular problems to foreign writers of English. Even those who are proficient writers in their first language have to acquire a wide language base from which to make these choices. They may also find that confusing differences exist between the conventions of writing in their first language and English.

For example, the level of formality or patterns of presenting information in letters may differ, or the accepted method of setting out arguments in discursive writing may vary. We need to be sensitive to all these factors when our learners attempt their writing tasks.

Creating a Natural Learning Environment for Writing

In order to create a non-threatening and conducive atmosphere in the classroom so that children feel free to express themselves, the following guidelines may be useful:

Some Suggestive Guidelines

(1) We need to build our writing programme and the classroom environment around the child's need to convey something to a recipient audience. The primary drive for wanting to write comes from the need to communicate or convey an idea. In the process of exchanging written interactions, the child learns to understand other people's writings.

(2) We need to understand the importance of experimentation and risk taking in the process of learning to write. Through imitation of adult writing and their inner drives, children step into unfamiliar language areas. As they use the language, as they write and speak and read it, they become better equipped—they acquire new linguistic abilities. Their mistakes help a teacher to provide the formal instructions they need.

(3) We need to understand that children progress in different ways and at different pace. Background of experiences of the child influence the child's writing.

(4) We need to support children's experiments with the new language. Children must feel comfortable exploring the written form of the second language. They must relate to it and feel a sense of ownership about their writing, without being afraid to make mistakes. It is through this that each learner discovers the strategies that allow him/her to be effective language user.

(5) Children need to be gently led into the arena of writing in the second language. Since most children are reluctant to take risks and experiment with an unfamiliar language, the teacher should design or mould writing activities which begin within a structured framework. Gradually, as the child acquires competence over the lexical and syntactic structure of the second language, more open-minded communicative activities should be taken.

(6) We need to recognise the importance of having audience respond to what the child has written. Writing involves a constant sharing with others; talking and sharing about ideas and getting a feedback on whether those ideas have worked or not. Children need to write for many different purposes. They need to write for a real audience—for themselves, for the examiner, for both younger and older children, for adults they know and for some general unknown audience as well.

(7) We need to provide the importance of what is involved in being

a writer. We can provide demonstration of writing in action and being partners in their writing process.

Process of Writing

Much of the research and academic work in the field of writing has begun to recognise that writers follow a process when they work, just as scientists follow a systematic method. When we begin to understand this process we can help our students invent, use and adapt to effective writing strategies (Murray 1982, Graves 1991). Yet in most of our language classrooms we tend to only look at the end products of writing. We look at the end product in isolation. It has very little to do with the child. We expect the child to produce a perfect piece of writing in one sitting. We do not allow them the process of revising, improving, rethinking about their writing. As adults we always write a draft, then rework, it may be once or twice, we ask for a feedback from others. It is only after this whole process that we produce a final piece of writing. Removing the writing from the whole process of development does not help children to become actively involved with their writing.

Theorists have defined the writing process as different steps or stages that a writer goes through to produce a piece of writing. Broadly speaking, these are the stages of pre-writing, writing and rewriting, editing and then producing the final piece of writing. Murray refers to these as rehearsal, drafting, revision and editing, each stage is important. There are different skills required at each stage, and children need to go through each stage under the guidance of the teacher. The stages, however, do not occur in the linear order given above, there may be overlaps. It is shown in the following figure:

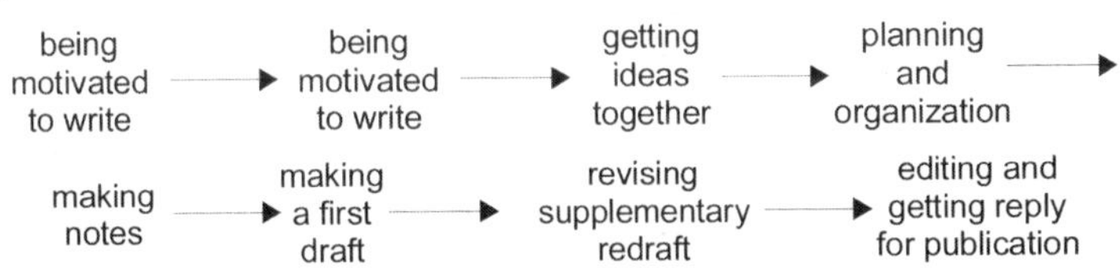

However, the figure oversimplifies matters because, although writing in general involve these stages, the process of composition is not a linear one, moving from planning to composing to revising and to editing. It would be more accurate to characterise writing as a recursive activity in which the writer moves backwards and forwards between drafting and revising, with stages of replanning in between. As Shauguessy (1977) describes it, it is "a messy process that leads to clarity".

The proces of writing consists of three activities.

1. Pre-writing

(a) What is the purpose of this piece of writing?

The writer must know the purpose of his/her writing, i.e., is she/he writing a report for action? Or is it a letter of invitation to some friend or a formal letter to the principal or a letter applying for job.

Identification of the purpose of writing would determine the choice of organisation and the style of the written piece.

(b) Who am I writing for ?

This question directly relates itself to the audience, the reader may be an acquaintance or an intimately known friend or a group of colleagues or an institutional head and so on. The information about the audience helps the writer to determine what to say and how to present the writing in the most appropriate style.

The good writer generally plans for writing at this stage, though the amount of planning varies as per the following scale:

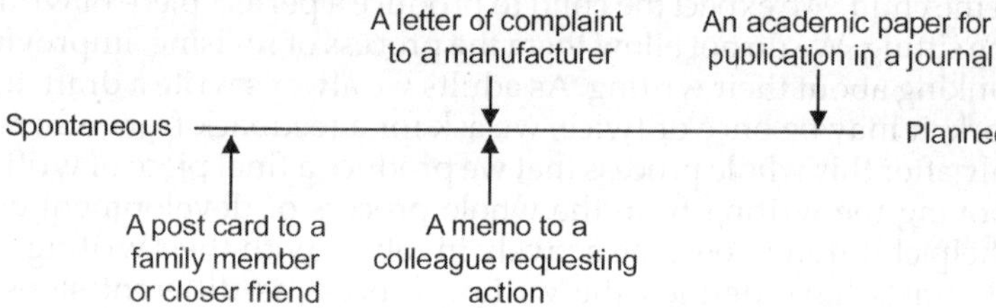

2. *Writing and Rewriting*

The second phase of activity is the writing itself, and with good writers this consists of making a first draft. But writing the first draft is often interrupted as the writer stops to read over and review, to get an idea of how the text is developing to revise plans, and bring in new ideas or rearrange those already expressed. There is a good deal of recycling in the process from planning to drafting, reviewing, replanning, revisiting, etc. Good writers tend to concentrate on getting the content right first and leave details like correcting spellings, punctuation and grammar until later.

In summary, the drafting process focusses primarily on what the writer wants to say, while redrafting progressively focusses on how to say it most effectively.

3. *Editing*

The post writing stage consists of reading through and trying to apply a reader's perspective in order to assess how clearly readers might follow the ideas. The editing process makes the final readjustments and checks accuracy so that the text is maximally accessible to the reader. Some lazy writers tend not to engage in editing but assume that their writing is clear to others because it is clear to them. Alternatively, some writers may concentrate throughout the whole writing process on accuracy in grammar, punctuation without considering whether or not the overall structure is clear. They continually move from drafting to editing without any in between stages of rethinking and reorganisation. It is a less than effective process that might well be unwittingly encouraged by teachers whose strategy for marking is to correct only minor problems on the surface of the writing without commenting on any major problems in structure. This is an understandable strategy on the part of teachers, given the amount of marking most of us have to do.

How can the teachers help?

1. Teachers can help to raise awareness of the process of composition by talking explicitly about the stages of writing as well as by restructuring tasks to take accounts of this.

2. Teacher can play a support role during the early stages of the writing process by helping students to get their ideas together. This can be done by talking about things to generate ideas, by pooling information, ideas or opinions in the class, by working from pictures, or by reading texts of various kinds.

3. Teachers can also provide good models for writing indirectly, by encouraging good reading habits and also directing, when appropriate, by analysing textual structure, particularly, with some types of more formal academic writing.

4. Planned activities structured by the teacher can be helpful, as it will provide a sense of direction in their writing.

5. Teachers can encourage the drafting process by creating a workshop atmosphere in their classrooms, to the extent of providing rough papers, scissors, paste, erasers, etc. Teachers can intervene quietly. Questioning and advising, in order to help students get their ideas down on paper in English. Rewriting is more motivating when it can be done quickly, easily and relatively painlessly by moving pieces of the text around. Alternatives can be evaluated and improvements immediately appreciated on the display screen.

6. Students need opportunities to engage in writing as a holistic process of composition. This means that they need practice in writing whole pieces of communication, not just controlled exercises in sentence structure, grammar or bits and pieces of paragraph development. These activities have their place, as students need to be accurate in their writing and they are sufficient in themselves.

Defects of Handwriting and Their Causes

S.S.M. Gaudar on the basis of his research work done in the composite school in Belgaum city has been able to discover the following handwriting defects and their causes:

Defects	*Causes*
(1) Too much slant	1. Writing too near the body.
	2. Thumb not mobile enough.
	3. Point of nib too far from fingers.
	4. Paper in the wrong position.
	5. Stroke in the wrong direction.
(2) Writing too heavy	1. Index finger pressing too heavy.
	2. Using the wrong pen.

	3. Pen holder too small in diameter.
(3) Writing too light	1. Pen held too obliquely or too straight.
	2. Eyelet of pen turned side ways.
	3. Penholder too large in diameter.
(4) Writing too angular	1. Thumb too stiff.
	2. Penholder too lightly held.
	3. Movement too slow.
(5) Writing too irregular	1. Lack of freedom or movement.
	2. Movement of hand too slow.
	3. Pen gripping.
	4. Incorrect or uncomfortable position.
(6) Spacing too wide	1. Pen progresses too fast to write.
	2. Too much lateral position.

Suggestions for Improving Handwriting

Bad handwriting is a wrong habit and once the bad habit is formed in the beginning it becomes difficult to get it removed and replace it. The following are the remedial measures for improving handwriting:

1. *Use of four-line notebooks*: The use of four-line notebooks will be extremely useful. If proper attention is paid by the teacher to the size and spacing of letters four-line notebooks result in good handwriting.

2. *Teacher's handwriting as model*: The teacher's handwriting should be model for the students. When he/she is writing on the chalkboard the students should be asked to watch his/her movements of hand and fingers. The pupils should be made to understand proper strokes, uniform size and proper spacing.

3. *Use of proper writing material*: The use of proper writing material at different stage of writing is an important consideration. They should be given pencil in the beginning and the pen later on.

4. *Development of proper posture*: Students should be guided to adopt a proper posture while writing. As good posture really helps in improving the handwriting. Constant use of this help the students in developing and getting control over hand muscles.

5. *Use of charts*: Charts written in good handwriting can be displayed on the walls. This will create interest among the students and they try to imitate the writing on the chart.

6. *Handwriting competition*: Frequent competition of good handwriting can motivate them to write well.

7. *Display of good handwriting*: Good writing of the students can be displayed and awarded.

8. *Language test*: Language tests conducted in the class are suggested as it will give special credit and appreciation to those who write in good handwriting.

9. *Individual attention*: The students who have poor handwriting

should be given special individual attention by the teacher in finding out the problems and suggesting measures.

10. *Seating arrangement*: Desk should be properly arranged as the proper height and breadth of desks help the learners in writing well.

The general considerations discussed above help the students a lot in the improvement of handwriting.

Writing Skills

Vocabulary Learning

You may think that whereas the structural approach emphasised the formal nature of language, focussing on grammar and structure of the language, functional and communicative approaches shifted emphasis to function of language and communicative needs of the learner. However, vocabulary did not get the attention it required in either of the approaches.

Researchers and linguists have again brought it to the forefront that vocabulary learning plays a crucial part in language learning.

Importance of Spellings

Correct spellings are essential for correct composition. Nothing offends more than the incorrect spellings. Moreover, it is a courtesy to spell correctly. You need to be aware of the correct spellings in order to appreciate the language and literature.

Let us talk about vocabulary learning. U.S. Tomkinson has remarked aptly: "Spelling is caught rather than taught".

Teaching of spelling should be incidental.

We can think of vocabulary learning in two ways: direct and indirect learning of vocabulary. By direct learning we mean concentrating on words as isolated items, focussing on their form, meaning may be used—in other words, paying attention to words through word exercises, vocabulary games or word puzzles. In indirect learning we imbibe the knowledge of words rather unconsciously, when we are interested in understanding the message.

Nature of Words

Following points should be considered:

- There are no exact equivalents between languages.
- Real meaning of a word depends on the context.
- There are no exact synonyms within a language.
- Words have more than one meaning.
- Words go on changing their meaning.

Role of Teacher

(i) Deciding and selecting vocabulary.
(ii) Maximising learner resources.
(iii) Extending vocabulary learning to phrases, fixed formulas, collections, etc.

(i) *Deciding and selecting vocabulary*: Validity, usefulness, frequency, universality, applicability, productivity and regional value of the words contribute in its prior selection for learning.

(ii) *Maximising learner resources*: The teachers have to help learners to maximise their resources so that students can learn vocabulary. For this purpose, teachers have to take the following things into account:

(a) Learners' prior experience and level.

(b) Making use of L_1.

(iii) *Extending vocabulary phrases, fixed expressions*: Words are not stored in the mind as single items alone but as parts of phrases, noun compounds, fixed formulas and larger chunks of speech. Moreover, this way the words take a firm grip in the mind and becomes a habit. And if we do not make a habit of using new words in our conversation they pass into our passive vocabulary from active vocabulary.

English Spellings

Techniques for learning vocabulary

1. Using a dictionary
2. Using contextual clues
3. Word games

Using a dictionary. Use of a dictionary is crucial for the second language learner. It is to help not only about pronunciation, spelling, meaning but also with grammar, collocations (words which co-occur) and frequency.

Using contextual clues. Guessing from context is a very useful way of discovering the meaning of new words. Every text develops an idea, or a situation and beginning from the topic itself. There are a number of clues to help the reader along, some of which are redundancy, parallelism, anaphora, examples, etc.

Word games. Crossword puzzles, association games, word building game, making pairs of words, recognition games, sorting out the synonyms and antonyms, choosing from jumbled words are some of the exercises which can be helpful for expansion of vocabulary.

They are useful for making the vocabulary rich moreover, it brings variety and interest, thus breaking the monotony in the class.

Writing Skills: Activities

Writing activities help the children in becoming good writers.

We give below different activity types that one can use to help the children to be good writers.

1. Dialogue Writing

Dialogue belongs to spoken English. But often they are included as part of the composition syllabus because it is quite difficult to test spoken English. Dialogues can be very simple and matter of fact as is day-to-day conversations. They could also be highly artistic and imaginative as in literary texts – especially novels. At the primary and secondary levels we could concentrate on simple dialogues.

What makes a dialogue natural, that is, very similar to the way we speak in our day-to-day life?

a) A piece of dialogue need not always be in a full sentence.
b) It is enough if simple vocabulary is used.
c) Short forms should be used e.g. 'can't don't etc.
d) Colloquial expressions are allowed e.g. tummy, oops, woe! Dad etc.

Some task types that you could use:

Task 1: The following is an incomplete conversation between a mother and her son.

Fill in the Blanks and complete the dialogue:

Son : Mom, our class is going on an excursion to Shimla.
Mother :
Son : In May, during the summer holidays.
Mother :
Son : For ten days. Two teachers are coming with us.
Mother :
Son : Not much – only Rs. 500 per head. Mom, Can I go ?
Mother :
Son : Thanks Mom, You're a pet, aren't you ?

Task 2: The following is a part of a telephone conversation between Mohan and Sohan. Reconstruct the whole conversation.

Mohan :
Sohan :
Mohan : And you know, the maths teacher was also on leave today.
Sohan : So you had two free periods ? That means I didn't miss much after all !
Mohan : Oh, we had a 'cool' time ! How I wish you had come to school today. You and your silly 'flu' .
Sohan :
Mohan :

Task 3: Imagine, that on your way to school, a stranger asks you the way to the Railway Station.

Write the dialogue between you and the stranger.

Task 4: Group Composition.

A picture is displayed so that the whole class can see it. Each group studies it and then creates a five minute drama based on the picture. They act out the drama in front of the whole class. The other groups watch the drama and because the same picture is referred to, their interest is retained.

Diary Writing

It is an important activity for developing writing skills. It is a personal record. One need not write full sentences. One can use abbreviations. Thoughts and feelings can be expressed in discontinuity also.

The language of diary is often close to the language of a telegram.

Read the following entry from the diary of an eleven year old girl Zlata from Goa.

Sat. Sept. 3rd 2016

Today is the big day— my birthday. Happy Birthday to me !!!!! But alas! I' am sick. My sinuses are inflamed and my throat aches. Nothing hurts really, but I have to take antibiotics and some disgusting nose drops. Why did this have to happen on my birthday ? Oh ! I am unlucky ! {Don't be such a pessimist, Zlata, things aren't so bad.]

Diary entries are not just a record of what happened during the day. It is a record of the writer's thoughts and feelings about what happened during the course of the day. A diary entry reflects the writer's fears, joy, expectations, disappointments and hopes about what happened and what might happen.

Everything expressed in a diary entry is very personal and is meant only for the writer. But this is an excellent device to get the children in the habit of writing.

Newspaper Article/Report Writing

A Newspaper report follows different sequence from a regular report. A sequence from a regular report. A regular report describes the events in a sequential manner.

A Newspaper report is in the form of an inverted pyramid way.

HEADLINE
BYLINE
DATE AND PLACE LINE

The first paragraph of report is the LEAD— which gives answers to the four questions:

Who, what, where and when

Then in the remaining paragraphs the information drawn from the lead is retold in more detail according to the order of importance.

Newspaper Report – A Sample Draft

Two Mango Fest Visitors with Trips to Bangkok

Times News Network

New Delhi, 9th July: The lucky draw to select winners among the people who visited the mango festival was held on Tuesday. The two winners got free tickets to Bangkok and Kuala Lampur.

The tickets have been sponsored by Air India. Visited by over 12,000 people, DTTDC claimed the event a big hit.

DTTDC chairman Ramesh Sabharwal said that at least one cultural festival would be organized in the city every month.

Notice that the first paragraph answers the four questions.
Then the information is organized in order of importance.

Narratives Using Stories

No one can deny the primacy of narrative. 'Story telling – the most ancient and compelling of human activities' according to John Morgan and Mario Rinvolucri.

All the races and rulers/ tribes of this world have their repertoire of tales that have come down through generations. They were initially transmitted orally and only much later came to be recorded in the written form.

Describing things and story-telling actions are being performed by everyone of us in one way or another. For small children it works as a mode of mental organization as it helps them to recall things and further gives them practice to describe them in their own language. The following are the main features of narrative:

- Underline emotions.
- A thematic structure.
- Cause and effect.
- Problem and its solution.
- Organization of events in time.

The person while telling the story has to keep in mind the above mentioned features in order to maintain the interest and attention of the listener.

In brief, the storyteller 'must' visualize the scene the characters, their speeches, and movements. See it all happening as a coloured film in your mind. On the part of the learner it is essential to keep in mind the grammatical aspects like tense, use of clauses and verb etc. After telling a story, the narrator/teacher can ask question from any part why do you think so? Was it right? Or some sentences can be given to the students, asking who said it, where and why and so on?

Teacher's Role

To make it an effective activity the teacher has to see, what is his/her target group? What type of stories should be selected for this group? Pictures related to story should be selected carefully, statement should be selected intelligently, as it should generate analytical thinking and ability of discussion among listeners. It should motivate them to express their opinion frankly.

Encouraging the Learners to Tell Stories: It is often difficult to recall a story and narrates it well without preparation, if one is asked on the spur of the moment. But providing some support by way of word, characters or a skeleton of the sequence of events can and does help the learner to imagine and narrate a story that can hold the listener's interest.

Writing Skills: Study Skills

The study skills help the learner to study more effectively. These enable him/her to gain knowledge of the subject-matter and learn other subjects independently.

Whereas 'linguistic skills' help learners to communicate while 'study skills' enable learners to study. This process involves four operations.

1. Perception
2. Comprehension
3. Retention
4. Retrieval

It is required that the teacher selects the material as per his/her utility. One can not read every word in the book. After selection the reader must focus on understanding. All learning is for understanding. Everything which is understood, is not in memory, something may be forgotten. For retention, one has to make specific efforts. Weak students memorize blindly, bright students learn with understanding, make short notes, which could be paraphrased later on.

The last stage in the learning process involves the retrieval of what has been learnt, when required. For example, in the examination hall, the learner should be able to retrieve all that s/he has learnt throughout the year.

Three major type of 'study skills' are—

a) Gathering Skills (perception, comprehension)
b) Storing Skills (Retention)
c) Retrieval Skills (Retrieval)

a) Gathering Skills

These are also known as reference skills and enable a learner to gather information as quickly as possible. This requires two sub-skills—locating and comprehending information.

For this knowledge of sources available e.g. books, journals, etc. is a must. After identification of sources the learner should make effective use of them.

A major source of information is Dictionary. It is deplorable that most of students do not even know how to use a dictionary. They are not aware of the rich information available in dictionary e.g. meaning, pronunciation, grammar, etymology derivations etc. of the words.

A student must know how to consult catalogue, content page and index at the end of the book. After locating the relevant pages the student must learn how to skin through them and perhaps scan only these sections which are useful for his/her assignment. Most students today do not want to go through these laborious processes, with the result that Xeroxed materials pile up but nothing gets assimilated. The gathering skills may be summed up as follows:

- *Locating Information*: Through reference to dictionaries, library catalogues, Tables of content, index, etc.
- *Comprehending Information*: Through mastering the sub-skills of reading, like skimming, scanning etc.

b) Storage Skills

It means what is learnt, should be retained. One may ask questions, when something is understood, is it automatically stored in the memory? The answer is partly yes, partly no. Most students are in habit of copying down every word spoken or dictated by the teacher. But when before the examination that information is required to be retrieved students may forget it.

They should have brief and precise notes, ready for quick reference. In fact, each student adopt his/her own way of storing information. However, S/he will benefit greatly from a training in storing skills.

Storing skills are of two major categories:

(i) *Note-taking*: It involves listening to lectures and taking down notes, i.e. the main and subordinate points. This is a skill every student needs to master. In fact, since students do not master this skill adequately, teachers are forced to resort to dictating notes after we have finished lecturing on a topic.

(ii) *Note-making*: It is very similar to note-taking except for the fact that note-making involves reading books and making notes. Note-making is a more leisurely activity.

Both the skills may be divided into the following sub-skills.

(i) Comprehension of the text/lecture
(ii) Identification of the main points.
(iii) Distinguishing main factors from subordinate ones.
(iv) Deciding on the order of priority among the various points.
(v) Identifying the organization of points.
(vi) Organizing the points into a visual display.

Note making and note-taking are meant only for the student's private use, hence S/he is free to use any abbreviation, symbol etc., although it would be a good idea to tell the students about certain abbreviation devices.

(c) Retrieval Skills

After gathering and storing information, students are required to express or summarize their ideas in lucid and coherent manner that it is understood by all.

The notes prepared by students at an earlier stage help them to make summarise the topic. The length of the summary depends on their purpose. Especially if students are to make précis, it should be 1/3rd of the content, but in making summary, one has to keep the purpose of doing so in view.

Reference Skills

Use of Dictionary

A dictionary is a reference book that focuses on defining words and phrases including multiple meanings. Whenever a language teacher or a student of language is in doubt about the meaning of a word or its right use, s/he turns to dictionary for gathering relevant information. The most frequently used dictionary is a language dictionary that includes the majority of frequently used words in a language. Language dictionaries are made for different types of users—scholars, office workers, schools and second language learners.

In the case of foreign language teaching, the general problem is that not only students but also teachers are not aware of all the words and facts of the language. They have to consult a dictionary when they comes across words phrases and idioms which require detailed explanation to understand. In a foreign language class students always find themselves in a position of disadvantage. Even the teachers are ill informed. As their own knowledge of the language is very poor, they have to consistently consult a dictionary for clarity and understanding of new vocabulary items.

Benefits of Dictionary

1. It helps in improving pronunciation.
2. It enhances the mental level and vocabulary of a student.
3. It inculcates the habit of good learning and self study.
4. It enables the student to write correct spellings.
5. It enriches different aspects of grammar.
6. It improves the quality of distinction between parts of speech.
7. It helps in learning correct stress and intonation.

How to Use a Dictionary

There are some students who do not know how to consult a dictionary. All standard dictionaries have a whole section of detailed information wherein the method of consulting it is given. The editor of a dictionary chooses to make use of certain abbreviations, symbols and relevant entries. He takes care to explain them for the benefit of users. The scholar must get acquainted with these details before he comes to use the dictionary.

As a number of dictionaries are available in the market, care should be taken in selecting a good dictionary. The names of some popular dictionaries are given below.

1) *Oxford Advanced Learner's Dictionary of Current English* by A.S. Hornby
2) *Bhargava's Dictionary*
3) *Oxford Dictionary*
4) *Webster's Dictionary*
5) *Chamber's Dictionary*

For learning a language the use of a dictionary is helpful, but using a bilingual dictionary is not recommended. The paraphrasing and circumlocution of L1 into L2 is not desirable, the monolingual dictionary by Longman is recommended for the purpose. Even if it is in a roundabout way, a monolingual dictionary such as *Longman Dictionary of Contemporary English* (which uses a basic 2000 words defining vocabulary) is intended to help the learner with not just pronunciation, spelling, meaning(s), but also with grammar, collocations and other relevant information about its appropriateness in certain contexts, its frequency, the speaker's attitudes associated with it. Bilingual dictionaries are more often applied at the initial stages of learning. Monolingual dictionaries written for non-native speakers concentrates on providing information. It teaches how to produce and pronounce a word. Monolingual dictionaries can be helpful in learning the inflectional form and grammar of words. But it is deplorable that a dictionary is not fully utilized by learners though it can increase their vocabulary and detailed knowledge also about words.

The use of a dictionary just to check the meaning is valid but there are other uses also. Every dictionary comes with a section at the beginning telling us how to use it with detailed annotated examples. However, these introductory sections remain to be read. It is almost peremptory for learners to know that an entry for a word is made up of several parts. Different symbols and typefaces indicate key features of the word — e.g. its pronunciation and how to spell its various forms – as well as it definitions and grammatical information. Here is word, from the *Longman Active Study Dictionary.*

accessible

accessible/ ek'sTsible/ adj easy to get

The island is accessible only by boat — opposite – inaccessible – accessibility / n (u)

The headword is **accessible**, the space without the two slanting lines tells us about the pronunciation for which phonetic symbols are used. (As teachers we must acquaint our learners with the symbols and sounds they stand for.) After the pronunciation comes the information about the word class (i.e. the parts of speech) it belongs to. The abbreviation adj. tells us that accessible is an adjective. This is followed by the meaning after which is given an example illustrating the use of the word in a particular context. Then we get the opposite of the word. Last of all another word *accessibility* is mentioned, which is a derivative from *accessible.* We are given information about its word class, i.e. n (own). We are told that it is an uncountable noun, indicated by U in square brackets. The meaning is not repeated the font size for *inaccessible* and *accessibility* is smaller than the one used for the headword *accessible.*

We give below a few tasks through which learner can be taught how to exploit the fall potential of a dictionary. (We are using the Longman Active Study, Dictionary of English for the tasks.)

Task 1: Alphabetical Ordering

The words are given in the dictionary in simple alphabetical order. You should be able to decide which word comes after or before another word.

Find the word in each column, which is not in alphabetical order. Put it in its correct place.

A	B
Destroy	Savior
Devil	Soldier
Dangerous	Save
Dutiful	Social
Doctor	Stratification

Task 2: Spelling and Pronunciation

The dictionary gives the spelling and pronunciation of the words. The pronunciation is given in the phonetic script. You should make yours self familiar with the phonetic symbols and the sounds they represent.

(i) Two of the following words i.e. have been wrongly used in place of '" use a dictionary to find them.
Fair, fare, steal, steel

(ii) Use a dictionary to find the silent letters in the words given below, i.e. the letter which is not pronounced. The letter ' h' is not pronounced in 'honest'
Hour, adjective, island, chemistry

Task 3 : Word Class Labels

The dictionary mentions the word class for every entry in the dictionary, its sources etc. which tells us whether a word is an adjective, a verb or a preposition.

Consult a dictionary to see which word class the following words belong to (some of the words may belong to more than one word class.): mind, chair, please, in, vegetable, game

Task 4 : Grammar

The Dictionary gives us the information whether a particular noun is countable or uncountable. It tells us whether a verb is used with or without an object, or whether an adjective is or is not followed by a noun and many other kinds of information about the grammar of a word.

(i) Use a dictionary to find out which of the following words are used in singular, in plural or both (if in plural, then also find the spellings and the pronunciation:
house , milk, news, progress, in –laws

(ii) Look up the following verbs in a dictionary and say whether they are used with an object, without an object or in either way: bring, cross, fill, keep, remain.

Task 5: Meaning

There may be more than one meaning of a word in a dictionary. You can choose the meaning according to the context :

sound

1. Your answer sounds well.
2. The sound of this instrument is harsh.

Task 6: Collections and idioms

The Dictionary gives us information about the way certain words collocate with certain other words the dictionary also makes available to us idioms (i.e. combinations of words with a fixed meaning is not deducible from the combination of the given words

(i) Match the words or phrases in column A with a word or phrase from column B

	A	B
(i)	A series	a purpose
(ii)	to exert	pain
(iii)	a practical	improvement
(iv)	a slight	of events
(v)	to inflict	pressure
(vi)	to serve	suggestion

(a) Read the following sentences and spot the idioms used in them. Guess the key word and look up the idiom in a dictionary.

(i) The island has been a bone of contention between the two countries for many years.
(ii) The little girl is the apple of her father's eye.
(iii) The man would hit the roof at the slightest of provocation .
(iv) The boy keeps rubbing the teacher the wrong way.
(v) You' ve had a hectic time now; it is time to let your hair down.

Using a Thesaurus

The word Thesaurus means 'a treasure house' in Latin . And it is indeed a treasure house of words for a writer. But it needs careful handling.

The basic point to keep in mind is that a thesaurus is not a substitute for a Dictionary. It is a word-finder. It is a handling tool to help recall a word that has slipped out of the mind. It gives us alternative ways of writing when we want to express ourselves more elegantly and effectively. But we should remember that a thesaurus does not tell the use of a particular word or expression. For that we need a dictionary.

So far the best known and used thesaurus is *Roget's Thesaurus*, which is not organized in n alphabetical order, rather the entries have been organized using a scheme of universal concepts. Suppose, a user is trying to recall a word such as 'inarticulate'. He would have to go to the section headed 'intellect' , then the subsection, 'Means of communicating ideas, and soon down until they reached that group of words including the word.

The *Longman Lexicon of Contemporary English* is another attempt in this tradition. The organization is based on fourteen semantic fields covering topics of everyday nature, for example 'Life and Living Things' , 'People and Family Life' and so on and so forth. It is a better reference tool for the learner of English for it provides detailed definitions and citations in the entries. In this way the Longman Lexicon also combines some of the features of a learner's dictionary. However, it is not exhaustive, it contains only about 15000 entries.

How to Use Encyclopaedia

An 'Encyclopedia' is a book or set of books giving information on many subjects. It contains general information about many topics and areas. The word 'Encyclopedia' is derived from the 'Greek' word enkyklia paideia which means ' a general knowledge '. The word has been in use for many years. It was used in print for the first time in Encyclopedia or knowledge of the world of disciplines, which was published in 1559. The first encyclopedia was written by Pling the Elder. The work consisted of 37 volumes and covered everything from anthropology and human physiology to agriculture, painting and pharmacology. During the following centuries, encyclopedias adopted as religious overtone. The first Christian encyclopedia was published in 560 AD, and the first Muslim encyclopedia came to light soon after. In 1403, the *Yongle Encyclopedia* was published in China. It consisted of 11000 handwritten volumes. Most of the original work has been lost through centuries and less than 400 volumes survive today.

Difference between Dictionary and Encyclopedia

An encyclopedia is often confused with a dictionary, although they are inherently different. A dictionary offers definition of words, while an encyclopedia explores topics more in depth and often includes illustration maps and photographs. While most encyclopedias are organized alphabetically some are organized by categories or cross-referenced articles.

Inferences, Analysis and Extrapolation

Inferences: After reading a story, essay or paragraph when one arrives at a conclusion, it is what we mean by inference. But here one has to be careful. While making inferences, the central idea should be kept in mind.

Analysis: When the content is long, it is divided into small portions for understanding, this process is called analysis. It can be said that analysis is a detailed study of a subject.

Extrapolation: Extrapolation means forming an opinion or make a judgment about a situation by using facts that we know from a different situation.

The concept of inferences is related to extensive reading whereas the concept of analysis is related to intensive reading. So we should be aware of intensive reading and intensive reading for better understanding of inferences and analysis.

(1) Intensive Reading: Intensive reading means detailed study of the passage in the type of reading, the reader has to be careful with the different language items i.e. words, grammar, language, expression, ideas etc. S/he tries to understand anything and everything contained in the paragraph.

(2) Extensive Reading: Here the reader is concerned with overall meaning and not the language. Here reading pleasure and enjoyment is more important, so that s/he can read fluently.

Generally in the lower classes, books are prescribed for intensive reading. But in the higher classes, extensive reading, on the part of the students, is as important as is intensive reading. In intensive reading the student cannot ignore the meaning of any word. S/he has to follow each word or structure contained in the paragraph. But in extensive reading, s/he can skip over a line a word or a structure which he fails to follow.

☞Points to Remember

(A) Listening Skill

1. Listening skill lays the very foundation of language learning.
2. To speak correctly, pupils should listen attentively.
3. You should present good models before the learners so that they can acquire correct pattern.
4. It must be clear to you that adequate methods, approaches and techniques will help the learners to develop listening skill.

(B) Speaking Skill

1. To learn a language, one has to speak correctly.
2. R.P. is considered to be the model pronunciation through out the world.
3. Pronunciation is the use of sound system, stress, rhythm intonation, fluency and pause in speaking.
4. You must help your students to understand about different speech organs and articulation of sounds.
5. Make it possible that your students can listen to native speakers may be on T.V. Radio, cassette or directly.
6. Pattern Practice is rapid oral drill on problem attention on something other than the problem itself.

(C) Reading Skill

1. Reading ability is an intellectual advancement and a source of pleasure as well.
2. You as a teacher should try to know what are the mechanics of reading.
3. There are various methods of Teaching Reading.
4. Try to know why the students have poor reading habits.
5. You should take care that proper guidance, correct model, self reading habit, regularity of spellings along with so many others are the ways to develop proper reading habits.
6. There are various ways of reading intensive reading, extensive reading, loud reading and silent reading.
7. Four levels of reading are literal, inferential, critical and creative reading.
8. How to use the sources, Dictionary and Encyclopedia etc.

(D) Writing Skill

1. Writing is a means of preserving the knowledge and physical expression of what you think.
2. Legibility, distinctiveness, spacing, simplicity, letter style, size and uniformity are the main characteristics of good handwriting.
3. You must be careful to create a natural learning environment for writing.
4. You as a teacher can try to know the causes of poor handwriting like bad posture, improper pen, holding of pen in a wrong manner, and careless attitude etc.
5. Role of the teacher is very significant in making the writing good.
6. You can adopt various techniques to improve the vocabulary of your learners like: using a dictionary using contextual clues and word games etc.
7. Major type of study skills are
   (i) Gathering skills,
   (ii) Storing skills,
   (iii) Retrieval skills.
8. A Dictionary is a reference book.
9. Thesaurus is not a substitute of Dictionary it is a word finder
10. An Encyclopedia is a book or set book giving information on many subjects.
11. Dialogue help in speaking skill.
12. Short story, Article, Speech all are useful activities in learning English.

17

Instructional Material

"It is easier to believe what you see than what you hear but if you both see and hear then you can understand more readily and retain more lastingly."

—Albert Duret

IMPORTANCE OF INSTRUCTIONAL MATERIAL AND THEIR EFFECTIVE USE

Meaning of Audio-Visual Aids

The word 'audio' refers to hearing and the word 'visual' refers to seeing. It means, the audio-visual aids are those things which appeal to our senses.

To understand the meaning of audio-visual aids more clearly let us see some definitions.

According to *Good's Dictionary of Education*, "Anything by means of which learning process may be encouraged or carried on through the sense of hearing or sense of sight".

McKown and Robert say, "Audio-visual aids are supplementary devices which the teacher, through the utilisation of more than one sensory channels, keep to clarify, establish and correlate concepts interpretation and appreciation".

According to *Comenius*, "The foundation of all learning consists in representing clearly to the senses the sensible objects so that they can be appreciated easily.

Kothari Education Commission (1966) has remarked, "The supply of teaching aids to every school is essential for the improvement of the quality of teaching. It should indeed bring about an educational revolution in the country".

According to *Dr. Sumer*, "The eye is the most important gateway to mind. For most people the visual impression is the one which can be most easily interpreted, is the most lasting and relates more readily to other sensory experiences".

Importance of Teaching Aids

To make the things easy and adjustable the audio-visual aids play an important role. With the help of these, the teacher can provide a clear cut idea of the words, phrases content or ideas to his students more easily. As *Wesley* has said rightly, "Audio-visual aids provide experiences. The relation between words and objects is easily established with their help. The time of the students is saved easily and correctly". Maximum learning occurs when our maximum number of senses are involved. The use of teaching aids has always helped in the development of human mind.

Some of the points are highlighted below.

1. *Clarity*: Audio-visual aids bring clarity and understanding to the various difficult and abstract concepts in language.
2. *Variety*: Mere chalk and talk do not help. Audio-visual aids give variety and provide different tools in the hands of the teacher.
3. *Novelty*: Audio-visual aids bring novelty in the teaching. Education through audio-visual aids has an element of novelty. It brings healthy changes in the general activities of the school like reading, writing and hearing, etc.
4. *Create situations*: Instructional aids would help create situations to illustrate the meaning of words and structures thus, making teaching-learning process meaningful.
5. *Best motivators*: Audio-visual aids are the best motivators. The students work with more interest and zeal. They pay more attention to the classroom activities.
6. *Based on maxims of teaching*: The use of audio-visual aids enables the teacher to follow the maxims of teaching like "concrete to abstract", "known to unknown", and "learning by doing".
7. *Time and energy saver*: With the help of teaching aids, the teacher can explain the things to the students quickly, clearly and abruptly. Moreover, this saves the energy of the teacher and the students.
8. *Meeting individual differences*: There are wide individual differences among the learners. Varied teaching aids can be selected and used according to the requirements of the learners.
9. *Reinforcement of the learners*: Audio-visual aids prove effective reinforcers, by increasing the probability of re-occurrence of the responses associated with them and thus render valuable help in the teaching-learning process.
10. *Useful in developing various skills*: These aids help in the development of various skills among the students. They learn, at a time, how to draw a diagram and the use of apparatus in solving the problems.

Use of Audio-Visual Aids

It is important for a teacher to know how the students can learn effectively. The maximum learning takes place when our maximum numbers of senses are involved in the process of learning. Following are the points why a teacher should use teaching aids in presentation of lesson.

1. According to human nature, when a teacher finds difficulty in explaining things or concepts in words, takes the help of teaching aids to create interest.
2. To realise actual or real experiences with the use of audio-visual aids students can be helped to realise the real experiences. The pupils can teach, smell, taste or draw pictures to gain knowledge.
3. Useful for slow learners. Individual differences among the children always occur. So the teacher can use the teaching aids to make the lesson effective according to the level of the students.
4. Knowledge is related to various sense organs. The sense organs are the gateways of knowledge and audio-visual aids help these sense organs to gain more knowledge. The more the sense organs are involved in learning, more the permanent learning would be.
5. Change in the traditional education. Use of audio-visual aids has brought a change in the traditional classroom teaching. Use of audio-visual aids make the teaching more systematic and impressive.

Principles in the Use of Audio-Visual Aids

1. *Principle of Aim*: Audio-visual aids should help the teacher in achieving the aims and objectives.
2. *Principle of Selection*: Teaching aids should be according to age level, and grade level of the learners. Along with element of interest and motivation they should fulfill the educational value.
3. *Principle of Preparation*: Locally available Teaching aids should be given preference and low cost teaching aids can be prepared with the help of students.
4. *Principle of Physical Control*: This principle relates to the arrangement of keeping aids safely and to facilitate their lending to the students for their use.
5. *Principle of Presentation*: The aids should be displayed properly and distraction of all kinds should be eliminated.

Precautions to be taken into consideration while selecting audio-visual aids

1. *Related to the topic*: A teacher should select the aids which are related to the topic.
2. *Approximate size*: Teaching aids should be of appropriate size so that every students can see it.
3. Teaching aids should not be very costly.
4. They should be portable.
5. They should be meaningful and purposeful.
6. The audio-visual aids should motivate the learners to learn more.
7. The aids must be used at the proper time.
8. Too many aids should not be used unnecessarily.

USE OF THE FOLLOWING TEACHING AIDS

Various Types of Teaching Aids

Aids can be classified on the basis of senses they make use of. Thus aids can be classified into three parts.

(I) *Visual Aids*: These are generally those aids which make use of visuals. The following aids are included in it:

(a) Chalkboard
(b) Pictures
(c) Charts
(d) Models
(e) Rolling board
(f) Textbook
(g) Film strips
(h) Museum
(i) Actual things (objects)
(j) Outlines
(k) Maps
(l) Magic lantern
(m) Epidiascope
(n) Specimen
(o) Collections
(p) Bulletin board
(q) Silent pictures
(r) Globe
(s) Class Magazine
(t) Projects

(II) *Audio-Aids*: These are generally those aids which make use of auditory senses. These can be.

(a) Gramophone
(b) Tape recorder
(c) Radio
(d) Lingua Phone
(e) Phonograph

(III) *Audio-Visual Aids*: These are generally those aids which make use of both auditory and visual senses. These can be:

(a) Television
(b) Motion pictures
(c) Dramatisation

These visual aids can further be divided into two sub-sections.

(i) *Non-Projective Aids*

- Models
- Charts
- Pictures
- Maps
- Graphs
- Bulletin boards
- Flannel board
- Museum
- Poster
- Photos
- Globe
- Specimen
- Textbook illustrations

(ii) *Projective Aids*: Those are the aids in which something or a process is projected in the form of pictures. These aids are:

- Silent pictures
- Film strips
- Epidiascope
- Episcope
- Magic lantern
- Micro projector
- Overhead projector
- Opaque projector

Let us discuss some important Teaching aids in detail:

1. *Flannel Board*

It is also sometimes referred to as Flannel graph or felt board. It is made of wood, card board or straw board covered with coloured flannel or woollen cloth. Display materials like cut-outs, pictures, drawings and light objects backed with rough surfaces like sand paper strips are used.

How to Use a Flannel Board?

Following points should be kept in view:

(i) The teacher may collect a large number of pictures or wall cut diagrams, etc. and back them with sand paper pieces. He/she may then use one by one.
(ii) While displaying, sequence should be observed.
(iii) Display material on the board should be changed as frequently as possible.

Advantages of Flannel Board

(i) It is quite economical and easy to handle.
(ii) The pictures or cuttings can be easily fixed and removed when required without spoiling the material.
(iii) Interest of the students can be sustained.
(iv) It helps in the clarity of the concepts.

Some Precautions

(1) *Numbering*: There should be proper numbering behind the pictures.
(2) *Related to the topic*: The cuttings and pictures should be related to the topic.
(3) Too many items should not be used at a time.
(4) Sand paper and flannel cloth should be of good quality.
(5) Selection of items to be displayed should be made with great precaution.

2. *Pictures*

Attractive, colourful pictures attract children as well as adults. A picture may help at the introductory stage of the lesson by making students have a visual image of the ensuing lesson as described by the teacher. It is said that a picture is worth thousand words and can be used in different ways as described below.

- Understanding of the lesson is facilitated with the help of pictures.
- *Vocabulary*. New words can be explained by associating them with appropriate pictures.
- *Structures*. New structures can be presented and drilled with the help of pictures. Pictures can be used for practising the tenses.

- *Composition*. The teacher can develop oral and written composition through pictures. In the junior classes the composition may be oral. It should be developed by putting questions on pictures. In the senior classes, pictures can be used to develop written composition.
- For developing imagination of the students. Pictures can be used for developing the imagination of the students. Here a picture is shown to the class and the students are asked to speak about it. This type of exercise makes the students creative and imaginative.

Principles for the effective use of pictures

- Pictures should be used for specific purposes.
- They should be hung at a place from where the students can see them easily.
- They should be integrated in the lesson.
- The teacher should point out what each picture is explaining.
- Pictures should be used judiciously, over–use of pictures should be avoided.
- Sufficient time should be given to the students to see and understand pictures.
- Size of the pictures should be large.
- It should not be loaded with informational material rather the maxim of 'one picture one idea' be followed.
- Pictures should not be used in every lesson as a fashion, instead only on the requirement of the topic, these should be used.

3. Chalk Board

It is one of the most common visual aids in use. It is a slightly abrasive writing surface made of wood, ply, hardboard, cement, ground glass asbestos, slate, plastic, etc. with black, green or bluish green paint on it. It has been termed as the most versatile visual aids. They can be fixed, roller or movable. Coloured chalk sticks are also used for better illustration.

Effective Use of Chalkboard

We find that chalkboard is the most common teaching aid used by the teacher for writing important points, drawing illustrations, solving problems etc. Following considerations should be kept in view while teaching:

(a) Writing should be clear and legible.
(b) The letters on board should not be less than one inch in height. The recommended height of letters on a chalkboard is between 6 cm. to 8 cm.
(c) There should be proper arrangement of light.
(d) Pointer should be used.

Advantages of Chalk Board

(a) It is a very convenient teaching aid for group teaching.
(b) It is the cheapest aid.
(c) Illustrations can be drawn on it to capture the attention of the students.
(d) Spellings, vocabulary and pronunciation of the students can be improved
(e) Quick revision of the lesson is made possible by writing the main points on the chalkboard.
(f) The teacher should write in straight lines.
(g) The teacher should also stand in right posture, he/she should not come, between the board and the students.

Limitations of the Chalkboard

(1) Dependence on the teacher is increased.
(2) It makes the lesson teacher paced.
(3) It makes the lesson dull.
(4) Individual attention to the students is not given.

4. Charts

Chart is another type of graphic aid which is a non-mechanical and non-projected visual aid that helps visualise a situation, concept or idea. As a matter of fact, charts expand the circle of contrived experiences where pictures, picture cut-outs and posters do not help introduce and/or develop a lesson for the simple reason that they are just not available and procurable. Charts may be resorted to achieve the same purpose, i.e., the clarity of concept and precepts, idea and image. Charts, therefore, are the visual and representative illustrations of things and processes which are otherwise not possible to be clearly transmitted to the students. To facilitate pupil-comprehension, charts simplify processes by presenting on analytic and synthetic view while dealing with a particular teaching-learning situation. Charts are especially useful in describing an on-going process/activity.

In the teaching of English, charts can be used for the following different purposes:

- Chronological events.
- To classify topics and to show relationship between words, word groups, sentences, their structure and patterns, structures and their substitutions, teaching of grammar specially tenses where verbs are described by means of a flow chart in teaching of poem by writing the poem on them—
  - in developing a story,
  - in fixing ideas and image,
  - in conducting pronunciation drill,
  - teaching paragraph composition,
  - meaning of difficult words.

Qualities of a Good Chart

- Charts should be simple, attractive, sequential and colourful.
- Letters on charts should be of big size to be seen even by the back-benchers.
- Charts should be used keeping in view the need and time available.
- Charts can be prepared by the help of students.

After use they should be kept properly.

5. Tape Recorder

It is a very useful audio-aid and occupies a key place in the audio-instruments meant for the educational purposes. Its main educational purposes are:

(i) Teacher can record his/her lesson with correct pronunciations, stress, intonation. But there should be no physical or environmental interference during the recording sessions, because any disturbance will affect the quality of input/output.

(ii) Fluency in speech is possible by recording the programmes. Doubts can be clarified and essential points can be discussed. Stopping, re-playing etc. is all possible and this makes the task of healthy interaction quite possible.

(iii) It may supplement the educational outputs of the radio and television broadcasts. The speeches and talks of renowned teachers, invited guest speakers and saying of the great men can be recorded and kept safe for future educational purposes.

- For correct pronunciation, poem, recitation, stress and intonation tapes can be useful.
- Spellings can be taught with the help of tape recorder.
- With its help drills can be given.

6. Lingua Phone (Record Player)

Record player is also an important audio-aid for teaching English. It may be a little costly, but its use are many. It is a kind of gramophone designed especially for correcting speech disorders, pronunciation and teaching sounds and sound combinations. A sound amplifier is filled in a lingua phone and also can be played upon it.

A record player is very useful for a teacher in diverse classroom situations. Some records on which the speech of important persons like—authors, poets, experienced teachers can be recorded and are made available to the students. And when they listen to these records with the help of a player, they enjoy learning a lot.

It can be used for teaching spellings, correct pronunciation, poem, prose, stress and intonation etc. Drills for vocabulary and structures can also be given with the help of a record player.

7. Television

Television has been described as "The queen of audio-visual aids". In addition to the sense of hearing it appeals to the sense of sight. Therefore, it is titled as "Electronic Blackboard of the future for the developing countries". Of late, its utility in educational process has been recognised. It has now become powerful means of communication of ideas all over the world. The teacher inculcates among the learners good viewing habits, critical and attentive listening. He also psychologically prepares them to receive the information from the television.

Kinds of Educational TV

1. *Open Circuit Television.* It is the usual type of telecast by commercial or non-commercial stations.

2. *Closed Circuit Television.* It is the selective telecasts which can be tuned in only by specially equipped receivers.

Types of Educational Programmes

The following are the type of educational programmes, commonly used on TV:

(i) *Demonstration Type.* It can be commercial as well as educational. Some outstanding classroom activities of a school is made known to others through television.

(ii) *Supplementary Type.* It provides such programmes which help the teachers and institutions in supplying that material which is required in a few problem areas. These programmes are also called as enrichment programmes.

(iii) *Direct Teaching Programmes.* It is the programme which is telecast in different type of schools. It can be utilised in elementary schools as well as in high and higher secondary school. Haryana Government had planned to give computer education to all the students of Haryana Board through this method at a time.

Advantages of TV

(i) A large number of students can be taught at a time.

(ii) It helps in improving linguistic skills of the learners.

(iii) The lectures and lessons by good teachers on the TV may prove a big help to the students as well as to the teacher.

(iv) On the television model type of handwriting can be shown. The students may look at it and they can improve their own handwriting.

(v) It is a time saving device.

(vi) It is very helpful in developing the skills of listening, speaking and understanding, reading and writing of the students at a time.

(vii) Speed of writing can be improved by writing, while listening to news.

(viii) The students who are not able to attend the class due to some reason can watch the TV lesson at their homes.

(ix) Gifted and brilliant students are benefited a lot.

8. Film and Film Strips

Film and film strips are very common but powerful audio-visual aids which can play more effective role. By watching English movie, the pronunciation and spoken English habits can be developed very easily, as these are combined with movement and sound. Thus, they provide very interesting and direct experience to the pupils. In films, there is a continuity, and thus arouses the interest of the students.

Film strips are more flexible than cinema. Slides are complete pictures in themselves and in the film strip some slides are shown in a fixed order. They make the things more clear and interesting. Variety can be brought. Some considerations are to be kept in view while using film strips.

- Proper sequence of slides.
- Proper seating arrangement.
- Careful explanation of film strips by the teacher.
- In between questions can be asked for more clarity.

9. Overhead Projector

The overhead projector represents one of the quite advanced type of projective equipments that may be properly used for projecting images of the transparencies on the screen. Image of the screen is projected over the shoulder of the teacher that is why its name is overhead projector. Light from a powerful lamp inside the box passed through a transparency (approximately 8 × 10 inches) placed on the stage. A lens and mirror system mounted on the stage on a bracket above the box turns the light beam 90 degrees and projects the image back over the shoulder of the presenter.

A variety of materials can be projected including cut-out silhouettes, small opaque objects, and in many types of transparent objects.

Projected materials can be manipulated by the presenter who can point important items, highlight them with coloured pens, add details by marking on the transparency with a pen. Large size slides of 21 × 25 cm can be used.

- No difficulty in changing the slides.
- Acts as a projector as well as a board.
- Handy and portable.

Limitations

The projection system is designed for large group presentation so it does not lend itself to independent study.

Printed material and other non-transparent items, such as magazine illustrations cannot be projected directly as is possible with the opaque projector.

Teacher should do it regularly because it is observed that use of OHP remains limited to illustrate drawings and papers read at professional conventions.

10. Language Laboratory

Technological aids in language teaching are a major force today, and among these aids, the language laboratory occupies the most prominent place. Two conflicting attitudes towards the role of the language laboratory are prevalent: one regards the lab as the centre of language teaching, with the teacher assisting the lab operation and adjusting to it; the other regards the lab as a teaching aid, with the class as the center.

Few would admit even to themselves then they look upon the lab operation as the central part of language teaching. Everyone is quick to state that the lab is not intended to replace the teacher but to take away the drudgery of drill so that the teacher may devote his time to more intellectual or literary activities. Yet the materials and plans produced may in fact be directed towards the lab as the order of teaching. Two criteria seem to characterise the lab as the center attitude: (1) the recorded materials are complete lessons, which attempt to do all the teaching; (2) the accompanying explanations and the advertisements state that the lessons do not require a trained teacher.

This point of view that the lab is the centre of teaching is rejected here for the following reasons: (1) it is more difficult and expensive to produce good materials that attempt to do everything than to produce materials that supplement the work of the teacher, (2) complete materials age rapidly and soon become dated, (3) such complete materials are inflexible and awkward without a teacher to control them and adapt them to the students.

The statement that such a lab will take the drudgery out of language teaching is problematical at best. Drudgery can never be completely taken out of teaching, because teaching will always involve working with those who know less than the teacher. A teacher who feels so strongly that drill is baring chore should seriously consider whether he should remain in the profession. One of the chief satisfactions of teaching is observing how the students learn what to them is new material, however, old and familiar it may be to the teacher. By relegating all learning and drill to the language laboratory, the teacher can become merely a baby sitter and examiner.

In the lab as an aid point of view (1) the teacher is clearly thought of as the central figure teaching of student, (2) the lab is one more aid, not the central component of teaching, (3) the lab materials are designed to supplement class work selectively, (4) the materials are not complete lesson.

With the explosion in demand for more education for more people there is a critical shortage of good teachers everywhere. It is sometimes thought by providing language labs anybody will be able to teach a language and the teacher shortage will be solved. The fact is who can put the new equipment and techniques to good use as well as conduct a class. Labs do not solve the teacher shortage. When used properly, they can increase quality, the effectiveness of good teachers, whether or not they are native speakers of the target language.

Definition of a Language Lab

There are laboratories designed for research on the analysis and description of languages and labs designed for teaching of languages. The language research or speech research laboratory may contain such equipment as the sound spectrograph and the oscillograph. The language teaching laboratory usually contains playback and recording equipment for students to practice the languages they are studying. This chapter is concerned with language-teaching laboratories.

There is great variety in equipment and facilities in language laboratories. Some may have a single playing machine with earphones for the students, while others have semi-private booths with a tape recorder for each student. Some have a sound proof recording studio, and others are merely listening rooms.

The language lab is a special room for practice with sound equipment. The tape recorder used by the teacher in connection with the lesson in class does not constitute a lab although every teacher should have nearly access to a tape recorder for teaching. What constitutes a language lab is a special room with necessary equipment set aside for practice by the students. A separate room with a single tape or disc playback apparatus where the students may practice is the most rudimentary lab, but it is a lab. A classroom can become a lab after class hours, or the lab can be used as a classroom by the teacher, but the distinctive characteristic is the separate room where students may practice the language.

The Scope of the Lab

The language lab can provide good models of the speech of the target language for imitation and manipulation by the student. This increases the power of the teacher who is not a native speaker of the second language and who has not achieved complete native pronunciation. It also increases the power of the teacher who is a native speaker by permitting the students to hear a variety of speakers of the language.

The lab permits audio-lingual practice outside of class. When the lab allows individual selection of exercise, it provides for individual differences so that each student can repeat an exercise as many times as necessary. Labs with recording equipment for the students permit recording the students for more objectives and accurate criticism and correction by the teacher labs that have the proper equipment can be sued for listening tests given individually or in groups and for group speaking tests, which the teacher can correct individually later.

It can be concluded from the above discussion that language

laboratory occupies the most prominent place among the technological aids in language teaching. It is one of the recent innovations in language teaching. It is not a place where learners perform language experiments, the same way as they do in physics and chemistry lab. It is a special room where students may practise speaking and listening with the help of sound equipment. It consists of the latest technological equipment in the field of audio-visual education including the facility of CCTV, computer aided learning and objective based instructional programmes with regard to English Teaching.

There are cabins in the lab for learners which are interconnected with the monitor head cabin through inter-communication system. From the cabin of the monitor board, the whole teaching-learning process is controlled. Here with the help of the tape scripts, pronunciation drills, dialogues, controlled conversation, the students are given ear training and planned practice.

Central Institute of English and Foreign Language, Hyderabad and Regional Institute of English, Chandigarh are worth seeing.

From the above discussion it is clear that there are two divergent views about the status and functioning of language laboratory.

Firstly, according to Robert Lado, the language laboratory is "the centre of language teaching" and the teacher helps its operational activities by providing suitable materials and learning situations.

Secondly, that the language laboratory is an additional 'teaching aid' with class as its centre. Experiments are not conducted here; rather it is a functional arrangement of teaching English, specifically its linguistic aspects and the skill component. It is equipped with electronic devise for recording and reproducing speech sounds with correct vowel-consonant element, intonation, stress and articulation. The teacher remains central as he/she regulates and monitors the linguistic activity going on in the laboratory in consonance with the age of the students. Language laboratory does not teach the whole range of linguistic material. It is selective and collective teaching. Laboratory exercise can involve the following activities.

Listening, listening-repeating, mimicry-memorisation, listening and identifying by number, listening and comprehending, pattern, substitution, addition, synthesis, oral composition, transformation, dictation, reading paced by a recording etc.

As the new pattern of language teaching become mere clearly established, language laboratory will become part and parcel of language teaching programme. A skillful teacher can give deeper understanding to his pupils of the true nature of the language skills. But as far as possible the teacher should prepare copies or tape scripts based on linguistic facts and psychological laws of learning. Drills should be pre-selected and based on the criterion of the pupil usage.

How to Use the Lab

We have stated that lab materials which attempt to teach complete lessons are expensive to produce, become dated quickly, and will not succeed ultimately direction by a teacher, who cannot be relegated to the role of baby-sitter. For these reasons, the materials for the language lab should be partial materials rather than complete lessons.

The Myth of a Lab Method

The idea that electronic recorders in the lab constitute a revolutionary method of teaching a special and second language is a myth. A forty five minute commentary on the subjunctive in Spanish without a single example and therefore without practice by the students is bad teaching whether in a classroom or in a modern lab.

Lab materials have to be prepared with as much if not more care than any other materials for teaching; they must be clear, graded, purposeful and based on linguistic facts and psychological laws of learning. Merely recording something for use in the lab does not make it a good exercise.

How to Prepare Lab Materials

There are commercially available tapes and records to accompany language textbooks or the supplement the language course. They usually have adequate instructions for the teacher and need no further elaboration here. Publishers often give the user the choice between purchasing a set of the tapes or records or borrowing the master tapes for the purpose of making one's own copies. It is preferable to purchase the commercially made copies unless one has superior copying equipment and technical assistants. Making one's own copies will take considerable time and they may not be of the best technical quality. Many schools do not have the money to buy expensive sets of materials, however, and the teacher will then have to make the copies for his students.

In addition to the regular tapes, the teacher will need to prepare supplementary tapes top be used as a regular part of the course, an extra assignment for slow students, a bonus for the better students, etc. The language teacher should, therefore, be able to prepare such tapes. The following discussion gives step-by-step suggestions and examples. They are intended to be suggestive rather than restrictive. As his experience develops, the teacher will be able to introduce variations and original ideas to suit a particular class or problem and to explore more effective materials.

The discussion is divided into the following steps: (1) identify the problem that needs lab practice, (2) choose the type of drill best suited for the purpose, (3) prepare the tape script, (4) make the recording, (5) check it, (6) evaluate the exercise in actual use with the class.

As you know individual differences occur, one can learn according to his/her own speed and learning ability.

Shy or introvert students can learn in a better way.

Tape can be organised and replayed accordingly.

Limitations

In a language laboratory the emphasis is only on one aspect of the language i.e. speaking. Other skills are ignored.

It requires adequate funds to establish a language laboratory.

11. Projects

Dr. Kilpatrick rightly defines a project as a "whole hearted purposeful activity, proceeding in 'a social environment'". According to Stevenson, we may define project as 'a problematic act carried to completion in a natural setting "Thus a project is a kind of life 'experience which is motivated by a strong desire and teaching by the project method is based upon the use of this desire.'" You are aware that planning, executing and evaluating play an important role in carrying out an organized programme for effective teaching. In fact, project is directly related to life, Professors Ballard's interpretation of project seems to be quite correct, "A project is a bit of real life that has been imparted into the school, 'learning by living' is a better description of the project method than is 'learning by doing'". Thus a project has four characteristics.

(i) Spontaneity: This means that children should not be forced to do anything. This is possible when we provide them with a situation in which they show eagerness to work.

(ii) Purpose: There must be a purpose behind a project. The purpose ought to be clear to the pupils. This clearness of purpose will act as a strong stimulus for them.

(iii) Significance: The project must be significant. It means that the purpose must be of lasting importance for the pupils.

(iv) Interest: The project must be interesting. It must be clear to you that spontaneity purpose and significance all will be accompanied only when the principle of interest is at work.

Designing a Project

We ought to bear in mind that besides providing situation, planning, executing and evaluating it are also important. As the project may demand various activities like reading, writing, correcting, oral discussion, collecting material etc., it will afford varieties of learning.

It would be good if pupils are asked to make a diary of their own and write out the name of the project, the date and time (beginning and finishing) of the project, the objections of the project the original plan and his own evaluation of his own work and also that of others.

12. Class Magazine

Class magazine is an important means to enable the students to express their inner feelings. It also helps them in developing the positive and desirable qualities. They can be of two types—

(a) Wall magazine.

(b) Annual or Half yearly magazine.

It is good to start with wall magazine. Students can be asked to write some articles, poems and some knowledgeable thoughts/facts on their own. They can draw some sketches, cartoons, designs and paintings.

All these cartoons etc. or articles should be screened by the Committee or incharge teacher. After scrutiny selected ones can be published in class magazine. There should be variety in the content e.g. short stories, essays, poems, cartoons, painting and sketches. Besides these important facts, good thoughts, Comedy skit, jokes, information about Co-curricular activities.

However the teacher may check the complete material and then it can also be included.

It should bear a suitable title and attractive cover page.

Objective of Class Magazine

(1) Providing opportunities for expression in writing.
(2) To develop literary interest and reading habits.
(3) To provide training for the utilization of leasure time.
(4) To develop (*Nishtha*) commitment towards school and feel proud of class achievement.
(5) To help in developing the model of good character.
(6) To make the society aware about class achievement.
(7) To help in enhancing the knowledge of students.
(8) It will also help the students to increase their vocabulary among general knowledge and ability of expression.
(9) To identify and nurture the creativity among students.

How to organize class magazine activities—

(1) Teacher can divide the class in groups and motivate them to write for wall magazine and class magazine.
(2) Student Editor should be selected on the basis of quality.
(3) Permission from the Head should be sought and proper name can be given to the magazine. Section wise or class wise magazine can motivate the students to excel in writing.
(4) Students should be given enough time meaning by prior intimation should be given.
(5) Class teacher or teacher Editor can give them proper directions.
(6) Editor Board should give proper attention in the selection of language, style and content.
(7) A very nominal fee can be charged by each student for class magazine at the time of admission fee. Care should be taken that each student gets the class magazine.
(8) Magazine should be sent to the agencies of social welfare and educational authorities.

(9) Previous copies of the magazine should be kept carefully as a record and guideline also.

13. Language Games

There are a number of games which can be played with students to teach the language. For your convenience various games are discussed. It depends on the efficiency of the teacher for selection of a particular game for particular level. Following are the various games—

- Question games.
- Spelling completion game.
- Sentence completion game
- Story completion game.
- Sentence building game.
- Missing words.
- Description game.
- Word memory game.

☛Points to Remember

1. The use of Teaching Aids makes the teaching-learning process interesting and effective.
2. You as a teacher must be careful in their selection and presentation.
3. Teaching Aids help the teacher in developing all the four skills : listening, speaking, reading and writing.
4. Prior planning regarding the use of Teaching Aids is essential.
5. Class wall newspaper is a marvellous teaching aid as it helps the learners to contribute their articles.

18

Co-curricular Activities

CO-CURRICULAR ACTIVITIES

Concept

Earlier, the term extra-curricular activities were used. But now-a-days along with the instruction of various subjects, activities undertaken side by side are named as co-curricular activities. These are considered as an integral part of the curriculum. In the past, also these were organised in order to bring healthy development of the child. But in the present education system it has drawn much attention. The Secondary Education Commission has very rightly stated, "Given a clean, pleasant and well maintained school building, we would like the school to see if it can provide a richly varied, pattern of activities to cater, to the development of their children's entire personality. It has to formulate a scheme of hobbies, occupations and projects that will appeal to, draw out the powers of children of varying temperaments and aptitudes".

According to Thompkin we can divide the co-curricular activities:

1. Individual Outcomes

(i) Constructive use of leisure times;
(ii) Development of personality;
(iii) Enriching of personality;
(iv) Achieving self-understanding;
(v) Taking initiative per individual responsibility and functioning;
(vi) Learning how to organise a meeting or conference and how one can participate in it;
(vii) Providing opportunity to the individual for self-evaluation.

2. Social Outcomes

(i) Providing physical and mental entertainment;
(ii) Getting practice for working with others;
(iii) Developing the democratic responsibility;
(iv) Learning to practice good human relations;
(v) Understanding group processes;
(vi) Encouraging good student-teacher relations;
(vii) Increasing social contacts.

(3) Civil and Ethical Outcomes

(i) Establishing the bonds of understanding of each other without any racial, religious or economic or intellectual differences;
(ii) Putting natural values and ideas in practical use;
(iii) Providing meaning to curriculum and diversifying it;
(iv) Helping the students in their liking of the school.

IMPORTANCE

- Students' interest is sustained.
- Help them to lead better social life.
- Democratic spirit is developed.
- Leadership quality is inculcated.
- Leisure time is spent fruitfully.
- Participation in physical activities leads towards better health.
- 'We feeling' is developed among students.
- Gives opportunities to develop interest in learning the language while playing with fellow students.
- To help in releasing the energy in learning activities.

THE WRITTEN ASPECT: WALL PAPER, MANUSCRIPTS AND MAGAZINES

Language has a two-fold function to perform in an individual's daily life:

Communicate Through Speech and Through Writing

When we talk of teaching English, we have to take into account, both the spoken and the written form. The aim of every school is to inculcate in the children the powers of good expression both oral and written.

Various exercises and expression of children. Even the most conscientious teacher of English will admit that normal school activities are rather inadequate in encouraging the children to express their views in writing. Even the maximum number of essays and composition exercises done in class inefficient in providing the child a free rein to express his ideas and opinions on a subject of his choice.

The school wallpaper provides an excellent opportunity for the display of such articles written by the children in a sincere and original manner. In such efforts, the the child is not constrained by limitations of classroom discussions or of subjects by the teachers. He can write on any thing that catches his fancy, or he may express an opinion on any subject that is dear to his heart. The fact that good efforts by the student will have the honour of being displayed on the school wall-paper. It encourages the child to put in all his best efforts in producing a flawless piece of writing. The wall paper also encourages the poetic talents of some students which would otherwise have died a natural death in the absence of any favourable wind to nurture the flame of talent. Thus a wall paper provides tremendous opportunities and encouragement of children to express their ideas originally and in presentable manner. A good teacher of English should exploit this part of school's activities to encourage the children to write as often as they feel the inclination.

The school magazine has all the advantages of the wall papters and even more. Since all children are greatly interested in what their friends write, the magazine will have a tremendous popular appeal to the children. The teacher of English can exploit this by including some articles on famous books or pieces of literature or poems in such a manner that the children's curiosity is aroused and they are encouraged to go to the source. In this manner, children can be led to great works of literature. The latest book is available in the library and other such useful information can be transmitted through the school magazine.

Moreover the school magazine has the added advantage of having a wider circulation. Hence the standard of articles and poems published can be maintained at a much higher standard. This automatically will raise the standard of writing the pupils also. Thus a well-produced school magazine fosters good habits of both reading and writing in the students.

Usefulness of language games, quiz, debate, group discussions and other co-curricular activities in the teaching-learning of English

It has been discussed earlier that there is a need of functional language. English language can be best understood in situations. So a teacher has to facilitate the learners by creating the best situations. It is a living language and our students are supposed to use it in almost every walk of life. A large number of co-curricular activities can be organised to enrich the experiences of teachers as well as learners. For better understanding some activities are being discussed in detail.

ASSOCIATION OF ENGLISH TEACHERS

It is good if English teachers form an association for academic purpose, to discuss problems, exchange ideas and find out the common solutions to various problems. Such associations may be formed at city level or district level. Various group activities such as lectures by experts, exhibitions and seminars etc. can be organised.

Since it is not our native language why our students should lag behind due to poor performance in this language. It is the utmost duty of language teacher to develop the interest, competency and enthusiasm of the students. To fulfil this purpose various co-curricular activities can be organised.

DRAMATICS OR DRAMATISATION

Dramatics is a synthetic art which involves the purposive coordination of speech and muscles of the body combined with a sense of rhythm and music, ideas and emotions, diction and movements.

Dramatics provides opportunities for the catharsis of emotions through expression of innate urges. It releases pent-up energies. The pupils play different roles and satisfy his innate tendency to play, to imitate, to express himself and to enjoy.

Speech and vocabulary both can be improved by dramatics. One learns better pronunciation, intonation, tone, accent, pause, rhythm and other qualities of elocution. From social point of view also it provides the opportunity of team work.

It is the activity liked most by the young learners which not only makes them to take initiative but motivates them to imagine that too in right direction. Shy and introvert students are also benefited by this activity.

Mime, 'Do' and 'Say' exercise, dialogue, short stories, fables, original plays etc. are the suggested activities.

Mental level and age of the students have to be kept in mind by the teacher. This activity can bring wonderful result with careful planning and organisation.

USEFULNESS OF LANGUAGE GAMES

The following word games are very useful for the teaching and expanding of vocabulary:

(i) Preparing a Word Dictionary

The children may be encouraged to enlist new words under different heads. For example, school, home, hospital, etc. This will inspire and encourage them to have new words and ultimately it will lead to the expansion of vocabulary.

(ii) Movable Strips

A large number of new words can be taught if the teacher is in a position to make use of prefixes and suffixes. The device of movable strips is very useful for this purpose.

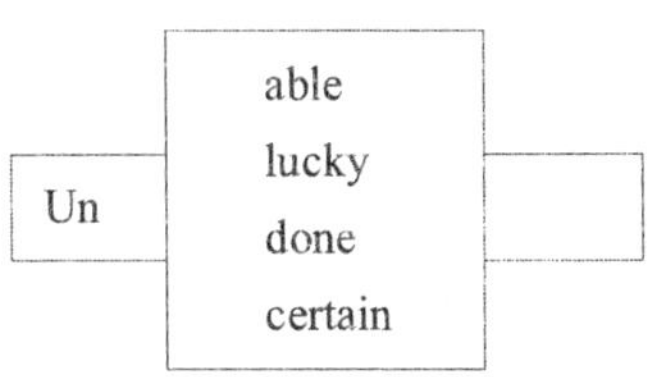

(iii) Miscellaneous Games

Here are a few more word games which have been given by a pamphlet published by the Department of Extension Services, Government Training College, Trichur:

(a) The students will be asked to frame a new word by rearranging the letters of the word in capital e.g. MILES: Smile.

(i) Thieves STEAL at the …… opportunity (least)
(ii) Parents should TEACH children not to …… (cheat)

(b) Fill in the blanks. Example: Something which causes destruction is ……. ive (destructive).
(i) A person who talks a lot is …… ive (talkative).
(ii) A thing which attracts people's attention is ……. ive (attractive).

(c) Each word in this test begins with the letter 'h' give them:
(i) A place of shelter for boats and ships (harbour).
(ii) The floor of a fire place (hearth).

Pairing

The words in the list A are of the same or nearly the same meaning as the words in list B. Pair them.

A	B
anger	abundant
disappear	vanish
swift	prevent
forbid	wrath
plentiful	rapid

Write down as many suitable words as you can find to complete each of these phrases:

(i) A lot of ……….
(ii) A piece of …….
(iii) A group of ……
(iv) A room of …….

Students may be asked to build nouns from verbs, nouns from adjectives, verbs from nouns, verbs from adjectives, adjectives from nouns and adjectives from verb.

Nouns from Verbs (by adding)

- ment → amusement, improvement, punishment
- al → arrival, refusal, withdrawal
- ure → closure, departure, pressure
- ation → inspiration, motivation, examination

Nouns from Adjectives

- ness → seriousness, weakness, ugliness
- ity → activity, hospitality
- ce → absence, excellence, difference
- th → depth, truth

Verbs from Nouns

- ize → economize, sympathize
- en → encircle, encourage, enjoy
- be → before, behead, befriend

- ify → terrify, beautify

Verbs from Adjectives

- en → deepen, widen
- en → enable, endear, enlarge

Adjectives from Nouns

- y → airy, cloudy
- al → emotional, parental
- ly → weekly, worldly
- ous → dangerous, nervous

Adjectives from Verbs

- able — laughable, consumable
- ant — pleasant, different
- ed — aged

In a given set of words, pick out the one which is out of the class.

(i) book, pencil, pen, shoe, notebook.

(ii) Soldier, battle, tank, gum, farmer, sword

Expansion of vocabulary through association

Vocabulary may be enlarged by telling synonymous, words connected with a chosen subject or by forming compound words with one part common. Pupils may also be given homonyms i.e. words having the same pronunciation but different spellings and meanings e.g. hair: hare, fair: fare.

Word Chains

Word chains are chains of word. Each word suggested by the one before it, either by meaning or similarity in sound.

Kin's Game

A list of words is written on the chalk-board out of sight of the class. For it, the teacher may use standing board with side reversed towards the students or he may write on roll-up board or chart in advance. If anything is not possible, students may be asked to have their heads down. There should not be more than 25 words. When the words are written students are asked to look at them for 2 to 5 minutes. When the time is up the words are removed or rubbed from their sight. The students are required to write the words on the basis of their memory. One mark is given for each correct word. The game is suitable for the students of junior classes.

However, a variation of the game may be applied in higher classes. Instead of words, sentences or idioms are written on chalkboard and students are required to write them. This game is a very good aid to memory.

Quiz

Quiz contributes significantly in student's performance. Quiz can be held without prior announcement. If the subject teacher, after entering in the classroom, says write a question, which you have to attempt in this period. Teacher can select the topic which has been taught during last days. The teacher has to score out the answers and has to show to the students. The records of quiz's marks are also maintained by the teacher. The obtained marks can be included in the internal assessment of final examination.

You must be knowing that such quiz tests are organised in G.B. Pant Agriculture University, Pantnagar (Nainital).

Need of Quiz Test

- It is an improvement over the conventional examination.
- The quiz are informal tests while traditional are formal examination.
- The quiz tests encourage students for regular studies in their subjects.
- Attendance can be given to the students for attending quiz.
- Quiz test makes the classroom teaching valuable.

Principles of Quizzes

Quizzes are based on the following principles:

- It provides the regular feedback for the regular study of the subject.
- It enables the students to get involve in their work seriously.
- It eliminates the fear of examination.
- Teaching and testing processes go side by side.

Types of Quiz

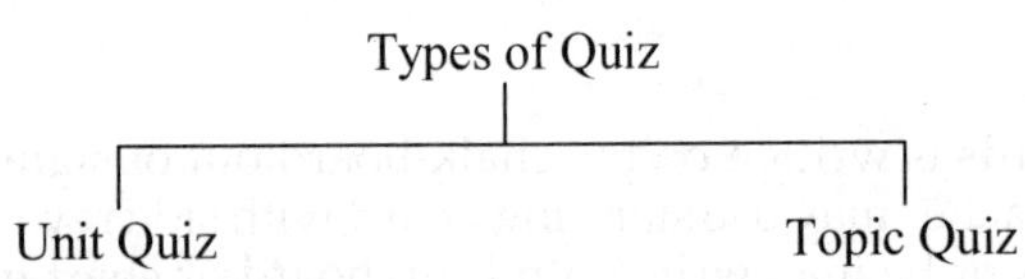

(i) *Unit Quiz*: When a teacher completes one unit of teaching subject he/she may give a quiz test on the unit at the end of teaching. It depends when the teacher feels its requirement.

(ii) *Topic Quiz*: The topic quiz can be administered on the topic of unit on any day after completion of topic. Sometime teacher announces that more time will be required for completion of topic, quiz will be held later on. But you may ask questions concerned to this topic. The basic idea behind it is to make the students regular in the studies.

The teacher has to score out their answers and has to show evaluated answer books. The students can compare their answers with other students, who have scored more.

Advantages of Quiz

- They become regular in the study.
- They are reinforced continuously.
- They acquire the mastery on the subject.
- Quiz prepares the students for final examination.
- Fear of examination is eliminated.

Suggestions

- Quiz should be based on what has been taught.
- It should be specific and pinpointed.
- Result should be announced verbally.
- If it is written type, then their answer books should be evaluated quickly and shown to the students.

LANGUAGE ACTIVITY

Dialogues Learning

Dialogue learning/dramatisation is particularly well-suited for developing linguistic competence and social insight in students of all ages. Pupils gain control not only on pronunciation, structure and vocabulary but also of the cultural situations in which various features of language are used by Native English Speakers. Well prepared dialogues and their dramatisations duplicate the communication situations in which individuals use English normally in their everyday lives.

Dialogues may be used to introduce features of pronunciation and grammar or to reinforce them. Their primary value lies, however, in showing pupils how the elements of language, they are learning fit together in actual use.

The dialogues prepared for beginning teaching should be short – two or three utterances perhaps. At intermediate or advanced levels they may be longer – eight to twelve utterances – but these need not be learned in one lesson. The teacher may introduce the entire dialogue first time it is presented but have student learn only the first two or three lines during that lesson.

Following are some suggestions for presenting and practising the entire dialogue or the portion of it to be taught in the lesson for the day. The teacher:

1. Gives the situation in simple English, pointing to each of the figures of the speakers (which have been placed on the black – or flannel board) as he tells about what each one is saying (hand puppets may also be used effectively to indicate the person speaking the particular line of dialogue).
2. Teachers new expressions and concepts in the dialogue through dramatisation pictures etc.
3. Says the part of dialogue he is going to present intensively three or four times. The first two times he stands near the board and

points to each figure as he or she speaks (or he has the puppet nod). The next time or two, the teacher walks to various parts of the room so that his mouth and gestures will be visible to all the class members.

4. Say each utterance several times and engages the entire class in choral repetition.
5. Takes one role and has the class the other. He then reverses the roles.
6. Divides the class in half and helps each group take a role. He then reverses the roles (This procedure is repeated several times).
7. Dramatised the dialogue with one of his more able students and then reverses the roles as above.
8. Has pairs of students dramatise the dialogue either from their seats or at the front of the room.

It is important to keep the dialogues alive and to keep adding to them. They can be dramatised during warm up, review or summary segments of the lesson. When introducing some features of grammar or pronunciation for intensive study, the teacher will remind the students that they have previously met in a dialogue. As the students learn new features of English, they can be helped to extend or change a whole utterance in a previous learned dialogues by adding new phrases or sentences when these fit logically. In addition to being dramatised, dialogues may be read, written, summarised into narrative paragraphs varied – to talk of different people, places or times – adapted to talk about oneself, and used naturally, as the basis for many oral practice activities.

CLASS DEBATES

Most often student's oral skills are assessed in inter-class, inter-school debates. It will be useful to first organise these debates at the school level.

Teachers can take up relevant topics for debates which are linked to the student's life at school and home. As students move into the middle school and their knowledge of the words increases, learners can debate on wider issues.

Short reading texts, letters to the editor, a newspaper cartoon and all kinds of verbal and visual stimulus can be used to start off the student's thinking processes.

Teacher's Role

The teacher can involve the learners in not only participating in the debate but also at the organisational level.

Once the debate is organised, the teacher can include the learners in the panel of judges who will assess the debates. The criteria of judging a debate can be spelt out or elicited from the students at the very beginning. The participants can prepare for the debate keeping the criteria in mind. Thus weightage for content ideas, delivery of speech, intonation and pronunciation can be collaboratively finalised.

Once the debate is over the teacher can declare the results. Later, useful feedback can be given.

DISCUSSION

Discussion can precede or follow reading texts. In the first case, discussion can prepare students for the reading task. In the second the reading text can enable learners to delve into the theme and thus participate more effectively in the discussions that follow. The reading text can give a fillip to the imagination of students and also give the less confident learners support in terms of content.

Teacher's Role

The teacher's role, while the discussion is on, is of an observer, a manager and a facilitator. If the speaking activity focuses on the use of specific language structures, then the teacher can direct the attention of learners in advance to these structures. They may be listed in the text. Once the discussion begins however, the teacher could allow it to develop rather than arbitrarily call the attention of the learners to grammatical details.

The teacher can move about unobstructively observing and monitoring the groups. Common errors in grammar and usage can be noted for remedial work to be done later on. At times the dominating student can be tactfully advised so that each student in a group gets a turn. The teacher can, if need be, join a group.

The discussion must lead to a clear task. Very often, discussions tend to wilt and collapse, if they are not planned out meticulously. The activity must have a sense of completion. Nothing is more demotivating for learners than to be left to drag on a discussion interminably, without a clear purpose and goal.

The activity or discussion can be rounded off by inviting one member from each group to report on the group's discussion. If sufficient time is not available, then some groups may be asked to put up posters with a summary of their group's ideas. An oral activity which is well planned, organised, executed efficiently, timed correctly with a feedback and follow-up session gives the learners a sense of achievement. Thus, in turn will motivate them to participate whole heartedly in the oral activities in future.

THINK-TANK SESSIONS

It is a collective type thinking on a common issue or problem. The theme selected could be real or hypothetical.

Play-cards with questions phrases and statements on the selected topic are prepared with the help of students. This activity stimulates the thinking skill of the students. Students sit in groups to deliberate in-depth on the given theme. Each group has its own play-cards on the same theme.

Students think, discuss, analyse, suggests alternative solutions, exchange views without any heated debate or arguments. It enhances reflective thinking among the students. Each student is required to explain the meaning of the content of his/her play-card. Play-cards are also circulated among different groups for encouraging different view points on the same issue. In this way students come to learn how the same problem can be viewed from different angles. This activity enables the learners to think and express speaking skill if the students can be improved by this activity.

PHOTO LANGUAGE SESSION

Some students hesitate to give expression to their thoughts, ideas and feelings. To develop the expression, power of such students this activity viz. 'Photo language session' is very useful.

The collection of pictures, photographs are shown to the students. They try to analyse mentally what the picture/photograph depict. Time for such activity can be fixed that depends on the teacher how he/she decides keeping in view the mental level and age of the students.

Process

Sets of pictures/photographs related to the theme are given to each group. The leader of group shows the pictures/photographs one by one to the whole group. Students are given time to observe them and jot down. The leader then asks the students to give their reactions to the details observed in the pictures without any inhibitions or reservations. The students then individually write observations. These observations are then compiled picture wise. The pictures and photographs are then circulated to the other groups where the same operation is repeated. All the groups then come together. Each picture or photograph is then presented one by one and each group presents its report on that one by one. The variation in the perception of different groups about the same picture or photograph is by themselves enriching experiences. If time permits a discussion on each could also follow.

The Gains

The exercise promotes the habit of close observation and the ability to mentally translate the depictions/details into feelings, and these into words. The exercise empowers students to reach out their thoughts to the affective domain and thereby to sensitise the students to certain needs and situations. This also helps students to channelize emotions and to communicate them.

THE PICTURE FILE

A picture file should be an integral part of every classroom where there are pupils learning a second language. The organisation of the file may be a cooperative activity of the teacher and all the pupils in each class or may be a group project for those pupils who will derive the greatest benefit from finding, sorting and inventing pictures. The very selection and mounting of pictures can be used as teaching lessons which will help pupils acquire language. Sentence patterns such as "can you find...?" We need (glue). "Let's look for ....." will be practised naturally during these lessons.

If teachers find it difficult to organise a complete file, the director of the learning centre or school may set up a Central file, in the general office, in the teachers' work room, or in the library, school service squads of civic-minded community members may be trained to mount, file and distribute pictures. As the teacher approaches a special unit, he should plan to borrow the folder containing pictures related to the unit so that it will be available for the entire lesson development, from motivation through culmination.

A file of flat pictures will be found available in:

(i) Ensuring motivation and stimulation
(ii) Providing for economical learning.
(iii) Vitalising any of the steps in teaching.
(iv) Providing uniformity of concept among pupils.
(v) Presenting initial concepts which are correct, real, complete and clear.
(vi) Overcoming the limitations of restricted personal experiences of the pupils.
(vii) Clarifying words and concepts which permit pupils to get ideas of proper perspective and proportion. For example, a picture showing the relative size of an elephant and a dog is much more valuable than plastic or clay models a dog and an elephant.
(viii) Overcoming the narrow limits of the classroom.
(ix) Providing for the direct interaction of the pupils with the realities of the social and physical environment.
(x) Reducing teaching and learning time by attracting the immediate attention of the public and by making possible fewer and shorter explanations of words and concepts.
(xi) Furnishing varied practice for making automatic the structural arrangements of English.

CLASS INQUIRY OFFICE

Similar to dramatisation is class inquiry office. It is an activity which helps the learners to visualise a common, familiar, everyday scene variations in the activity may be amusing to the learners. For example, students are familiar with the ticket window and inquiry window at the railway stations. The class may be given the shape of ticket window and inquiry window. Some students may be given the charge of windows and rest of the students act as passengers. Some of them asking for tickets, while rest of them are inquiring about the timings of the train. In this way, some important sentence structures may be practised. Some aids like a model telephone, posters and notices may add beauty to the activity. Students may in advance be asked to make these preliminary arrangements. When this whole activity takes place, only some students by rotation participate in it and rest of them closely observe it and make notes. When the activity is over, al the students discuss and provide valuable suggestions for improvement. This activity may provide an opportunity for the teacher to train his students in active listening and critical thinking.

ORIGINAL STORY WRITING

The teacher may motivate the learners to write original stories. A group of two or three students may be asked to write jointly. However, the teacher may tell them certain rules about it such as – the story should not have any impossible situations etc. in order to have accuracy in writing, the teacher may encourage students to use dictionaries etc. The completed stories can be bound into a volume and kept in the class library. The best story may be awarded. This activity will not only bring novelty in teaching but also develop imagination and creativity.

FIELD TRIPS

A well organised trip may provide an efficient language teacher many opportunities of teaching various language skills. Children, generally, love to go on excursions. This interest of students can best be utilised by making excursions or language field-trip.

Visit to certain nearby places like bank, post office, railway station, public library, museum etc. may be organised. Students may be asked to observe the activities taking place. Later on in this class the same dialogue may be enacted in the form of 'class inquiry office' or students may be asked to narrate it orally or in writing whatever they have seen there. Every field trip should be followed by an intensive discussion session; otherwise, the main purpose of such visits will be lost. Somaratne (1955) suggests the following questions, which a teacher must ask to himself before and after the field trip.

Before the trip—

(1) Is this trip really necessary?
(2) Is there any other better teaching method to teach the topic?
(3) What do I need to plan before hand?
(4) What are the various types of material that are available on this subject?
(5) How should I use them?
(6) Will the time spent on preparing, planning and undertaking the trip be worthwhile?
(7) What effect will this trip have on the students?

After The Trip

(1) Did the trip serve the aims and purpose?
(2) Were the students interested in the trip?
(3) Did it help the students to think?
(4) Was the spirit of inquiry and curiosity aroused in the students?
(5) What effects did it have on their conduct and behaviour?
(6) Did the trip provide experiences that could not be arranged in a more expedient manner?

The answers to these questions will provide an overall assessment of the activity, so that, it can be made more fruitful and purposeful in future.

ENGLISH CLUB

For the students of secondary level and senior secondary level, English clubs can be organised. The main purpose of these clubs is to develop interest and fluency in the use of language.

To organise a club, the teacher should give the knowledge about its purpose, working system and usefulness. When the students give their consent to participate, then rules and regulations regarding membership can be decided. Various office bearers can be elected among the students. When the club comes in existence, meetings should be held to chalk out the programme of the year. In every activity of the club, presence of the teacher is must. Somaratne in his book 'Aids and Tests in the Teaching of English as a Second Language' suggests the following model programme for an English club. It may serve as a guide to those teachers who wish to form such clubs.

July	1.	Party games and sing-songs.
	2.	Programme on the education box.
August	1.	Pen friends.
	2.	An evening with the tape recorder.
September	1.	Play reading.
	2.	Prepared speeches.
October	1.	Extempore speech.
	2.	Debate
	3.	Word games.
November	1.	A dinner with after dinner speeches.
	2.	Educational excursions.
December	1.	Epidiascope lesson or T.V. lesson
	2.	Lecture by Mr. X.
January	1.	Discussion about annual function.
	2.	Parent's day.
February	1.	Book reviews.
	2.	Elocution contest.
March	1.	True adventures.
	2.	Great explorers.

THE SCHOOL ASSEMBLY

A well planned assembly may provide a language teacher immense opportunities to teach the language. The first and foremost use of assembly is training in listening skill. Students are trained to comprehend selected prose and verse pieces read in the assembly. When the assembly is over, English class students may discuss it with their teacher.

Those students who participate actively in such activities are benefited more in comparison to those who are passive listeners. To provide equal opportunity to all, it must be made compulsory for each student to participate actively by rotation. The teacher may provide a helping hand to shy and weak students. The task given to each student should be in accordance with their abilities. Thus, besides educational value, it develops confidence in students. They learn to read properly with speed and intelligence.

THE HOUSE SYSTEM

To teach language in natural set-up house system is also a good technique. You can divide the classes into houses, and are named after great scholars while allocating the students to different houses, the teacher should keep in mind that each house must have certain bright average and dull students i.e. there must be a balance in the structure of the houses when the houses are allotted to the students, various inter-house competitions like debate extempore speech elocution etc. are organised. In these activities language developing themes can be chosen and selected by the house teacher which motivates the students to learn and speak new words in English. In this way, opportunity is provided to the students to show their talent.

INTERPRETING

Interpreting is a popular profession amongst language learners. It can also be called liaison interpreting which one sometimes has to do when there is a foreign visitor or a visitor from another region whose language you alone know in the given situation. One has to interpret when the visitor mingles with the people of the host country, goes shopping or sightseeing.

You can say interpreting in the language classroom is a good co-curricular activity because it would be a simulation exercise where one of the participants of the conversation pretends not to know English. You need to create a situation and role cards will be given to all participants. The scene may be a market place, or hospital etc. Hopefully this kind of simulation will create interest for the learners.

Other learners should not interrupt in between visitor himself/herself can do when he/she chose the sentence of the interpreter. Sometimes, if the interpreter has not interpreted (correctly something that the visitor has been able to make out) the visitor can refuse to understand and seek clarification. The teacher should explain the activity to the learners by involving few volunteers.

S/he needs to assure the learners who are playing the role of the interpreters that pauses, repetition, hesitation and regression are common in day-to-day speech and that ought not to inhibit them.

Listening activity can be improved by it.

Use of tape recorder is also helpful as later on 'interpretation' can be discussed.

The learners would be using a lot of noun clauses like "He says that..../He means that ...../He wants to tell you that.....".

Since nothing in this activity is rehearsed, it is a challenging activity involving the mental processes of providing immediate equivalent to what one said.

Resource Book for Speaking Activities

The teacher needs to have a collection of speaking activities based on various aspects of the learner's lives. The reading list given below would provide the teacher with many activities for the second language learner. There are certain activities, which the teacher would have to adapt for his/her class.

Reports of school events, newspaper clippings, advertisements, posters and fliers of various programmes also can go into the file which could be used at the opportune moment for an activity.

- School events
- Neighbourhood events
- School trips
- Neighbourhood tabloids
- Periodicals
- Interviews for selection as perfects and editorial board member
- Topics of current interest
- Letters to the editors
- Television programmes
- News

The Newspaper

The class newspaper is a marvellous aid and helps in improving the language ability of children. Since students feel it as their own newspaper, they have enthusiasm in contributing to it. To bring out a class newspaper an editorial board must be elected including students of various talents and abilities. In the beginning the teacher should help students in the selection and publication of articles. All the students of the class may be asked to contribute jokes, anecdotes, proverb, quotations, short stories, poems, special news, etc. To create interest in the life of school and its environment a section of it may be devoted to relevant notices, reports of the school etc. The newspaper may be hand written or typed. If possible, photostat copies may be distributed. Issue should be published once a month and rest of the days editorial board selects suitable articles. A suitable title such as *Ryan International* (name of the school) *Times* may be given to it, the regular publishing of the newspaper will bring diversity and joy to the routine teaching and help students in the development of their language.

Class Library

The class library plays an important role in developing reading habits of students, whereas visits to the main library cannot be effectively arranged for all students. Class library may be formed under the charge of the class teacher or the subject teacher. For this purpose it should be ensured that a large variety of books is provided to students to make free selection of books. For a class of 40 students at least 150 books should be provided in the class library.

It is not necessary to have all different titles in the library. There may be ten to fifteen copies of each title. There would be about fifteen different titles which may be given to students by turn. The book should be arranged according to the requirement of students.

Importance of Class Library

(1) Class library is helpful in developing the reading habit of students. If a student develops the habit of reading, S/he will continue to learn and gain knowledge throughout life.
(2) Reading at convenience is possible.
(3) It arouses students' will to read.
(4) Their reading interest is aroused.

In this way we can say that there is an important role of class library in developing reading skill. It saves students from going to the central or main library.

A class library is of immense help to the teacher. With well-equipped library, he can encourage his students to read relevant books. In this regard, a language teacher, with the help of the school librarian, may have a classroom library with certain selected reading material.

The classroom library is the responsibility of a language teacher. The main purpose of having such a library is to develop the interest of students towards reading. In the library, there may be books in different areas. In such a library the teacher may have a collection of books, magazines, photographs flash cards, coins, objects etc..

There should be regular library periods under the supervision of the teacher. In higher classes, to make the reading period all the more purposeful, the teacher may give them suitable topics. In this way, students would learn to read extensively in order to select relevant material. Students of lower classes may be asked to keep a record of their library reading by making a chart showing the day of the week, the number of pages they have read, the speed of reading, list of new words, etc. The teacher may use this chart to find out the progress they make in vocabulary expansion and reading skill.

Listening to Telephone Call and Writing the Message

Learner at the middle school are often required to make telephone calls for formal and informal purposes. Listening forms a key element in telephone skills. In the activity the teacher is introduced to a situation where Sunita has to give an important message to her friend Mona. It is the mother, Mrs. Sharma, who receives the message. She notes important details of the school trip. In case you wish to use the word 'itinerary' in the listening work sheet, you may wish to deal with it in the pre-listening stage or you may use the word in the listening passage in such a way that its meaning becomes clear. If you find the word too difficult for your learners to grasp, you may not use it at all, and use the term 'tour programme' instead. These are decisions you will have to take keeping in mind your learner's level and experience.

Listening Passage

Listening to a Telephone call and writing down the message—

Sunita : Hello—is that 9121628?

Mrs. Sharma : Yes, who's speaking please?

Sunita : Good evening Aunt... this is Sunita here. May I speak to Mona?

Mrs. Sharma : She's gone out for a walk. Anything important?

Sunita : Yes Aunty. It's very important. You see. Mona was absent today and our Trip-in-charge was asking for her.

Mrs. Sharma : But, I did send the cheque for the trip. I remember signing it yesterday.

Sunita : No Aunt–it is not the cheque. We're all supposed to hand in a consent slip.

Mrs. Sharma : Really, how careless of Mona to have forgotten!

Sunita : Aunt please ask Mona to get it tomorrow– it's the last day. We leave the day after.

Mrs. Sharma : What about the itinerary?

Sunita : Well –we leave the day after, that is an 19th July. It's a Monday. Then–on Tuesday we reach Shimla. We have three days at Shimla for travelling and sight seeing. We return on the 23rd evening– that's Friday night.

Mrs. Sharma : That sounds exciting. Sunita , has your teacher given you a list of things to take along?

Sunita : Yes Aunt. Mona's has got one too. But she's added a few more things—so we all need to carry a sleeping bag.

Mrs. Sharma : Yes, just a minute– I'll note down the things. What else?

Sunita : Well—we need to carry a torch and — I forgot– it's rained in Shimla. So she said we must carry raincoats.

Mrs. Sharma : A raincoat–okay–I' ve got that. Anything else?
Sunita : Yes–an extra pair of shoes too–yes, Aunt I think that's all she told us.
Mrs. Sharma : Thank you Sunita you' ve been a real help.

Logs

Learning the use of log books is simple and straight forward way to help students integrate content, process and personal feelings. By learning log book operation students learn how to write rather than writing what they have learned. The common application is to have students make entries in their logs during the last five minutes of the class or after each completed week of the class. The message here is that short, frequent bursts of writing are more productive over time than are infrequent, longer assignments.

Learning logs are most commonly used in assessing learning but there are many crossovers into content areas other than those associated with reading and writing. Properly understood and used, learning logs becomes a vehicle for exchange among parents, teachers and students.

There are some overlaps between portfolios and learning logs. In fact, both journal and learning logs frequently provide artifacts for students portfolio. The most valuable result of learning logs is that as students write to learn, they also learn to recognize their own and other's good work. Both learning logs and journals assist the learning process. Journal are free flowing, subjective relying on opinion and personal experience. Learning logs are concise, objective, factual and impersonal in tone.

The following questions could be used to guide students in making thoughtful entries in their learning log books:

1. What did I do in the class today?
2. What did I learn?
3. What did I find interesting?
4. What questions do I have about what I learnt?
5. What was the point of today's lesson?

☛Points to Remember

1. Co-curricular activities are considered as an integral part of the curriculum.
2. Leisure time is spent fruitfully.
3. Teachers can guide and help the students to take part in various co-curricular activities.
4. Class library stimulates children to read.
5. Listening forms a key element in telephone skills.
6. The most valuable result of learning logs is that is students write to learn they also learn to recognize their own and other's good work.

19

Basic Principles of Testing English

"A Language learing is largely a matter of forming habits and skills in the use of that language, the test must cover a wide range of skills and knowledge.

—B.S. Bloom

The main purpose of educative process is to improve the performance of the students. The learning outcomes of the students are measured with the help of achievement tests. Performance assessment is the process of measuring the terminal behaviours of the students at the end of teaching or instruction. It is the job of the teacher to measure whether the students have acquired the level of attainment in the subject matter. The achievement is the end product of the instruction usually verbal or written performance.

There are two concepts which are used in the performance assessment of the students:

(I) *Measurement and*

(II) *Evaluation.*

These terms are used interchangeably but these are two different concepts in this context and shall be discussed in this chapter.

As stated the purpose of testing is to assess the workability and effectiveness of teaching activity. B.S. Bloom has emphasised that testing should be based on teaching. The purpose of teaching and testing is to realise the objectives of education. Herbert has emphasised the presentation of content by teaching in the classroom and it should be tested by examination. Most of the approaches of education have suggested that teaching and testing should go side by side. Therefore, it is important to consider the principles of teaching for testing.

General Principles of Testing English

1. ***Principle of Continuity***: Evaluation is a continuous process which is an integral part of teaching. It is not merely a test at the end of an English lesson or unit. Instead, evaluation goes on constantly. It makes the students regular, punctual and systematic. Teaching-learning process and the evaluation procedure go on together.

Language learning is a matter of practice so it should be evaluated throughout. This will enable the students to have better command over the skills.

2. ***Principle of Comprehensiveness.*** It aims at evaluation of the total personality of the child. Following are the constituents of evaluation:

(a) Formulation of aims.

(b) Changes in the behaviour patterns of the pupils through these aims.

(c) To formulate reliable tools to observe the behaviour patterns, knowledge of skill.

It can be said that growth and development of the child, physically, morally, socially, culturally and politically etc. are assessed. Moreover, evaluation is done keeping in view the ability, capacity and inclination of an individual towards English language.

In this regard Secondary Education Commission says, "The schools of today concerns itself not only with the intellectual pursuits but also with the emotional and social development of the child, his physical and mental health, his social adjustment and other equally important aspects of his life, in a word with an all round development of his personality".

3. ***Principle of Objectives*****:** Evaluation/testing English is based on the principle of objectives. It tries to know how different objectives of personality are being achieved. For teaching English lesson, first the objectives are fixed up and then efforts, on the part of teacher, are taken to achieve them.

4. ***Principle of Totality*****:** Unlike examinations which take into account one side of things, evaluation is considered with the total process of education. It is committed to all types of learning exercises and at all levels of learning. All significant and insignificant things concerned with the process of education come under the purview of evaluation.

In the teaching-learning of English, totality means overall—how much has the student been able to acquire on the whole, learning of the language includes all the four skills.

5. ***Principle of Broadness*****:** Here total learning done by the students is considered broadly. It is no way confined to the assessment of limited parts of learning experiences.

6. ***Principle of Quantity and Quality*****:** Principle of quantity is the base of examination. To have a better evaluation quantitative and qualitative aspect of human personality are to be considered.

7. ***Principle of Learning Experiences*****:** As evaluation is directly linked with the learning of students, it gives main importance to the child and his learning experiences instead of content matter. This principle is very helpful in creating conducive environment in the school.

8. ***Principle of Application*****:** The principle of application is also very important. Evaluation adjudges that student is better who can apply his knowledge and understanding in different situations.

In English testing we lay emphasis on four different aspects. The ability of listening, speaking, reading and writing capabilities of an individual are to be evaluated. This compels us to test the English language on four basic principles. These are:

1. *Principle of Listening English*: In the learning of a language listening is the basis of everything. Naturally, this is the first principle of language, learning and testing. To learn a language means the learner should be exposed to the listening of a language. News telecasts on TV, broadcasts on Radio, tape recorder, lectures of eminent scholars will be useful. Students should be encouraged to reproduce the listened material. Pronunciation should be correct. The teacher should note that RP pattern of pronunciation is followed. Testing listening skill is very challenging. The teacher can evaluate this skill in the class orally. He can explain a paragraph and give out the meanings of new words with correct pronunciation. Then he can ask a number of questions to recall the meaning of paragraph, reproduce the new words and likes.

2. *Principle of Spoken English*: The second principle of testing and learning English is that of spoken English. The child learns his mother tongue (Hindi) in natural environment and speaks as he imitates in daily routine. But in case of learning English, there is less exposure. In our examination system there is no provision for testing English, that is why this skill remains ignored. Opportunities should be provided to test this ability in the form of delivering lectures, holding debates, organising group discussions, imitating the good models of spoken English. Even our English teacher is not the native speaker of English language. So the exchange programme of teachers with foreign countries can be helpful. The students should be encouraged to participate in these programmes and thus can be evaluated through their participation in various programmes.

3. *Principle of Reading English*: The third principle of testing English is principle of reading English. Reading comes next to listening and speaking. This is to test the ability to understand written English. Therefore, it is the testing of the comprehension of written material in the form of text in books, magazines and newspapers. It is the testing of vocabulary, structures, tenses and the subject matter. So it is reading with comprehension as well as reading with correct pronunciation. For this, we have so many techniques of testing the knowledge of reading. We can arrange oral and written test for testing this skill.

4. *Principle of Writing English*: The fourth and the last general principle of testing English is the principle of writing English. Listening comprehension precedes speaking and reading process writing. Writing skill is postponed till the listening, speaking and reading ability take firm grip in the mind. It comes at last but is equally important. Correct writing is a great trait of good personality. One should be proficient enough to pen down his own ideas in the form of better writing, paragraph writing, summarising the lesson and other composition work etc. The knowledge of grammar, correct sentences, filling up blanks with appropriate form of verb, preposition, conjunction, determiners and pronouns are tested with the help of objective type tests. The assessment can be internal as well as external. It can be in the form of objective type tests, short answer type tests and essay type tests.

In the process of teaching-learning tests, examination and evaluation are the terms which are commonly used. There is a difference between test, examination and evaluation. Let us first understand their meanings.

Test

The word 'test' is derived from the Latin word '*testum*' which means some special type of earthen pot. These pots were used for testing the authenticity of other metals. Therefore, it was called testing pot. Nowadays, it is used in the same respect but in different circumstances. The test is now conducted only to scan the knowledge of the students and to check whether the taught material is still in the minds of students or not. Tests can be conducted along with the teaching process while testing the knowledge, the questions from the taught material are asked in the direct form. Test can be held in less time. The teacher may teach something and thereafter he can test the students—their understanding, their grasping ability, intelligence etc. by putting some questions. Tests are, thus, informal because the teachers need not undergo any sort of formality. In tests only those questions are put which have been taught, so the teacher comes to know whether the students have learnt them or not.

Examination

The word 'examination' is formed out of the word 'examine'. The term 'examine' is derived from the Latin word '*examen*' which means the pointer of a balance. The pointer of a balance indicates whether the weights in the two pans are equal or not. Standard weights are put in one pan and the thing that is to be weighed is put into the second pan. Thus, a comparison of a thing is made with the standard weights like 50 gms., 1 kg. etc. Similarly, in the case of examinations, there are standards fixed by the higher authorities like the Education Department, the University, etc., the students are expected to come up to those expectations by way of standard. Only then we say that such and such student has passed a particular examination.

To differentiate between test and examination following points come to the forefront:

1. Tests unlike examinations, can be held without observing any formality.
2. For holding tests, it is not essential to give intimation before hand. But in the case of examination, intimation has to be given before hand.
3. To hold test we need less time in comparison to examination.
4. Examination is a broader term than the test.

5. In a test, you cannot ask about what is not taught. But in the examination, any sort of the question can be put of course it is up to the standard of that particular class.

Measurement

Measurement is a process by which the developed abilities of the pupils are expressed in the quantitative form. The measurement is directly concerned with quantity. By measuring the content, skill and the results of abilities are expressed in numbers, scores, percentage and average so that the provision of education of the pupils may be made according to their present achievement. By measurement the variable, groups, capacities, time and distance etc. can be tested very conveniently. In short, according to Campbell "measurement is the assignment of numerals to objects or events, according to rules".

It measures something in numbers. It means it is quantitative evaluation. In the process of measurement, numerals are used to represent quantities of an attribute. In other words, measurement involves the process of quantification.

Quantification indicates 'how much' or 'to what extent' that attribute is present in a particular object. Following are some of the definitions of measurement:

- *Stevenson*: "Measurement is the process of assigning number to objects according to certain agreed rules".
- *J.P. Guilford*: "Measurement means the description of data in terms of numbers and this, in turn, means taking advantage of the many benefits that operate with numbers and mathematical thinking provide".
- *Thorndike*: "Anything that exists at all exists in some quantity. Anything that exists in some quantity is capable of being measured".

Therefore, measurement is part of evaluation, which is related to numbers in the form of averages, median, mode, central tendency and percentage. It gives out the result of a thing in numbers. We cannot measure a man or an object.

Characteristics of Measurement

1. Measurement is related to numbers.
2. Measurement is related to mathematics.
3. Measurement categorises things.
4. Measurement categorises numbers.
5. Measurement gives number to value, interests, aptitudes, attitudes and quality.

Functions of Measurement

1. *Selection*: Selection of an individual to an institution as a student or teacher is done with the help of measurement. Achievement tests or

interviews are conducted and marks are awarded. Meritorious candidates are selected.

2. *Classification*: We can classify with the help of measurement. Tests are conducted. Numbers or marks are awarded. So any type of classification can be done with the measurement.

3. *Diagnosis*: The weakness of a student can be diagnosed by conducting various types of test in a particular subject. And then remedial work can be carried out.

4. *Research*: In research area the raw data is collected and given statistical treatment for analysis and final conclusions. So it helps in research work.

Methods of Measurement

(1) *Test Method*: It involves a defined task and testing period in which the situations are such that it may be right or wrong. One score is assigned to the correct answer and zero to the wrong answer. It tests covert behaviour of a subject. Permanent record is needed for scoring and process must be observed and evaluated. These methods are applicable for quantifying abilities and aptitude.

(2) *Observation Method*: In this method behaviour is observed in the natural situations. There are various techniques of observation. It tests overt behaviour of a subject.

(a) *Self Observation,* in which the individual reports on his own reactions as far as he is aware of them. It can be planned observation to cover a specified period. It can be retrospective observation which is based on present memory and evaluation of past reactions.

(b) *Observation by others,* in which the other person like friend, relative, employer or teacher reports on the individual reaction. Such type of observation may be planned observation or retrospective observation. This method is used to measure abilities, attitudes and traits.

(3) *Mixed Methods*: In it following can be taken:

(a) Inventories
(b) Situational tests
(c) Rating and projective techniques

These methods are used to measure the traits like personality, attitude, interest and adjustment. Their various forms are:

(a) Appraisal by tests *v/s* appraisal by observation in natural situations.
(b) External observation *v/s* self observation.
(c) Planned *v/s* retrospective observation.
(d) Observation combined with test.

Evaluation

Evaluation is a broader term than test and examination. It is a social and psychological activity which is applied to every individual whether one is purchasing something or reading a book.

Old Concept: Old concept of evaluation was narrow and was limited up to the academic aspect of the personality. It was concerned with subject matter and teaching was assessed on priority basis.

New Concept: The new concept of evaluation is a complete changed aspect of old concept. Now, instead of subject matter, the personality of child is considered for the purpose of assessment. Thus, modern evaluation tries to measure the objectives of school curriculum through different procedures and methods. The term evaluation has been defined by various educationists in following manner:

1. According to T.W. Wringtstone, "Evaluation is a new technical term introduced to design a more comprehensive concept of measurement".

2. According to Bradfield and Moredock, "Evaluation is an assignment of symbols to a phenomenon in order to characterise the worth or value of a phenomena usually with reference to some social, cultural or scientific standard".

3. Clara M. Brown defines evaluation as, "Evaluation is essential in the never ending cycle of formulating goals which emerge as a result of new warning. Evaluation involves measurement which means objectives, quantitative evidence. But it is broader than measurement and implies that considerations have been given to certain values, standards and that interpretation of the evidence has been made in light of the particular situation".

The Secondary Education Commission writes, "The school of today concerns itself not only with the intellectual pursuits but also with the emotional and social development of the child, his physical and mental health, his school adjustment with other equally important aspects of his life in a world, with all round development of his personality".

The evaluation cycle is completed on the basis of following elements:

(a) Objectives
(b) Learning Experiences
(c) Tools and Devices of Evaluation

The relationship between these three is clear in the diagram given below:

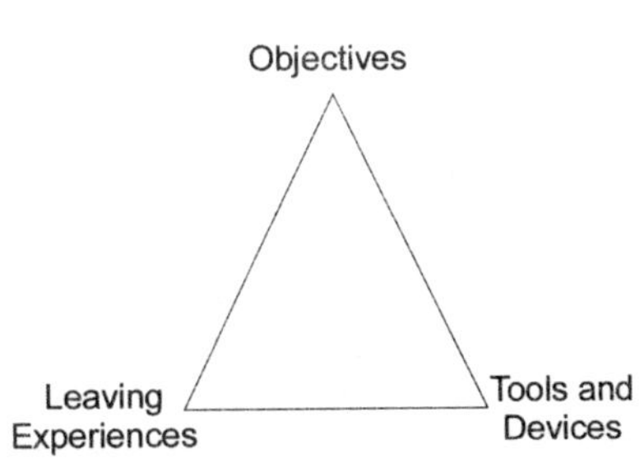

In every educational system, we find that there are some objectives through which it aims at bringing about some changes in the pupils. In order to bring about those changes, learning experiences are provided in the schools. The success of the learning experiences is judged on the basis of behavioural changes noticed in the students. For this different types of evaluation tools and devices are used.

Thus objectives (ends), learning experiences (means) and evaluation are interrelated with each other.

Characteristics of Evaluation

1. Educational evaluation is the estimation of the growth and progress of pupils towards objectives in the curriculum.
2. It is a means to an end and end in itself.
3. It is a continuous process. Teaching-learning process and the evaluation procedure go together.
4. It is very systematic and scientific.
5. Its concentration is more on learning than teaching process.
6. Evaluation is a cooperative process involving students, teachers and parents.
7. It is concerned with the total personality of the student, i.e., physical, moral, social, cultural, academic etc.

Purpose of Evaluation

1. *Diagnostic*: Evaluation helps the teachers in finding out the different causes that hinder the all round development of the child. Evaluation means so much to a teacher in the teaching process. Students also come to know about their weak points. So it makes the teaching-learning process better
2. *Remedial*: To overcome the weak points, required remedial programmes can be organised. As we know that evaluation is a continuous process evils can be cured in the beginning.
3. *Guidance*: Guidance is a very important purpose of evaluation. Evaluation of the child helps the teacher in knowing about the learner. He can know about the attitude, interest, aptitude of the students and guide them properly. Thus proper guidance can be given to bring full growth and development of the learners.

Evaluation Devices

Testing the academic achievement of the students is only a part of evaluation. In case of teaching-learning English language, it is essential to evaluate the achievements of students in all aspects of learning. For evaluation following types of tests can be adopted:

1. *Oral Test or Viva-voce*: This type of examination is very popular in the lower classes. In fact, this type of examination is very important because the examiner comes face to face with the student and examines him/her by putting questions orally.

This type of oral examination is of immense value in the case of those subjects where pronunciation and spoken language of the students need to be considered. In case of foreign language like English, oral examination helps in acquiring mastery over spoken language. Oral examination are of great significance in subjects like English. There is a need of making them compulsory for all the learners of English right from standard I to M.A. Because only through oral tests listening and speaking abilities of the students can be tested properly.

Thus, it will make the teaching-learning of the language more meaningful and it will also help in raising the standard of English.

2. *Practical Examination*: This type of examination is purely of practical nature where the students have to do something with their hands and show it to the examiner. Usually there are practical examinations in science subjects like physics, chemistry, botany, zoology. Practical examinations are also there in subjects like Geography, Home Science and Music etc. In the case of technical courses like Engineering and Medicine, practical examination is attached with every subject. In B.Ed. (specially in M.D. University, Rohtak) practical examination is attached almost with every subject. During practical examination viva-voce of the student is also held side by side.

For teaching English effectively, language laboratory is being made available in most of the institutions. Aural oral practice can be done here.

Practical examination combined with oral examination will help the examining authorities adjudge the students better as far as their proficiency in the language is concerned.

3. *Written Examination*: Generally a question paper for written examination is divided into three parts:

(i) Grammar Work
(ii) Textual Questions
(iii) Reading Skill.

(i) Grammar Work

Through the various questions on grammar, knowledge of students can be tested. Few examples are given below:

(a) Change the voice of the following:
She sings a song.
Who gives the punishment?
Boys are playing football.
Go there.

(b) Change the following sentences in negative and interrogative:
He is a poor fellow.
He has a good moral character.
He always helps the needy.
He is writing a letter.

(c) Change the following sentence into indirect speech:
He says, "India is a great country".
Ram said to me, "My mother will rebuke you for mischief".
I said to my son, "Honesty is the best policy".

(d) Fill in the blanks with the correct form of the verb:
My brother (go) to Bombay tomorrow.
She (writes) this paragraph since past 10 minutes.
All except Anil (be) playing.
He (attend) the meeting yesterday.

(e) Rewrite the following sentences making corrections where required:
He died with cholera.
He is blind with one eye.
The cat jumped in the well.
He entered in the room.

(f) Fill in the blanks with appropriate modals:
You ...... consult the teacher.
You ...... obey the parents.
How ...... you speak against me?

(ii) Textual Questions

In written question paper, the question from the textbooks are also included. They are based on—

a. *Essay Type*. They are descriptive in nature. Students have freedom to express their own.

Advantages

- Opportunity to express own views.
- Increases creativity.
- Develop students' writing skill.
- Enable the students to coordinate their thoughts and expression.

Disadvantages

- Students may go astray from the given topic.
- It becomes boring and dull.
- It is time consuming.

b. *Short Answer Type Question*. Students are supposed to answer in 30 to 40 words. Only those students can answer satisfactorily who have gone through the text thoroughly.

These questions are less subjective as compared to essay type questions.

(iii) Objective Type Questions

(a) Multiple Choice Questions
Tick the right answer

- It was good for a house
  (a) cite (b) site
  (c) sight (d) scene

(b) Match the column
Match the word opposite/antonym in meaning in the column A and B given below:

A	*B*
Shut	White
Sit	Happy
Black	Open
Sad	Stand

(c) Recall Type
Students are asked to fill the blanks with the appropriate word:
(a) The poem True Love is written by ....
(b) The poem Daffodil is written by ....
(c) Macbeth is written by ....

(d) Completion Form
Students are asked to fill the blanks with the given words:
fast, aloud, sweetly
Geeta sang ....
The horse ran ......
She spoke ....

(e) True or False
(a) Shakespeare was a great poet.
(b) Akbar was a great Hindu Emperor.
(c) America was discovered by Columbus.

Merits

- ➢ Whole of the syllabus is covered.
- ➢ Subjectivity is less
- ➢ Interesting, useful and time saving.

Demerits

- ➢ Chances of cheating are more.
- ➢ Guess work is enhanced.
- ➢ Setting of question paper is difficult.

Rightstone has rightly said, "Evaluation is a new technical term used to design a more comprehensive concept to measurement". It means measurement. Concentrate on one aspect at a time whereas evaluation is comprehensive measurement, which aims at totality. Evaluation is continuous and gradual. Measurement measures in terms of number whereas evaluation in spite of measuring in number also evaluates in terms of interests, abilities and capabilities. Evaluation is a qualitative term. It results in something good or bad.

The evaluation is an informal and continuous process. It takes place every time in every walk of life. The objectives, facts, events and behaviours are continuously evaluated

Measurement is the formal process which is used in planned and objective way. The measurement is the process of quantification of a trait or characteristics or assigning numerals. The direct measurement is used in physical and biosciences while measurement is indirect in psychology and education. Because the traits and attributes are abstract. We cannot perceive them through our senses such as intelligence, attitude, aptitude, achievement and personality.

Difference can be understood in the following ways:

Difference between Measurement and Evaluation

The term "measurement" and "evaluation" are often used interchangeably. However, in psychological, sociological and educational researches these two terms are used separately because they cannot stand for two different meanings. Measurement refers to the process of assigning numerals to events, objectives etc. according to certain rules.

Basically measurement is a part of the process of evaluation. When we assign a score on a given task performed by a learner, we are doing an act of measurement. When we compare this score with those of other learners and judge whether it is good/bad/average/satisfactory/ unsatisfactory. We are doing the act of evaluation. Thus evaluation is a wider and more inclusive term than measurement.

According to Nunnally (1970) "Measurement consists of rules for assigning numbers to objects in such a way as to represent quantities of attributes". On the other hand evaluation as defined by Tuckman (1975) "is a process where in the parts, process or outcomes of a programme are examined to see whether they are satisfactory, particularly with reference to the other programmes in stating objectives, our own expectations, or our own standards of 'excellence'."

Difference between Measurement and Evaluation

Item	*Measurement*	*Evaluation*
1. Purpose	Quantification assigning numerals for a variable	Quantitative and qualitative both assigning grade and level
2. Functions	Prognosis, diagnosis and research	Selection, grading, guidance prediction and diagnosis
3. Nature	Formal process planned, more precise or accurate	Formal and informal planned and unplanned continuous less accurate
4. Methods	Testing and observation method	Observation, interview, questionnaires, records
5. Technique	Tests, observation and written tests	Records, rating scales observation, check list, oral, practical and written tests
6. Scope	Narrow and formal	Wider and informal
7. Use	Physical sciences, behavioural sciences education and vocational guidance, testing hypothesis	Education for the assessment, career guidance, educational vocational guidance administration
8. Tools	Intelligence, achievement and aptitude tests	Inventories, rating scales, questionnaire, interviews, situational test, check list, observation

☛Points to Remember

1. The purpose of testing is to assess the workability and effectiveness of teaching activity.
2. Various principles of testing English should be always considered.
3. In 'test' only those questions are put which have been taught.
4. Examination is a broader term than test. You have to intimate students before hand.
5. Measurement is a process by which the developed abilities of the pupils are expressed in quantitative terms.

20

Comprehensive and Continuous Evaluation in English

"Assessment of performance is an integral part of any process of learning and teaching. As a part of sound Educational strategy, examinations should be employed to bring about qualitative improvement in education."

"Comprehensive and continuous evaluation in English." —NPE (1986)

The role and status of English language has changed vastly in the last three decades. It is increasingly being used for technical, scientific and business communication and specially for international contacts. English, today, is undoubtedly the most important and widely used world language. Being also the language of information technology, English serves as "Window on the world" as the language in which the latest developments in different field of knowledge are available with the change in the role and function of English language in an average Indian's life, the approach of teaching English in schools has also changed. In the syllabi for secondary stage of education brought out by the NCERT it was mentioned that, "English has been assigned functional role in our educational system. It is primarily a library language through which the learner gains an access to the ever-growing accretions to different fields of knowledge". (Syllabi for Classes IX-X, NCERT P. 26) Consequently the focus of English language teaching in schools has been mainly on reading and writing skills, rather than on overall communication skill".

With the increasing role of the language, English is no longer considered a library language in India. The emphasis has shifted from only reading and writing to other communication skills of listening and speaking.

Considering the change in the perspective of English language it has been realised that language learning is a continuous process and correspondingly the evaluation process is also envisaged to be continuous at the school level.

Meaning of Continuous Evaluation

The term 'Continuous Evaluation' involves two terms 'Continuous' and 'Evaluation'.

The term 'continuous' refers to regularity in assessment. The growth of a child is a continuous process. Therefore, the students progress should be evaluated continuously which means that evaluation has to be completely integrated with the teaching and learning process.

'Evaluation' is the process of finding out the extent to which the desired changes have taken place in the pupils. It, therefore, requires collection of evidence regarding growth or progress, so as to use that information for decision making.

In this way, information gathering, judgement making and decision making are the three phases of the process of evaluation.

Thus, continuous evaluation means a regular assessment of the pupils' development in school. Besides, being a continuous experience, evaluation is cumulative and thus becomes comprehensive. When we have it fully internal without the help of external agencies, it is called internal evaluation. Teachers are supposed to judge the performance of the students. All types of achievements of the students, scholastic and non-scholastic are evaluated continuously for the whole session. In all spheres of life, learner's acquisition of four skills of language learning, i.e., listening, speaking, reading and writing are taken care of in evaluation.

The whole record of the student is maintained properly in the cumulative record register and on that basis student's performance is adjudged.

Continuous comprehensive internal evaluation seems to be the panacea of all the ills. It is high time that we make evaluation an integral part of the total teaching-learning process. That way our testing will become comprehensive as it will take care of all the three domains for all round development of the learner in both the scholastic and non-scholastic areas. The current system of giving divisions in the examinations and thus classifying the learners into classes should be ousted. It should give place to unit tests which should be administered regularly to judge over all personality of the child in the light of objectives fixed up.

The objectives of teaching English are framed in the light of overall environment of the child which includes social, political, national, cultural and economic aspects of life. Those objectives naturally include scholastic and non-scholastic areas. Through continuous evaluation judgement about the child is made continuously. The objective and the efforts to achieve those objectives remain in the process of review and revision till the desired ends are achieved.

Characteristics of Continuous Evaluation

1. Continuous evaluation is basically formative in nature and is school based. It is, to be carried out by the teachers teaching a particular class.
2. The purpose of continuous evaluation is mainly improvement

in leaning. For this learning gaps and weaknesses are diagnosed so that remedial measures can be provided.

3. Continuous evaluation is informally carried out in the classroom. There is no need of making lengthy arrangements required for a formal examination like printing of question papers, seating arrangements, etc.
4. Multiple techniques of evaluation need to be used for continuous evaluation. These include not only written tests but oral tests assignments projects, observation, peer evaluation, self-appraisal etc.
5. Continuous evaluation is built into total teaching-learning programme and is a part of the daily routine for a teacher.
6. In continuous evaluation analysis and interpretation of evidence collected may be made at three different levels:
   (a) With reference to the student himself/herself, that is, how is the student progressing, what are the hard spots and what are the learning gaps. This helps the learner improve his/her learning.
   (b) With reference to the peer group, that is where does a particular student stand with reference to his/her class. This means that the performance of a student can be compared with the performance of other students in the class. This motivates the students to do better.
   (c) With reference to the criteria set by the teacher, that is, the teacher finds out whether the student has attained the expected level of performance or not. Those who do not reach the expected level need to be the given remedial instruction so as to bring them at par with their counterparts.

Advantages of Continuous Evaluation

There are several advantages of Continuous Evaluation.

The purpose of Continuous Evaluation is to improve learning by making evaluation an integral part of the teaching-learning process. Traditionally the evaluation of students has been used for a number of purposes like classification ranking/grading, selection, certification and promotion of the students. Evaluation has been used to discriminate between good achievers and low achievers. But in continuous evaluation the focus is on three Ps—Progress, process and product. Through this evaluation the teacher continuously monitors the progress of the student in different areas of learning. The process of learning is also monitored and if need be altered according to the requirement of the individual student. It also assesses the quality of the product of learning. It indicates the interests of students in particular subjects on the basis of which decision can be made about the future vocation of a student.

We know that individual differences exist. By evaluation they can be identified thus allowing the learners to learn at their own speed. So a teacher can provide individual attention to students according to their needs.

To operationalise Continuous Evaluation, different steps are to be followed. On the basis of the feedback from the tests, diagnosis of the hard spots of learning is made. After diagnosing the gaps in learning, remedial instruction is provided so that weaknesses can be removed. Sometimes this process may demand the re-teaching of the whole unit or a change in the strategy of teaching. The students are then retested to find out the improvement in learning. Thus, evaluation also helps the teacher in taking a relook at his/her transactional strategies and redesigning them in order to be more efficient and effective.

Continuous evaluation can be used at all stages of education and in all the subject areas. In English language evaluation, it is still more advantageous as the weaknesses and errors of students in different skills can be removed before they become a habit with them. Right from the beginning, from Class I when English is introduced as second language, the teacher should monitor the students continuously so that wrong language habits are not formed.

Continuous Evaluation and Techniques of Assessment

Continuous evaluation allows for the use of multiple techniques of assessment. Multiple methods are best to improve the reliability of evaluation. In the traditional system students are assessed mainly through written technique at the end of the term. The one shot examination is not enough to test all the skills and activities developed during the session. Continuous evaluation using varied techniques makes it possible to evaluate the process of learning in all the four language skills through oral testing, observation as well as written technique.

For assessing the process of learning, it is important to involve the learners in the assessment of their own work. While the assessment of product is very often undertaken by a third person or the teacher, assessment of process necessarily involves those involved in that process. Therefore, self-assessment and peer assessment motivates the students to do better. Self-appraisal helps increase pupil's awareness at their strengths and weaknesses.

Evaluation in English

For evaluating the four language skills of listening, speaking reading and writing continuous assessment is necessary as the progress and processes of the development of these skills can be evaluated only through continuous assessment which is formative in nature. The purpose of this kind of evaluation is the assessment during the process of learning for its improvement.

The continuous assessment in English includes assessment of conversational skills which is to be done using oral technique and also observation technique. It also includes unit tests, half yearly exams and assignments which use the written mode.

Informal continuous evaluation helps the teacher to cover all the language skills, which are not possible to be tested through the formal final written examination. It involves students in self/peer evaluation and also uses a variety of means for assessment. Some of the techniques of such evaluation are given below:

Oral Technique

For testing the skills of listening and speaking oral technique is to be used. For example: Pronunciation, speed and accuracy of reading a book, comprehension and verbal questions etc. These tasks can be set up either formally or informally. Some formal activities are given below.

(a) *Answering questions*: This is a good device for testing the use of vocabulary and various structures alongwith pronunciation and intonation. In this test the student is asked questions of various types and he/she is required to answer them. Some questions may be simple, requiring one word to one sentence answer, whereas others may require long answers consisting of 3 to 4 sentences.

(b) *Talk*: A short presentation is also useful to test the oral skill of the students. A clue can be given so that they can speak 5 to 6 sentences on that topic.

(c) *Story telling*: In this test the testee is told a story by the teacher or she/he is given a story for reading. After this, she/he is asked to tell the story in his/her own words and assessment is made.

(d) *Reading aloud*: Students can be asked to read aloud the dialogues, short conversational pieces, parts of a play or passages from the textbook. Assessment can be made on the basis of their pronunciation of vowel sounds and consonants, intonation patterns, stress etc.

(e) *Describing things, actions etc.*: Students are asked to describe an object picture or an action. Description can be up to 4 to 5 sentences. Vocabulary and pronunciation of students can be tested this way.

For the purpose of grading or marking a rating scale may be used consisting of 4-5 points on each component or oral expression. For example, the following grid can be used for rating oral production

	1	2	3	4	5
Production				√	
Vocabulary			√		
Structure			√		
General fluency				√	

Maximum Marks: 20
Score: 14

According to this grid each component is evaluated on a five point scale—5 being the best and 1 being the poorest performance, with 3 as an average. Then a mark or score is given by adding the points that the testee gets.

Other activities like panel discussion, debate, role-play, extempore talk, interviews etc. can also be used with secondary and higher secondary classes for testing oral skills.

Observation Technique

For testing the listening and speaking skills informal observation technique can be used. The teacher can observe the students' use of language while participating in the English classes. Whenever in the course work the students are required to discuss, role play, simulate, express a point of view, or answer questions, etc. The teacher should monitor the activities and quietly observe each student's participation.

It is important that this kind of informal assessment conversational skills, should be a regular on going activity throughout this term. The teacher should organise pair work, group work etc. and set up oral activity in the class so as to give an opportunity to the students to engage in oral activity.

For evaluating oral skills, the students can be rated on specific points using the rating scale as described above.

Written Technique

All teacher are familiar with written technique as it is the most commonly used technique for evaluating the skills of reading and writing. This is used for unit tests/class tests, term tests, half yearly and annual examinations. These tests can be designed according to the guidelines for designing good question papers, class work and assignments/home work involving written work, so as to assess students' writing ability. These activities are ideal for continuous assessment. If required, certain weightage may also be allotted to the assignments and homework to be utilised in the final assessment.

The skill of reading should also be tested which involves reading of a story, extracts from reports, poems, biography, asking short question answer, table completion, description, etc. They should not be lengthy one. In classroom exercise true/false type of question can be asked but not in the examination as they involve guess work.

While making the answers for reading tasks, a teacher should ignore students' spelling, punctuation and grammatical mistakes. As this exercise is meant for comprehension ability of the students.

While assessing the writing ability three points are to be considered *viz.* content, accuracy and fluency.

Self Evaluation

In Continuous Evaluation students themselves are supposed to evaluate. This gives the students a sense of involvement in learning. They can be guided in the following way:

1. Asking students to write what they like or dislike about the English syllabi and why.
2. Ask them to note down difficult areas where improvement is required.
3. Maintaining diary and noting down their learning, strengths and weaknesses with exercise will ensure them better performance in future.

Peer Evaluation

Discussion with peer group brings improvement. In fact, in a language classroom, conversational skills are to be taught with interaction among peers wherein a continuous peer evaluation goes on consciously or unconsciously. Teacher may have a check that it should be a healthy discussion.

Thus Continuous Evaluation allows for using multiple techniques of evaluation and keeps the students away from fear, anxiety and tension which they feel during formal testing.

Self Assessment and Peer Assessment

Self and peer assessment are the strategies which make students responsible for learning. They make learning experiences rich and wide. Students are made to realize its value for them. It saves the time of teachers. Students must take it as a natural part of their learning.

What is Self and Peer Assessment

Students are involved in monitoring and making judgements about aspects of their own or peer's learning.

- students can learn to evaluate their thinking skills.
- they learn to think indepently
- Their critical thinking is also improved.

Students must be made to realize that the main focus is on improvement rather than on judgement. Constructive feedback is a must for students. In this manner they get constructive suggestions. They must know that comments of others are a step towards their improvement.

Need and Importance of Self and Peer Assessment

1. Thelearning style is improved.
2. The critical evaluation skill is developed.
3. The sensitivity towards task is increased .
4. The learning from feedback is increased.

Suggestions for Improvement of Peer and Self Assessment

- Feedback must be given.
- More discussion should be held.
- Meeting with old students is beneficial.
- The provision for online assessment is helpful.
- Work of previous students can be presented online.
- Details of assessment criteria and their level of performance should be known to students.
- The plan should be reviewed before implementation.

Using Portfolio for Subjective Assessment

A portfolio is a collection of students work which gives evidence to show how they can meet the specified learning outcomes. In practical terms, a student portfolio for assessment purpose is a compendium of reports, papers and other material, together with the students reflection on his/her learning and on their strength and weaknesses. A typical portfolio consists of work selected by the student. Portfolio is a developmental process, it is not only the product that the students or teacher assess upon but also the learning process in which the student develops during the given period. Portfolio is an assessment method that monitors the growth and development of students' learning .

The portfolio demonstrates the students' progress towards the achievement of curriculum outcomes overtime. Portfolio assessment is a continuous assessment, charting students' progress towards the expected standards in each exit learning outcome. For each candidate to benefit from such ongoing assessment, his/her portfolio supervisor must have regular review sessions to discuss the rating with the students and monitor the student's progress towards the curriculum learning outcomes.

Portfolio assessment is carried out where the students learn and practise what they will do in their future professional career.

Advantages of Portfolio

1. Students get opportunities to become responsible to learn.
2. Improvement through self reflection is possible.
3. It promotes diversity in the assessment method.
4. It promotes creativity, individuality and uniqueness in the assessment.
5. Moreover it has high validity.

Disadvantages of Portfolio

1. Portfolio is a time consuming assessment method in terms of planning, responding, correcting and providing feedback.
2. It is a subjective assessment method.
3. It has less reliability.
4. It is a time consuming method.
5. Sometime an actual idea may be overlooked.

Cloze Test

Evaluation is essential for diagnostic and remedial purposes. A Cloze test is an important technique to fulfill this objective. In this technique a passage is presented to students and they are asked to fill the blank or delete words from the passage to complete the idea. In this way their proficiency can be diagnosed and reading problems can be tested and improved. Following are the uses of the Cloze Test:

- Students' understanding and knowledge can be tested by administering it.
- The vocabulary power of students can be increased.
- The comprehension power can be developed.
- They are motivated to think analytically and judge critically.
- Students can go into the deeper idea of the author.

Procedure

Select a paragraph in which every 7th word is deleted, for example, and students are asked to fill it up. Or other kind of exercises can be given like on the use of punctuation marks, preposition or omitted content words. Students are asked to fill it up. Give them guidelines, and ask them to read well before filling it. Time should be noted. This is a good exercise to sharpen the mind of students .

Examples: The Cloze test is an exercise test or assessment consisting of a portion with certain words removed (cloze text) where the participant is asked to fill up the missing words. Cloze tests require the ability to use vocabulary in appropriate contexts in order to identify the correct words. This exercise is commonly administered for the assessment of native and second language learners.

Examples:

1. Supply choices for the blanks.
   We need umbrella in .... and coat in .... (rain /winter).
2. When learners have used the technique described above and can replace the appropriate words from the choices supplied, provide passages in which every fifth word or every tenth word is arbitrarily deleted and only a letter of two of the correct word is available perhaps a beginning consonant or consonant blend.
3. When the learners do well with this task, indicate only the blanks with the additional clues. Accept any words that seem to fit.
4. A language teacher may give the following passage to students.
   I went to .... without taking .... to examination hall. I knew it was .... but I was thinking to buy .... but shop was ....

Students would then be needed to fill in the blanks with words that would best complete the passage. Context is essential to fill in language and content terms in most, if not all, cloze test. The first blank is preceded by ' school', therefore a noun, an adjective or an adverb must follow. Although, a noun follows the blank, thus sentence would not be grammatically correct if anything other than a noun were in the blank. The words pen, shop and close are significant for deciding which noun to put in the blank.

Assessment

The definition of success in a given cloze test varies, depending on the broader goals behind the exercise. Assessment may rely on whether the exercise is objective (i.e. students are provided a list or words to use in a cloze) or subjective (i.e. students are to fill in a cloze with words that would make the given sentence grammatically correct)

Group Evaluation

"Group is a social units of interacting personalities who think, feel and act together and who have some common aims, interest, stimulations, emotions and loyalties. "

According to Sheriff and Sheriff "a group is a social unit consisting of a number of individuals who stand in role and status relationship to one another, stabilize in some degree at the time and who possess a set of values and norms of their own, regulating their behavior, at least, in matters of consequences to the group."

According to Cattel "a group is a collection of organisms in which the existence of their relationship is necessary to the satisfaction of certain individual needs of each and again as a set of people who satisfy their needs consciously or unconsciously."

"Group Evaluation is an effective technique for achieving certain kinds of intellectual and social learning goals. It is a superior technique for conceptual learning, for creative problem solving and for increasing oral language proficiency."

According to Groning, an abstract subject through group evaluation can become more concrete and easier for the students to understand.

When students are placed in a group, their proficiency is better. It is good for teachers as well as learners, the following are the merits.

Merits of Group Evaluation

1. Students learn in cooperative manner as they help one another in a group and can be tested as well.
2. A healthy competition in a group motivates them to learn and their performance can be evaluated.
3. Creativity of students is highlighted when they work in a group and can be judged easily.
4. Different learning styles can be evaluated.
5. Cultural sensitivity is essential which is possible to be tested in a group.

Using Assessment Rubrics

A rubric for assessment, usually in the form of a matrix or grid, is a tool used to interpret and grade 'students' Rubrics are against criteria and standards. Rubrics are sometimes call 'criteria sheets' 'grading schemes' or 'scoring guides'. Rubrics can be designed for any content domain .

A rubric makes explicit a range of assessment criteria and expected performance standards. Assessors evaluate a student's performance against all of them rather than assigning a single subjective score.

A rubric handed out to students during an assessment task briefing makes them aware of all expectations related to the task. It helps them evaluate their own work as it progresses.

By using rubrics teacher can maintain consistent standards when assessing qualitative task. Through rubrics we can organize discussions in which the level of performance can be noticed. Rubrics are useful in self-assessment and peer assessment. Once students come to know the concept, need and procedure of rubrics, assessment becomes easy and better.

Rubrics can be used during Peer Assessment and Self Assessment to generate and justify assessment. Once you have familiarized students with the idea of rubrics, you can have them assessed in the rubric, design process, thus taking more responsibilities for their own learning.

Students can set goals and come to decide the responsibility. Thus feeling motivated to work in the required direction. When rubrics are used for self and peer assessment it is helpful for learners to judge quality and improve it if required.

By using rubrics learners as well as teachers can assess their performance. Students can design rubrics themselves as it helps them to become self directed learners. Moreover it is a way of empowering oneself.

By using rubrics learners receive feedback. They come to know their strengths and weakness. In this way their performance is likely to improve. This technique enables them to adjust according to work so that they can check it before submitting.

Record Keeping

Record keeping is an important part of any evaluation process.

The teacher should prepare a record sheet for each student indicating the different skills to be tested, number of tests taken and the students grades or marks in each test. Home assignment done by the student, use of library, practical work done on the language laboratory.

A Scheme of Continuous Evaluation in English

As it is not possible to test all the skills through formal time bound examination, each school should design a scheme of continuous assessment in English. A scheme of evaluation as suggested by Central Board of Secondary Education for its course A in English for Class IX is given below:

	Types of Assessment		*Weightage*
1.	Continuous assessment	—	60%
	(a) Conversational skills	20%	
	(b) Assignments	20%	
	(c) Formal unit tests	20%	
2.	Final Examination	—	40%

According to this scheme all the skills of listening, speaking, reading and writing will be evaluated throughout the session. The final examination will be used to evaluate the skills of reading and writing only.

Based on the above model, the teachers may design their own schemes for upper primary classes, secondary classes and even higher secondary classes.

Limitations of Comprehensive and Continuous Evaluation

- The Continuous and Comprehensive Evaluation may not be successful in a crowded classroom.
- It is not possible for a teacher to do Comprehensive and Continuous Evaluation without knowing the students and their background.
- It is time consuming.
- It can work only in a congenial environment.
- For its successful implementation dedicated teachers are required.
- The observations and judgement of teacher should be free from any prejudices which is really difficult.

☛Points to Remember

1. Evaluation is the process of finding out the extent to which the desired changes have taken place in the pupils.
2. Evaluation is continuous because of regular assessment of the pupils development in schools.
3. Evaluation is comprehensive because it takes care of all the three domains for all round development of the learners in both the scholastic and non-scholastic areas.
4. For its successful implementation dedicated teachers are required.
5. Students are involved in monitoring and making judgements about aspects of their own or peer learning.
6. Portfolio assessment is a continuous assessment, charting students progress towards the expected standards in each exit learning outcome.
7. Cloze test is an exercise test or assessment consisting of a portion where the participant is asked to replace the missing word.
8. Group evaluation is a superior technique for conceptual learning.
9. A rubric helps the teachers applying consistent standards when assessing qualitative tasks and promotes consistency in shared marking.

21

Digital Portfolio: Use of ICT

Earlier the choice of technology for education was limited to radio, television, overhead projector, slide projector etc. But now the scenario has changed. Instead of cost factor and potentiality, the insight and imagination counts more in selecting the mode of technology. Through integration, convergence and miniaturisation, technologies are becoming user friendly. Selection of technology for a particular lesson is important.

Digitalisation of many ICTs has made it possible to design, develop, deliver, manage and assess the learning and training process. The new digital technologies are combination of hardware and software, media and delivery systems. Following are some of the recently evolved digital technologies:

- Multimedia PC, laptop, notebook
- Digital video/still camera
- Local Area Networking (LAN) and other networks/mobile phone
- WWW (World Wide Web)
- CD-ROM and DVD
- E-mail and chat
- Digital libraries
- Computer mediated conferencing video/audio conferencing
- Virtual reality
- Application software as word processing, spreadsheets, power point and simulation and speech recognition

However, latest technology can be linked with the older one.

Richness and quality of teacher education can be enhanced by ICT. Which technology tool should be selected depends upon various factors like: technology infrastructure, access, cost, support personnel and facilities available to create digitised knowledge resources and individuals commitment to sustaining the venture.

USE OF ICT

Information in digital portfolios may also be used in a variety of media, such as text, diagrams, audio files, photographs, illustrations, web material, spread sheets and power point presentations. It has digital portfolio as a tool in technology and was given by Hartners-Young and Morris (1999), Barrett (2000) and Piper (2000). They opined that in this manner learners can increase their skill of understanding and presentations as well.

You should have a clear understanding of 'portfolio'.

The digital portfolio is a collection of all students' best work that has been saved to computer files. Links to these files are organised into a navigable format such as a power point presentation or a web page, making it easy for other people to explore and assess the work.

Digital portfolio can be combination of mixed media. It can be either off-line or on-line or both way. User must have control over it.

The multimedia portfolio is a multifaceted tool which can be used to fill several different purposes, but the most important is that it promotes learning among both students and teachers. This type of portfolio is an important asset to school and individual as society is heading into the digital age.

There are three types of Digital Portfolio:

- Developmental
- Reflective
- Representational

COMPETENCY

Technology is transforming education unlike any trend that has preceded it – but how do teachers take revolutionary tools and use them to optimise learning?

In the first place the curriculum should advocate a shift from a technology of teaching to a technology of learning. This can be easily made possible by transforming learning to a search for information, interpreting the information, and asking the right questions. Curriculum training questions are a major focus of classroom activity where teachers guide students an effective searching prospecting gathering and interpretations, questioning and information, literacy has become fundamental and powerful channels for learning and the students use the tools and information to explore solutions to contemporary issues.

The time has come for teachers to take a fresh look at assumptions about children and learning. Teachers around the world are trying to change their approach to learning and teaching. The teacher must learn to turn the power of technology into teaching tools that should help the students to tap internet resources, evaluate them, contact experts, work in groups and present their ideas more clearly and imaginatively.

The lessons should be prepared in such a way that will enhance student learning, meet challenging standards, supports the diverse needs of learners, and provide a deeper understanding of what they are learning. They should look beyond the conventional classroom, and plan for a working environment in which all the students can fully develop their abilities and interests within the confines of one unit.

Here teachers should interact with students as they complete a task is important to the students' ability to perform the activity. Scaffolding is an instructional technique that should be used by the teacher to provide help at specific points in the learning process. It would help the students to complete the task and once the desired learning has taken place the responsibility would gradually shift to the students.

Assessment should be one of the most important aspects of the curriculum and it should take many forms – from informal observations to a performance task to the evaluation of a final product with many things in between.

You will understand more genuinely when you put a glance on the comparative table given below of traditional approach to teaching and learning with technology supported approaches:

Traditional *v/s* Technology Supported Learning

Traditional Learning Model	*Technology Supported Learning*
• The teacher is the source of knowledge.	• Educators are guides to source of knowledge.
• Learners receive knowledge from the teacher.	• Learners learn by doing.
• Learners work by themselves.	• Learners learn in groups and from each other.
• Tests are given to prevent progress until students have completely mastered a set of skills and to ration access to further learning.	• Assessment is used to guide learning strategies and identify pathways for future learning.
• All learners do the same thing.	• Educators develop individualised learning plans.
• Teachers receive initial training plus adhoc in-service training.	• Educators are life long learners. Initial training and ongoing professional development are linked.
• 'Good' learners are identified and permitted to continue their education.	• People have access to learning opportunities over a life time.

In such a scenario where future skills are based on self-learning and life-long learning, technology and its integration to the learning process is no longer optional.

ICT is useful in following ways:

- Instruction become more effective.
- Time for learning is reduced.

- Individualisation of instruction is possible.
- It helps developing communication skills by using a variety of media and formats.
- Skills of organising, analysing, compiling and synthesising information is developed.
- Learning is self-directed.
- Collaborative learning reinforces the importance of teamwork. Communication becomes the key in a language classroom.
- Motivation levels are high and self-esteem is nurtured.
- Creativity is encouraged.
- It is more student-oriented.
- Students can add to content by locating information from other sources.
- It caters to diverse learners in terms of multiple intelligences as defined by Gardner—Spatial bodily—kinaesthetic, logical, mathematical, music, linguistic, inter-personal and intra-personal.

USE OF ICT— A CHALLENGE

ICT is affecting us as a teacher, as an individual, as a member of society. As a result, our options for education, entertainment and working are radically changing due to ICT revolution. All the modern day innovations have a common denominator – computers and internet. Traditional teacher-centred lecture method will not serve the purpose when you have to survive in the times of globalisation. A teacher has to use computer, mobile, TV and radio etc. for lesson presentation. It becomes more significant when you have to learn and teach English language. It has been already brought to your knowledge that you have to create environment for learning English language and technology. Supported presentation is really helpful to serve this purpose.

There is a great deal of discussion on the issue whether very young students should use computers. According to the National Educational Technology Standards (NETS) Project Overview "parents want their children to graduate with skills that prepare them to either get a job in today's market place or advance to higher levels of education and training. Employers want to hire employees who are honest, reliable, literate and able to reason, communicate make decisions and learn, communities want schools to prepare their children to become good citizens to become good citizens and productive members of society in an increasingly technological and information based world".

Young students can quickly adopt and adapt themselves to the use of technology and many organisations have designed curriculum series to provide schools from kindergarten to Class XII for technology based instruction.

HOW DOES ICT HELP TEACHERS

In the new technology era, the role of educator/teacher has changed and continues to change from being an instructor to a constructor, facilitator, coach and creator of a learning situation. An educator/teacher will be able to integrate the use of ICT's into training/teaching effectively if he develops various competencies like creativity, flexibility, logistic skills, skills for project work, administrative and organisational skills and collaborating skills.

ICT's can help educators/teachers in the following ways:

- ICT's enable to enhance the critical preparation by giving good teaching and/of training materials to use simulators, recording and feedback practices for teaching and micro-teaching, other training institutions experiences and working introducing trainees with resource and support on cyber space, and examples of the use of technologies for teaching training situation.
- With the help of ICT, educators/teachers can have access to colleagues, institutions and universities, centres of expertise, rich resources at cyber space and national organisations like UGC, NCTE, NCERT, and NAAC, etc.
- ICTs enable to interact with students over a physical distance.
- ICTs enable to access online libraries, journals and research to enable individual learning.
- Didactic software/courseware and intelligent tutoring systems can dramatically reduce the cost of teacher training.
- ICTs enable to give feedback and testing objectively and fast, without biases.
- ICTs provide life long and professionally developed courses at a virtual situation, training on demand, orientation and refresher courses through video conferencing on line.
- ICTs enable to facilitate sharing of ideas, experiences as well as collaborating on projects, exchange materials through virtual communities.

Some Examples

Word Processor

At the early levels the recognition of letters of the alphabet could be done by using the keyboard. Typing on the board and subsequently seeing the letters appear on the screen satisfies the child's desire for an immediate response. The addition of sound has an audio-visual impact. The teacher could move on from letters towards using phonics and pictures. The next step could be using the words in sentences and the final stage at the class V level would be where students compose creative stories.

At a later stage writing reports, writing projects and using vocabulary from the thesaurus effectively strengthen language skills. Learning to use the "spell check" and "grammar" tool would while lightening the teacher's load also help to motivate the students as there is a sense of achievement in self-correction and producing a piece of work without mistakes.

Modelling writing activities and taking up shared writing activities help students to see the process of writing and it can provide an excellent opportunity for writing frames. Some softwares, e.g. MS Word, Power Point are available for both group and independent work.

In English ICT can enhance teaching and learning by enabling pupils to:

1. Plan draft, revise and edit their own writing using as word process and other desktop publishing packages.
2. Easily locate and read significant parts of the texts by using search strategies.
3. Locate information quickly confidently and accurately.
4. Publish writing in a variety of forms and fonts.
5. Have access to a wider number of text online e.g. newspapers.
6. Communicate with a wider group of people e.g. e-mail, newspapers, online conferencing.
7. Integrate different media into one text.
8. Use a wider range of texts to—
    - compare the way information is presented.
    - identify the features of particular text types.
    - discuss the merits and limitations of particular text types.
    - investigate how reading strategies are adapted to suit different texts (DEFE) the national strategy 1988.

Database Management and Spreadsheet Applications

While these applications lend themselves to mathematics learning very well, the language learner can use them for effective development of comprehension. Students could be encouraged to collect data on various issues e.g. eating habits, activities during the day, weather reports, etc. These could then be put on the spreadsheet and graphs developed. A series of questions could be put up for students to answer, which require analysis and interpretation of the graphs. The expected answers could be typed out using the word processor or as a presentation in a talk before the class.

Besides recognising graphs as an important tool, the students would also be using the language skills of analysis, comprehension and presentation.

Multimedia Presentation

Multimedia offers the teachers ample scope to present lessons. It has an impact on every type of learners and caters to the concept of multiple responses. Multimedia involves three or more of the following media within a computer environment:

1. Speech or other sounds.
2. Drawings or diagrams.
3. Animation
4. Still photographs.
5. Video clips.
6. Text

Multimedia material could be in the form of a marketed CD, a slide presentation, a presentation on a floppy or from the world wide web. As the CD-rom can store huge quantities of information, it is a valuable tool for the teacher. A good multimedia presentation must not make the learner passive before the computer. It must push the leaner to do something and the results must be immediate e.g. worksheets that are self-corrective. The learner, not the computer should be in control. In this context, it is worthwhile to mention that the interactive video slide and the T.V. can also be an effective tool in learning.

Multimedia is also effective for students having difficulties in reading and writing. Pictures increasingly interact with words pictures and words work together and reinterpret each other. Sometimes assessing communication particularly at the elementary stage only on the basis of written texts may be demotivating with multimedia, non-textual sources can be used by the students to express themselves. This helps students to incorporate their own cultural, social or personal ideas in their work. The integration of individual expression empowers and motivates students beyond the confines of written word. Visual literacy is important not because verbal literacy is becoming obsolete but because "not only have pictures gained ground, but also language, where it is used leans further and further towards the meanings it derives from interaction with pictures" (Look 1992; 49). Images can be talked about and grammar, sentences, stories – the creative aspect of language can emerge. Given the chance children can really "talk a good picture". This is particularly helpful, given the fact that "learners can retain about 25% of what they hear and see and about 75% of what they hear and do".

(Brian Scenbean, 1993). Some of the activities studies could be given are "writing an autobiography", "keeping a daily journal", designing a newsletter". Do remember that the tasks must be suited to the learner levels.

Using the World Wide Web (www)

The internet is often defined as network of computers but it is also important to think of it as a network of people who use these computers. Some of the activities that could reinforce learning language skills are listed below:

- Using 'Talking Books' to teach reading students can see the text and pictures as well as hear the text being read. Students go through the same mechanics of the reading process-decoding, using phonics and seeing words in context. These books are easy and fun to use and children are motivated to read. Children can click on words, pictures etc. for the sound. Clear guidance from the teacher is necessary for using and downloading e-books.

- Students can link up with schools in other countries and they can share books, talks, ideas and letters. They can make "key pals".
- Students can write chain stories that helps link up with other countries. This provides students an opportunity to look and critique writing by other students.
- They could plan tourist brochures by actually visiting tourist's sites on the web; collecting material on them and choosing places to visit.
- Students could attempt web quotes which involves use of the internet.
- Students could publish their own work like stories and poems on the internet.
- Teachers can exchange common teaching problems as bilingual learners are now a part of school education all over the world.
- With adequate videoconferencing facilities, schools could link up to the native speakers of English and actually converse on the net while seeing the speakers at the other end. A group of Indian children learning English language becomes more meaningful to both and is truly communication in use.
- Pupils should e-mail to write to range of people. This could be to pupils in another schools involved in a joint e-mail project or an organisation from which they require information for the class topic. Pupils could exchange first drafts of stories, which are then reviewed by other pupils who send back their comments on how the story could be improved. They could jointly design a questionnaire which could be used to collect information in their respective schools.
- They should use web sites of national and local newspapers to read a variety of reports. They should look at the layout and common features. They could collect, list and compare opening sentences of articles on the same topic. They could compare several reports on the same subject and categorise what is fact and what is opinion. Pupils could write articles in pairs and amend them over a period of time. Their articles could then be used to produce a class newspaper. They should focus on the content of their articles and consider the layout and presentation later.
- Pupils could collaborate with others to write stories in chapters, with particular audience in mind e.g. horror stories for junior pupils.
- Pupils could locate information on CD-rom or on the internet by using the contents pages, indexes and bookmarks. Pupils in groups could compare and evaluate critically the information from different sources and be able to check the accuracy or reliability of the information.

Radio

It is a very important type of audio-aid. The advent of radio in 1917 triggered a thought that mass education can be achieved through radio broadcasts. In India, the first radio station was established in Bombay in July 1927, one in Calcutta, even in Delhi in 1936. School broadcasting was initiated in 1937 from Calcutta. The Central Institute for Educational Technology (CIET) under the NCERT produces radio broadcast—Quality audio programmes.

The radio is a valuable aid in language-learning. Its flexibility and immediacy makes it better than any other aid except television. The radio, as an aid in the teaching of English, has many advantages. It presents the true spoken English on which we can base all good English teaching. It can use the services of outstanding speakers and teachers of English. It can reach all kinds of listeners inside and outside the classroom. As compared to other audio-aids it is cheaper because one set can prove useful to the whole school.

Radio is the most popular mechanical audio aid available ever in the most remote areas of the country. Though other aids like television, video and VCR have been found more useful than it, but due to high cost, it is very difficult for every school to afford them. Besides, these equipments require electric light to run while radio can be easily run with cells only. A little careful planning may serve the purpose. Though, it may look odd to talk of radio in the age of computers but it is the cheapest mechanical aid and has the following advantages:

1. Radio presents and interprets the most current event to us, before it becomes a part of history. Any activity, taking place in any part of the world is made available to us within seconds. A person living in the most remote area may become aware with the current events.
2. It can give students a feeling of participation. It is not possible for a language teacher to organise field trips so often but radio can solve this problem. Students sitting in their classroom may listen the direct broadcast of the presidential speech. Thus, it helps in providing 'immediate knowledge' of many things.
3. A language teacher may use radio to develop a sense of discrimination among students. Students may be asked to listen a speech of a native speaker and after it, the speech of a person whose mother tongue is some other language. Students may be asked to discriminate in the ways of pronunciation.
4. It may not be possible for a language teacher of a remote area to get an opportunity to listen the president of America delivering inaugural speech at some function but international broadcasting may provide an opportunity to listen him, even sitting in the classroom.
5. Use of radio brings pleasure of strangeness and variety. If it is used intelligibly, it serves as a valuable aid in language teaching and learning.

Procedure

For effective and efficient use of radio, certain planning is needed. The entire learning programme can be divided into three categories:

(1) Preparatory Phase
(2) Listening Phase
(3) Follow-up Work

The following paragraphs describe in detail the whole procedure:

(1) *Preparatory Phase*: To use this aid properly some planning is needed. Information regarding the programme is made available in advance. The teacher may select the suitable programme and mentally prepare the learning to listen the programme. He may tell the learners the purpose of organising such programmes. He may write some questions in advance on blackboard, which students would have to answer after the speech is over. This would help students to focus on the required areas and they would listen the programme attentively. The purpose of this step is to make the learners mentally, prepared for the activity and develop their enthusiasm. This phase also provides background knowledge to students so that radio lessons may give best results. Below is given a list of activities compiles at Ohio State University, which may be done at the preparatory stage.

(a) Putting questions about the broadcast topic on the background.
(b) Discussing the topic with class.
(c) Telling the class what he knows about the topic.
(d) Listening things the class wants to know about the topic.
(e) Asking the students to read the reference material related to the topic.
(f) Asking the students to write out what they know about the topic.
(g) Writing and defining expected difficult vocabulary items (key words) related to the topics.
(h) Making books and magazines related to the topic readily available.
(i) Making all necessary seating arrangements in advance of a broadcast.
(k) Making plans to connect the broadcast with regular class work.

(2) *Listening Phase*: Proper seating arrangement is essential. Students are not required to talk in between. Radio station should be set in advance. To make the students listen attentively teacher also need to be involved. During the programme teacher can make observations of the reactions of the students to determine the extent of the success of the programme correct pronunciation of the R.P. pattern can be initiated by the students.

(3) *Follow-up Work*: Now comes the follow-up phase. When the programme is over teacher can write the words on chalkboard and ask them to pronounce the way they have listened spoken by the experts/English teachers/native speakers. An action research can be done how many errors have been reduced by the listeners. Students can be asked to make critical comments in writing on the broadcast.

They can be asked to make a list of new items and phrases used by the broadcaster. Summarising the main points of broadcast either in spoken or written form which will enhance their listening, speaking and writing skill as well.

For your understanding we will discuss some important measures for the effective use of radio in language teaching.

(1) Radio offers a wide variety of programmes. In selecting a suitable programme, age and interest of the students should be kept in mind.
(2) Some recorded audio-tapes of radio broadcast can be utilised by language teacher in the class.
(3) Students habit of knowing the schedule of radio broadcast through local newspaper must be inculcated.
(4) After knowing the schedule next step is to select the programme. Following criteria can be useful:
   (a) Length of the programme should be genuinely set according to the interest, urge, attention, span and physical needs of students.
   (b) Time of broadcasting should suit the scheduled periods.
   (c) Selected programme must fulfil the set objectives. Although occasionally, certain different programmes such as special newscast, spot broadcast, foreign broadcast, special event broadcast etc. may also be selected.
   (d) It is to be noted that a programme may be of utility but if poorly presented, can serve no purpose. Clarity of voice, simplicity, vividness of terminology and standard pronunciation are the pre-requisite of a good programme.
   (e) The place of keeping the radio set also needs attention. The best place is to keep the receiver at a table, facing the class. The learners should be free to raise their hands if there is difficulty in hearing so that the volume may be adjusted according to the need. The voice must be audible clearly, even to the students, sitting in the distant corner of the class, otherwise the very purpose of radio lessons would be defeated.
(5) The set should be tuned to the desired station. This exercise should be done in advance.
(6) Attempts should be made that no unnecessary disturbances should be there like in between students seek permission for refreshment or sometimes teacher gets some notice from office. It is better to put a signboard outside the class that a radio programme is going on.
(7) Note taking habit by the students is a matter of personal habit of the student. Teacher is not supposed to discourage or encourage for it.

From the above discussion, it is clear that "Radio" is a marvellous device and can be used profitably in English language teaching. A little effort on the part of the teacher can make the language learning lively and interesting.

Use of TV in Education has been discussed in Instructional Media.

Use of Language Laboratory has been discussed in Instructional Media.

Mobile Communication

Satellite based communication can help learners at two level. One, they can be provided electronic gadgets like radio, cellular phone etc. which will allow them to remain in touch with the teachers while they are on move from one place to another. It is expected that in future more number of learners would be mobile for their work or business purposes. Secondly, specially designed mobile van fitted with audio equipment, talk back facilities, etc. can be developed. These vans can move from one area to another to impact conduct on the spot education/ training. Interested groups can be created around a learning centre (preferably in a centrally located village) in the rural and remote area where learners in the adjoining locality can assemble and share their problems with resource persons/teachers located at block or district centres. They can interact with teachers located at different centres using satellite technology.

The number of mobile phone users has increased leap and bound in the recent years. As a result of various technological options the mobile phone users in the country has exceeded 23 million. According to TRAI (Telecommunication Regulatory Authority of India), if the same growth rate is maintained the target of tele-density will be really great.

Specially in the English language learning direct linkage with the native speakers is feasible which will improve the pronunciation of our learners. Every minute you are connected with the whole world. This type of learning English language on mobile can be helpful in diagnostic and remedial teaching.

Use of Mobile Phones in Education

Perhaps the most well-known and biggest programme exploring the use of mobile phones in education in a developing country is the text to teach project in the Philippines.

You should know that 28% of Africans have a mobile phone subscription, according to data released by the ITU earlier this year, part of a larger trend that sees two out of every three mobile subscribers around the world living in a developing country. The flagship ITU publication measuring the information society (pdf) notes that two thirds of the world's cell phone subscriptions are in developing nations, with Africa, which has a 2% subscriber rate as recently as 2000, growing the fastest, and it is not only adults who are making use of this new technology. Survey work at a low income high school in South Africa Samara Machel Township suggests that mobile penetration among youth in some places might be higher than one might suspect.

While the explosive use of mobile phones in developing countries is well documented and undeniable – and evidence is emerging that phones are slowly making their way into the hands of teens, just what this might mean for the delivery of education in developing countries is a little less clear. This topic first started to get clear attention among small groups of people in international donor agencies around 2005, with a mobile learning for the topic. The workshop report (published as mobile learning for expanding educational opportunities) is in many way typical of work around this time, focusing largely on the possible usage models and relevance for using mobile phones in a variety of ways to support new teaching and learning process. Further a field, DFID began to support work in this area in Africa and papers written on mobile learning in Africa sounded similar notes to what was being discussed in Asia, as revealed in titles like. The potential for using SMS to support learning and organisation in Sub-Saharan Africa (pdf) and transforming learning through technology. The case of using SMSs to support distance students in South Africa (pdf).

While the evidence base is still quite spotty, some lessons and usage models are slowly emerging from pilot projects in places as diverse as Thailand and Mongolia. The increasing ubiquity of mobile phones has helped through. Pilots looking at mobile gaming to support literacy in India.

Exploring what might be possible should smart phones drop greatly in price in the coming years projects like Duniya Moja, a joint initiative of Stanford University (USA) and partner universities in Southern and Eastern Africa, are exploring how communication and joint research between students and faculty on environmental issues can be facilitated and supported.

When we talk about the use of mobile phones in education sector, it is clear we are still in the very early stages of development, and we expect this will be an area of major research interest and activity in the coming years – and a recurring to the blog.

Opinion against Mobile

On the other hand someone opines that text to teach cannot solve the problem as an effective way of media of course it enriches the material by using SMS, then delivered via satellite, and downloaded to a digital video recorder connected to a TV set in the classroom. To being with, what is the need to send an SMS, to order for the material? Why not simply put all the media rich materials that will be used during the school year in a C.D. library or a server in the school? Why pay for (expensive) satellite transmission when these multimedia materials can be saved in CDs and delivered via mail to the school at the start of every year.

One other view point is also there that India is a developing country and lessons on mobile will be a costly affair. But you should understand that somewhere we have to take initiative in technology to shake hands with other developed countries.

Needless to say that we need expert teachers and trainers for such programming. In a nutshell, learning English on mobile is useful in following ways:

(1) Students can learn at their own speed.
(2) Expert views can be sought.
(3) Native speakers can be heard and imitated.
(4) One is not supposed to bind with the time factor and can learn at his/her convenience.
(5) Audio-video clippings on mobile can be very helpful for the learners specially in the area of pronunciation.

Lastly, it depends on the efficiency and attitude of the users.

Teacher's Role in Technology Integration

We shall look at how the teachers should be prepared for handling technology integration. Many teachers are not adequately prepared to use technology in their teaching. Some of them may have received some pre-service training in technology but may still not be comfortable with their computing skills. This can present a challenge to the introduction of technology integration. A new teacher with some technology know-how may feel unprepared to integrate technology without guidance and support. Here are some hints to help you to meet this challenge.

(1) Self-assessment of your skills and deficiencies is essential. Ask and be ready to learn.
(2) Find people in your school who are ready to share technology know-how and have the time as well.
(3) Plenty of books are available and these are cheaply priced.
(4) Ask students to help.
(5) Set your goals and push yourself to learn.
(6) Learn to use e-mail and share ideas.
(7) Be familiar with your school technology plan.
(8) Attend technology conferences and bring back ideas for the school.
(9) Join technology groups on the web. In English language teaching we have the ELTECS groups.
(10) Begin planning to use technology in your instruction.
(11) Get to know your school computers and the materials available at school.
(12) Get help from the school technology coordinator.
(13) Keep in touch with students' know-how on technology.
(14) Get parents help with technology.
(15) Improve your technology quotient (TQ) by periodic upgradation of technology skills.

As a teacher of English what are the technology skills that could be of importance for you in the context of student learning?

- Word processing database management and spreadsheet applications

- Ability to create multimedia presentations.
- Ability to access information.
- Ability to make presentations through power point.
- Ability to use audio and video conferencing for distance learning situation.

WHAT SHOULD YOUR MULTIMEDIA BASED LESSON PLAN INCLUDE?

What is Technology Planning?

A good technology plan should be based on six or seven basic principles—

- Be simple, organised and continuous.
- Take into account the mission of the organisation.
- Be realistic and economically viable.
- Involve all the stakeholders – administrators, teachers, parents, students, community and technology experts.
- Identify the strengths and weaknesses of the organisation and how these will effect the technology implementation plan.
- Develop procedures for purchasing and upgrading technology.
- Be related to educational goals e.g. creating lifelong learners.

Any technology plan should have two parts:

(1) Human Resource Development (professional development, learning and support)

(2) Technology (hardware and software facilities)

Connect Your Classroom to a World of Learning

We need to redesign and reshape our lessons more consciously and practically, so that learning becomes more meaningful and focussed on student inquiry. To make our students understand important ideas conveyed in a lesson/unit, we need to plan our lessons meticulously.

The lesson plan serves as one of the most effective curricular and instructional framework for classroom teachers for designing their lessons. It should help you to decide what the students will learn, the resources that you will use, how the lessons are related to students' interests and needs, the questions that you would ask them, and how technology can be integrated into your teaching.

Framing Questions

Curriculum involves not only teaching or covering portions, but helping students discover too. Our aim as teachers is not merely coverage, but also "un-coverage". We assume that when students learn lessons and answer questions. They have gained knowledge. Students are not given an opportunity to realise that knowledge is acquired and refined in response to questions and inquiry. We can make our teaching more authentic by revealing how knowledge is pursued and shaped by questioning. This will help the students recreate the processes by which the knowledge is created.

Questions are the doorways to understanding. Every question we answer leads to another question. They enable us to make changes in life, to invent new and better ways of doing things. They are the most powerful tools we have for making decisions and solving problems. Strong questioning skills help us to discover something new. They provoke thought and inspire reflection.

Now, in classrooms, the questioning process has been reduced and oversimplified to a search for pre-packaged answers. This helps in creating only superficial knowledge not insights. It could perhaps, help the students to go to greater depths, if they so desire.

How can we Make Learning more Meaningful for the Students?

One strategy is to build curriculum around questions that give rise to content knowledge. We need to ask provocative and multilevel questions that reveal the richness and complexities of a subject. They are umbrella-like organisers of what you want your students to remember for thirty years and longer.

These questions challenge students to use higher level thinking skills and help them to understand essential concepts. They are essence of what your students will examine and learn in the course of their study. They generate multiple plausible answers, perspectives and research directions – leading to other questions. They cast old knowledge, ideas and texts in a new light.

Let us differentiate between unit/lesson questions and essential questions. Unit/lessons questions work with the essential topical questions to provide background and guide the work on a particular unit of study. Unit questions tend to be more topic and subject specific. They frame a specific set of inquiries and lead the student to uncover the essential question. The facts obtained by finding the answers to the unit questions are used to build the answer to the essential question. Listing of unit questions will help students finally to answer their essential question.

Students Objectives/Learning Outcomes

To make sure your multimedia based lesson plan will teach exactly what you want it is, you need to develop clear and specific objectives. Please note that objectives should not be the activities that will be used in the lesson plan. They should instead be the learning outcomes of those activities. To classify objectives, Bloom's taxonomy has proved to be an invaluable tool for teachers. It provides a clear guide to levels of thinking, the processing of learning experiences and the needs of students with different levels of intelligence.

It gives a structure to learning and moves from the foundation levels of knowledge. Comprehension and application skills is higher order thinking skills of analysis, synthesis and evaluation.

BLOOM'S TAXONOMY

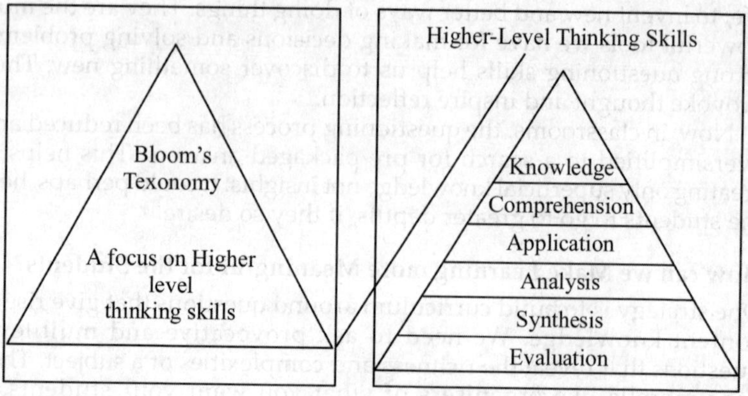

Knowledge[1]	*Comprehension*[2]	*Application*[3]	*Analysis*[4]	*Synthesis*[5]	*Evaluation*[6]
Define	Summarise	Solve	List	Design	Evaluate
Classify	Explain	Illustrate	Match	Support	Choose
Locate	Interpret	Calculate	Analyse	Write	Estimate
Outline	Describe	Interpret	Organise	Report	Judge
Give examples	Compare	Manipulate	Deduce	Combine	Defend
Distinguish opinion from fact	Convert	Predict	Choose	Comply	Appraise
Recall	Paraphrase	Classify	Diagram	Develop	Criticise
Describe	Differentiate	Modify	Discriminate	Discuss	Justify
Name	Demonstrate	Cut into practice	Contrast	Plan	Debate
Identify	Visualise	Demonstrate	Compare	Compare	Support your reasons
Show	Restate	Compute	Distinguish	Create	Conclude
Define	Rewrite	Operate	Categorise	Construct	Assess
Recognise	Give examples		Outcome	Rearrange	Rate
			Restate	Compose	
				Organise	

Notes:

1. Knowledge—Recall or Recognition of Information
2. Comprehension—Understand, Translate, Paraphrase, Interpret or Extrapolate Material.
3. Application—Use Information and Transfer Knowledge from One Setting to Another.
4. Analysis—Identify details and discover and differentiate the component parts of a situation or information.
5. Synthesis—Combine parts to create the big picture.
6. Evaluation—Judge the value or use information using appropriate criteria.

Objectives should reflect the progression of thinking and responding for knowledge to evaluation. Not all levels need to be developed for every topic. However, using multimedia in the classroom provides opportunities to the teachers to cater to all the levels of learning outcomes for the topic for the mixed ability groups being taught. Applying this in classroom changes the learning environment from teacher-directed to student-centred.

Procedures

For a multimedia lesson, a step-by-step description of how to replicate the lesson and achieve lesson plan objectives is written. This provides suggestions on how to proceed with the implementation of the lesson plan. It also focuses on what the teacher should do during the lesson. These don't have to involve every little thing the teacher will say and do, but they should list the relevant actions the teacher needs to perform for the success of the lesson.

Prerequisite Skills

This is useful in considering the readiness/state of your students for the multimedia based lesson activities. It allows you and other teachers, replicating your lesson plan, to prepare the students for the activities that will help them to accomplish the lesson objectives.

Materials and Resources

This helps you to quickly determine how much preparation, resources, and management will be involved in carrying out this plan, and what materials, books, equipment and resources you will need to have ready. In a multimedia lesson plan, we need to give full citation of textbooks/story books/CD-roms/websites/any other references used.

Student Support Materials

We now make you aware of a very important concept in supporting student effort in learning and specifically learning language i.e. concept of scaffolding.

Concept of Scaffolding

Teachers create scaffolds or organisational tools to guide students' learning. Scaffolding is a structure we give to students to help them organise and support their investigation or inquiry (e.g. concept maps, check lists, study guides, self-assessment tools, pre-formatted documents, presentations and publications/organisational charts).

In the beginning, students use scaffolds provided by the teachers. Later, students modify scaffolding to fit their own needs. Finally, they learn to create their own scaffolds to become independent learners.

What is Scaffolding?

Scaffolding is a temporary framework that supports a building during construction. When the structure is sturdy enough to stand on its own the scaffold is removed.

What does Scaffolding mean in the educational sense?

- Scaffolding is a temporary structure to help students understand a process or concept.
- It is an instructional tool that reduces ambiguity, thereby increasing growth opportunities.
- Scaffolding, in the form of coaching or modelling supports students as they develop new skills or learn new concepts.
- When the student achieves competence, the support is removed. The student contributes to develop the skills or knowledge on his/her own.

  Scaffolding essentially means doing some of the work for the student who isn't quite ready to accomplish a task independently scaffolding is intended to be temporary. It is there to aid the completion of a task and it is eventually removed as are the supports used by the construction workers.
- This technique of scaffolding works very well with technology based learning in which students are intended to become self-reliant learners. Scaffolding, in fact, leads them, gradually and logically towards self-reliance in the following way:
  - The teacher creates supporting structures initially to involve the students into the topic by generating their interest.
  - Once the students are interested, they gradually develop a hold on the topic.
  - With the hold on the topic they usually assume more responsibility.
  - When the student is in control of the topic and is achieving the laid down targets the teacher removes the scaffold.
  - With continued exposure and at a later stage of self-reliance in learning, the student learns to create his/her own scaffolds even at the initial stages of learning a topic and thus gradually gains independence in learning.

Examples of Scaffolding

- Field trips
- Organisational charts
- Check lists
- Concept maps
- Teacher's sample
- Prepared documents
- Self-assessment tools
- Study guides

☛Points to Remember

1. The new digital technologies are combination of hardware and software, media and delivery systems.
2. The digital portfolio is a collection of all a student's best work that has saved to computer files.
3. ICTs provide life long and professionally developed courses at a virtual situation, training on demand, orientation and refesher courses through video conferencing on line.

22

Characteristics of Good Text Book

"To make the best use of time in the classroom and to avoid unintended repetition or the neglect of essential language patterns, the teacher is wise to have a textbook, at least in the background of his mind". —F.L. Billows

Textbooks occupy an important place during primary and secondary education. In English teaching textbooks are all the more important. According to R.S. Trivedi, "In the absence of any other instructional materials the textbook becomes a potent tool in the hands of a teacher to teach the skill of a language and the more of a foreign language". It is not merely a source of information but a course of study, a set of unit plans and a learning guide. It helps to revise and reinforce the language material already taught. The teacher must be able to evaluate the textbook she/he has to use.

Importance of English Textbooks

If a textbook is properly planned and utilised, it can prove a useful tool both for the teacher and the taught. It can help them in the following manner:

1. It gives meaning and purpose to the teaching-learning of a language.
2. It keeps the teacher on guard against any unnecessary repetitions and omissions.
3. It makes the teaching systematic.
4. It helps students in self-study.
5. It facilitates and stabilises students' learning.
6. It serves as a memory aid for the pupils.
7. It prepares ground for writing.
8. It is a means of presenting selected and graded vocabulary.
9. The examples and illustrations given in the textbook help the pupils a lot.
10. It gives the knowledge of linguistic principles and experiences.
11. It also serves as an index for academic achievement.
12. It becomes a permanent record or measure of what has been learnt.

Characteristics of Good Textbooks

Following characteristics are desirable in a good English textbook:

1. *Adequate Subject Matter*

(i) It should be based on psychological needs and interest of the students.
(ii) It should be related to pupils' environment.
(iii) It should be according to the age of the students.
(iv) It should have a link with the Indian culture and tradition.
(v) It should have varied topics.
(vi) It should be of practical utility as well as informative.

2. *Style*

(i) The style should be based on the maxims of simple to difficult, known to unknown, concrete to abstract.
(ii) Logical manner should be adopted for the presentation of subject matter.
(iii) The style should appeal to the readers.

3. *Suitable Vocabulary and Structures*

(i) The vocabulary should be controlled.
(ii) It should be properly selected and graded.
(iii) The introduction of vocabulary should be progressive within series of Readers.
(iv) The new words and structures should be repeated.
(v) Every reader should give an index of words and structures at the end.
(vi) At the end of the book, a glossary of difficult words and structures should be given.

4. *Pictures and Illustrations*

(i) The illustrations should make the subject matter clear.
(ii) They should be sufficient in number.
(iii) The readers for junior level should have illustrations occupying more space and quite large in size.
(iv) They should be attractive.
(v) Too many ideas should not be conveyed in one illustration.

5. *Developing Language Skill*

It should provide necessary facilities for developing the necessary language skills of speaking, reading and writing in the young learners.

6. *Proportion and Order*

(i) A lesson should not be very long.
(ii) There should be plausible proportion between prose, poetry, story, biography, lessons etc.
(iii) Two topics of the same kind should not be in continuation.
(iv) Proportion of content and structural words should be maintained.

7. Exercises

(i) There should be sufficient number of exercises at the end of every lesson.
(ii) The instructions about the exercises should be brief and clear.
(iii) Varied exercises should be presented.
(iv) Exercises should be well selected and graded.

8. Opportunity of Oral Work

(i) It should provide sufficient opportunity for oral work.
(ii) The lessons should be based on the possibility of introductory oral work.

9. Technical Characteristics

(i) Paper should be of good quality.
(ii) Printing should be attractive.
(iii) Size of the type should be bold for juniors and small for seniors.
(iv) Binding should be proper.
(v) The cover should be thick and durable with some interesting illustration over it.
(vi) A jacket should be added to the cover.
(vii) The book should be handy.
(viii) Price should be moderate.

Teacher's Hand book

In addition to these characteristics, a good textbook of English should be supplemented by teacher's handbook. It will guide the teachers. Teaching of English can be made more effective and useful, and the teachers can go a long way in the improvement of linguistic attainment of the students with the help of teacher's handbook.

☛Points to Remember

1. Text Book is a useful tool both for the teacher and the taught.
2. A teacher must see that a text book possesses all the Academic and Technical characteristics.
3. A good text book will always keep the teacher and the taught on the track.

23

Development of Good Test Items in English
(*Objective Type, Short Answer Type and Essay Type*)

"To discover that a child is backward is of great value. But to analyze precisely where and for what reasons he is backward constitutes a problem of the highest practical importance." —*Burt*

Examinations have always been an important part of the total educational process. Examinations are designed and administered at different stages of education and their results are used for various purposes like improvement in learning, grading and classification of students, selection for admission to higher classes or for scholarship, certification and for providing guidance for future, etc.

In our country, written examinations are the most commonly used technique of testing student's achievement. But the challenge before everyone is the qualitative improvement of the teaching-learning programme. It is essential to fix the aims of teaching in order to make efforts to achieve them. How much the students have learnt and what is the effect of the teaching can only be judged through the exams, test and evaluation work. But more important than test is the content matter of the test.

There are the terminal and annual examination in the schools. Written tests are organised by school in each and every subject. In fact, the evaluation of students' scholastic achievement is based on these written tests and examinations.

Chronback defines test as "A test is a systematic procedure for comparing the behaviour of two or more persons".

A question paper is the basic tool used in a test or examination. It is usual for a teacher to prepare a test by assembling questions on the spur of the moment without taking into consideration the characteristics of a good test. A test must possess certain attributes.

Attributes of a Good Test

1. Validity

Validity is the most important characteristic of a good test. Validity of a test is the extent to which it measures what it attempts to measure. That is to say that a test should conform to the objectives of testing.

There are three types of validity:

(a) *Face validity*. Face validity means that a test, even at a simple glance, should look valid. For example, in a language test the following items is totally invalid, as it does not test language but the computation skill of the students.

The train starts from New Delhi at 8.10 hours and reaches Kanpur at 14.30 hours.

How much time does the train take to reach Kanpur from New Delhi?

To establish face validity of a test, the examiner or the teacher should go through the test and examine its content validity.

(b) *Content validity*. Content validity is very important in an achievement test as an achievement test tries to measure some specific skills or abilities through some specific content. The test should contain questions on every important area of the content in appropriate proportion and the questions should be framed in such a way that all the objectives of the course are tested properly.

(c) *Empirical validity*. Empirical validity is also known as statistical validity or criterion related validity as to ensure this a criterion is taken and the scores of the students are correlated with their scores on the criterion test. Empirical validity is important because it shows statistically that a test is valid, i.e., it measures well what it intends to measure.

2. *Reliability*

The higher the degree of reliability the results of a test have, the greater is considered the reliability of the test itself. And the reliability of its conclusion means that if the same test is performed upon the same individual more than once, results obtained in each individual lists should be the same with the first one, if it is modified by changed circumstances.

3. *Usability*

Usability or practicability is the third characteristic of a good test. There are a number of practical factors that are to be considered while preparing or selecting a test for use.

- Length of the test should be neither too long or too short.
- Test should be easy to administer.
- Scorability is also to be taken care of.

4. *Objectivity*

A test can achieve a high level of objectivity only if the answer to each of its various question is distinct and precise and if there is no difference of opinion regarding it among the various examiners. Its efficacy lies in the fact that the conclusion or result is in no way influenced by the examiner's personal thoughts or opinions, so that the conclusions or results are obtained, no matter what the number of examiners who examine the same subject. There should be no scope of subjectivity. There should be objectivity in evaluation procedure.

5. Comprehensiveness

In it, questions cover the quality in question as well as allied qualities so that no aspect of the measured or tested ability escaped attention.

6. Discriminating Power

This applies to the ability, which helps to distinguish between persons with greater or less ability so that they score more or less points or marks.

Characteristics of Good Test in English

1. Continuous evaluation is basically formative in nature and is school based. It is to be carried out by the teachers teaching a particular class.
2. The purpose of continuous evaluation is mainly improvement in learning. For this the learning gaps and weaknesses are diagnosed so that remedial measures can be provided.
3. Continuous evaluation is built into the total teaching-learning programme and is a part of the daily routine for a teacher.
4. There is no need of making formal arrangement.
5. Its language must be lucid and clear.
6. It should be from whole syllabus and easy to score.
7. The questions should be neither too difficult nor too easy.

Some Details about Questions

A. Objective Type Questions

In this form of question the answer is completely controlled thus, making its assessment 'objective' and 'impersonal'—the two charges always levelled against the 'traditional type of examinations/ evaluations'. These are called 'objective' firstly, because they are objective related and secondly because there is no element of subjectivity in assessment as the answers are externally 'controlled' leaving no scope for examiner's bias, prejudice and/or favour.

Classification of the type of objective test is given in a tabular form.

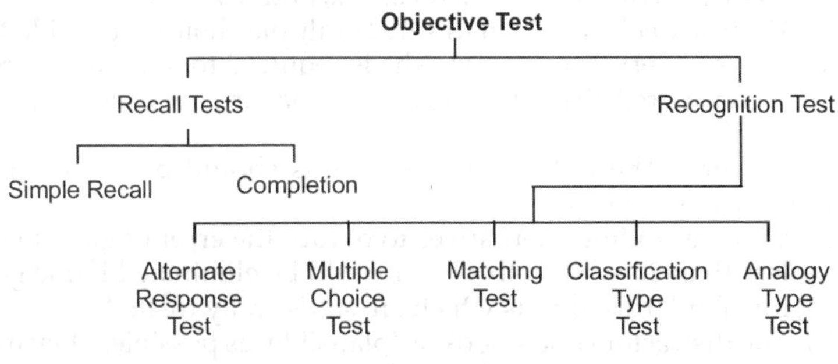

1. ***Simple Recall Test*****:** These tests are used to assess the factual knowledge of the pupils. The nature of these questions is simple and direct. Such types of test items are framed to replicate what the pupils have learnt already for example.

Test Item

(i) Who had composed the poem True love?
(ii) Name the writer of the book 'Robinson Crusoe'.
(iii) Who is the writer of 'Oliver Twist'?
(iv) Who had written the book 'Pilgrims Progress'?

Answers: (i) Shakespeare, (ii) Daniel Dofoe, (iii) Charles Dickens, and (iv) Leo Tolstoy.

2. ***Completion Tests*****:** In these tests, the 'teaching point' represented by words is left blank in a given sentence, or a number of sentences.

Test Items:

(i) Indira Gandhi was the daughter of ......
(ii) The major component of language teaching is .....
(iii) The functional grammar is evolved by .....
(iv) The opposite of Black is ....

Answers: (i) Nehru, (ii) Grammar, (iii) Chomsky, and (iv) White

3. ***Recognition Type*****:** These items are classified into five types:

(i) True and false type/alternative types
(ii) Multiple choice items
(iii) Matching type items
(iv) Classification type items
(v) Analogy type items

(i) *True and False Type/Alternative Items.* In this test mixture of true and false statement is given. Pupils are required to mark their correct nature. Such questions may have two or more alternate statements.

Test Items

(a) Pandit Jawaharlal Nehru was born at Allahabad. (True/False)
(b) Akbar lost the battle of Kalinga. (True/False)
(c) The sun revolves round the earth. (True/False)
(d) The prose and poetry are the major components of English literature. (True/False)

Answers: (a) True , (b) ...., (c) ...., and (d) ....

(ii) *Multiple Choice Items:* In this test multiple choice is provided to the pupils for every question. He/she is required to mark the correct one. It is considered absolutely correct. Dr. Ballard has called it a 'fool proof' test.

Precautions: The following precautions should be taken while framing such questions:

(a) Give fair to fine alternatives to reduce the error of guessing to less than 20%. Even this error could be eliminated if one goes for standardised tests which are statistically treated.
(b) The distractor should look as 'plausible' as possible. They may look correct, but are still not the right answer.

(c) The order of the right response in the alternative should be mixed up lest the students guess it right. Do not follow a set pattern.

(d) There should not be anything intrinsically in the right response that it stands out, e.g., its length of treatment or explanation, etc. Avoid catchwords.

(e) The responses should not be suggestive of the right answer.

Test Items

Four choices are given below. Select the best correct response.

(a) Well begun is half done. In the sentence the word well is:
 (1) Noun
 (2) Adverb
 (3) Participle
 (4) Gerund

(b) Mark the synonym of 'Popular':
 (1) Person
 (2) Friendly
 (3) Liked
 (4) Desirable

(c) What is the meaning of 'Big'?
 (1) Large
 (2) Complexion
 (3) Sweet
 (4) Small

(d) He has been ill ...... a number of days.
 (1) Since
 (2) For
 (3) From
 (4) Till

Answers: (a) 2, (b) 3, (c) 1, and (d) 2

(iii) *Matching Type Tests*: It is a type of recognition test. In this type of test item, two mismatched columns are given. The questions and answers given in two columns are required to be matched or compared by the students. By giving the pupils two columns and asking him to match the related items, the teacher can easily and quickly see if the students recognise the relationships that exist between the items. There is less of stress upon sheer memory or recall of fragmentary information because the materials are presented to the students for his correlation.

Because matching tests are generally focussed to measuring subject matter, it is not always indicative of the pupils' ability to perceive the deeper meaning or real understanding of the relationship between the items used on the tests stress upon mere verbalisation and memory of isolated bits of information should be avoided.

Match the following

A	*B*
Beautiful	Synonym
Lavish	Handsome
Zeal	Extravagant
Same	Zest

Answers 1:2, 2:3, 3:4, 4:1.

Cautions

1. The homogeneous material should be included in each item.
2. It should be checked that unwanted clues are not there for matching pairs.
3. The items should not be too easy or too difficult.

(iv) *Classification Type Test Items.* In this test several places, objects and persons are listed whereas all other words belong to the same class, one of them is odd. The pupils are required to underline/score out the 'odd'

Test items

(a) Poetry, prose, grammar, drama and story.
(b) Chair, sofa, settee, desk
(c) Apple, banana, guava, potato
(d) Adverb, preposition, imperative, adjective.

Answers: (a) Grammar, (b) Settee, (c) Potato, and (d) Imperative

This type of items are used for assessing the ability of seeing the relationship to form the group and power of discrimination to isolate one as correct response. There is twenty per cent probability for correct answer through guessing. The formula correction for guessing should be used.

(v) *Analogy Type Items.* In this type of item there are two parallel or similar situations. In the first situation two words are given having same specific relationship, the second situation is given incomplete form, only one word is provided. The second word is to be selected or to be recalled for establishing the same relationship by the examiner.

Test items

Complete the following by selecting a proper word.

(a) Poetry: Literature; Grammar: ……
(b) Well: Adverb; Near: …….
(c) Imperative: Sentence; Adverb: …….
(d) Gerund: Noun; Participle: ……

Answers: (a) Language, (b) Preposition, (c) Word, and (d) Adjective

The analogy type items are usually prepared in multi-choice form. Such items are used for assessing verbal reasoning and ability of relationship. They are used for measuring higher level than the earlier type of items rather than factual knowledge. These are used in the intelligence achievement and aptitude tests.

B. Short Answers Type

Answers in this type are brief, to the point, limited and short. Sometimes the number of words are specified. Naturally, in this type of questions, the freedom of the students attempting the answer is narrowed down. It is easy to score. But the subjectivity on the part of examiner is reduced.

Test Items

1. Write a paragraph of 150 words on Shakespearean Tragedy.
2. Justify the title of the novel 'Far from the Madding Crowd' in 200 words.
3. Write a dialogue between the teacher and the student in 4 to 6 sentences.
4. Why do you like the democracy? Write in 6 sentences.

C. Essay Type Test

Essay type questions are descriptive in nature. To answer such questions, the students may use their own views and ideas. This type of test is specifically useful for testing skills like written expression and organisation of matter, attitude of examinee towards problem.

For Example

1. Write an essay on the topic: Indian politics.
2. Highlight the role of cable TV.
3. How to check the danger on ozone layer?
4. Express your views on globalisation.

These type of tests are easy to construct and easy to carry out. Moreover there is full freedom of expression and originality of ideas are considered.

Limitation of Essay Type Tests

These tests have low validity, low reliability and are less comprehensive. There is full scope of subjectivity in marking.

But construction of a genuinely thought-provoking essay question however is required. Teachers must take pain for it and make efforts in the direction.

Conclusion

Keeping in view the advantages and disadvantages of Objective Tests, Short Answer Tests and Essay Tests, it will be good if we have their judicious combination to test the pupils' ability in language.

The teacher while testing the achievements of his/her pupils in English must use all these three types of tests. Essay type and Short answer type tests are essential for judging comprehension of subject matter, appreciation, originality, reasoning and written expression. Objective tests are a must for measuring the pupils' achievements in vocabulary, spelling grammar and spoken English. These scores combined judiciously, will give a fair indication of pupils' achievement in English.

Test Items

1. Testing Reading Comprehension

(a) In order to test the reading comprehension of the students, a paragraph is given and related questions are put. For example: We, who live in the present day world are proud to call ourselves civilised. Is it because we live and dress better than our forefathers? Of course, we have the advantages of the inventions of science which our ancestors had never known. But let us search our heart and ask ourselves, "Has science solved our problems?" Frankly speaking the answer is "No". In fact, science has added to our worries. Perhaps now we can kill more easily and swiftly than ever before. And we have not given up the old habit of fighting. That is why we have wars after a decade or two. If we wish to be really civilised let us learn to live in peace, let us achieve brotherhood of man.

Questions

1. Why do we call ourselves civilised?
2. Has science solved all our problems?
3. How can we become truly civilised?
4. Give other words for ancestors; decade.
5. What is meant by 'brotherhood of man'?

(b) Although religion does not inhibit the acquisition of wealth; although it does not hold up large fortunes as evil, the tenor of its teaching, by and large, is to induce an attitude of indifference to worldly things, things which gratify one's lower self and keep one engrossed in money-making. The student should be made to realise that the real goods of life are spiritual, love of things of the spirit and service of one's fellowness, joy of an ordered disciplined life. These are blessings money cannot buy. What is wealth before such things of the spirit? Of all religious teachers Jesus Christ has dealt more comprehensively than any other with the problem of wealth in all its aspects. He may be called the greatest exponent of the science of the wealth with only four words "Blessed are ye poor!" he changed altogether the values which man attached to human existence and human happiness and acquisition and acquisition of wealth.

Questions

1. What according to the author is the meaning of "indifference"? Is it applicable to all religions?
2. Which are some of the real goods of spiritual living? Is it easy to make the student realise this?
3. In what sense can it be said that Jesus Christ has dealt more comprehensively with the problem of wealth?
4. Give a suitable title to the passage.

2. Testing Items for Judging the Listening Ability

(i) To test the listening ability, first of all the teacher reads out a topic in the class then he revises it at least 2 times. Later he asks a few questions and asks to write.

(ii) Outline of the story is given. Teacher reads it, and students fill the blanks.

(iii) The teacher expresses some commands and students follow them, e.g., the teacher speaks, get up, go there, switch off the fan, open the door. The students perform the activities as per commands.

(iv) The teacher speaks a few sentences and shows pictures to the students. The students point to the right picture according to the statement.

3. Test Items for Judging the Speaking Ability

(i) Students are asked to produce different sounds. The teacher writes pairs of words related in sounds, such as, steal-steel, fair-fare, wine-vine, etc.

(ii) Students are shown the pictures and then they describe the pictures.

(iii) The teacher performs a few physical actions and the students are asked to describe them.

(iv) The teacher and the pupil have a conversation on some subject, object, animal or general topic.

4. Test Items for Judging the Reading Ability

Reading can be done in two ways—loudly and silently. In loud reading the students are asked to read a given passage loudly, while the teacher examine their reading skill regarding stress, pause and tone. Whereas in silent reading the students read whatever the teacher shows them. In doing so, they neither move their lips nor put fingers under the line. Then the teacher asks few questions to test.

5. Test Items for Writing Ability

To test the writing skill of the students, the teacher can use various methods at different levels. For example:

Recognition of letters and words, at primary stage, can be introduced. At higher stage writing ability of the students can be judged in following ways:

(a) *Punctuate the following sentences*:

(i) If you go to Delhi please see Mohan.

(ii) Take this letter and post it before three o'clock in the noon.

(iii) I said to him where are you going now.

(b) *Testing Vocabulary:*

(i) Meaning of words and phrases:

➢ Put in pairs, words of the same class, from the given list: drink, chair, pen, brother, sister.

➢ Put in pairs, words and phrase having the opposite

meaning from the given list: beautiful, forget, near, day, night, big, etc.

- Put in pairs, words and phrases of similar meaning from the given list: to oppose, to let in, to admit, to go against, to remember, to forget, etc.

(ii) Use of words and phrases

- Put 'a few' or 'a little' whichever is correct before 'men', 'furniture', 'sugar', 'people'.
- Use the appropriate word or group of words. He is the most handsome boy (of all the boys, than other boys).

(iii) Word building

- Make at least two new words (not verbs) from each of the following: angry, workable, improve.
- Make adjectives from blood, fear.
- Make verbs from: dark, fall, long.

(c) *Testing the Structures:*

I. Complete the following sentences:

(i) He is my ....
(ii) Mother is cooking .....
(iii) When she went ......
(iv) He rebuked .....

II. Change the following sentences into negative:

(i) She is singing.
(ii) He helps the poor.
(iii) She is washing the clothes.
(iv) He is writing neatly.

III. Convert the following sentences into interrogative:

(i) She is writing a letter.
(ii) I am reading a book.
(iii) They play cricket in the morning.

IV. Rearrange the following sentences in meaningful sentences:

(i) Boys going to school are.
(ii) Girls talking to are boys.
(iii) The opens school nine o'clock at.

(d) *Testing Composition*

(i) The teacher may narrate some incident and give key words to the students and then they are asked the report by using given words.
(ii) The teacher first shows a picture to the students. He may himself draw it on the blackboard or use a chart or a picture, later he asks the students to write at least 10 lines on that picture.
(iii) The teacher may narrate half of a story and rest of the story is left for the students for self-composition.
(iv) The students may be asked to develop a story on the given outline of the story.

(v) A substitution table can be used for testing students' writing ability.

It can be said that, if these tests are prepared and conducted properly, standard of teaching and learning will improve.

☛Points to Remember

1. It is essential to test what has been achieved by the students.
2. A good test must possess certain attributes like: reliability, validity, usability, objectivity and comprehensiveness.
3. While designing the question paper due place should be given to essay type short answer type and objective type questions.

24

Remedial and Enrichment Control of Aural, Oral, Reading and Writing Skills

"The language must be presented to the child, not as a subject of study, but as an accomplishment as necessary to the man who is going to live a full life as the ability to read, to write, to perform on musical instruments." —*Jesperson*

Remedial Teaching: Meaning

Remedial teaching is of great importance for the learners who are not native speakers of the language. As you are aware that individual differences exist. So students learn at their own pace. A teacher has to bring variation in teaching methodology. Sometimes wrong patterns are fixed. To correct them remedial teaching is essential.

Remedial teaching is educational activity aimed at removing deficiencies in knowledge or skills.

Objectives of Remedial Work

(a) To identify cases who are, in general backward in studies and fail in one subject.
(b) To identify 15 to 20 units in the subject area. To prepare new skeleton plan on each such unit containing all the rudiments involved in teaching one unit. From the first step to the final one the procedure along with the material should be clearly written down.
(c) To prepare suitable assignments including easy to difficult tasks.
(d) To prepare items to test the learning that should take place.
(e) Remedial classes should be handled by the capable energetic and imaginative teacher. A lot of patience is required to work with the students with such specific backwardness.

Who and How Much?

Certain forces create difficulties in learning a language. It is just natural that a pupil while learning a new language perceives some difficulties. Sooner the difficulties are detected and remedied, better it is for both the teacher and the taught with more advanced classes the defects grow to enormity.

The question arises when a teacher notices that in earlier years the mistakes and error has been transferred what s/he should do? Should s/he go on presenting the new structures and vocabulary items contained in the syllabus, should s/he handle earlier problems? The school administration forces him/her to complete the syllabus on time. Whereas one step forward for the teacher becomes impossible because the uncorrected bad learning in the learners steadily grow till the bad language habits is formed, threatened with a permanent damage. To save the learners from a colossal disaster, timing the remedial programme ought to be considered. The teacher cannot make reasonable amends if the urge to conduct remedial teaching is felt nearing the end of the session or when the children are to appear in an examination. Number of students timing, duration and place should be taken for teaching.

To diagnose what remedial teaching is itself requires a very clear understanding, a sort of unreputing zeal and a thinking, planning mind. Lastly, the procedure that need be followed in a remedial class may be varied as to defeat any previous foresight.

Errors in Reading

Some reading errors are following:

Miscues or Decoding Error

Through one to one oral reading (or individual oral reading), a teacher can identify and interpret a child's miscues, or decoding errors. Miscue analysis, or the analysis of a reader's error patterns, provides valuable clues to a reader's interaction with a text. If you study the error patterns systematically, you will realise that all errors are not equally significant. For example, the reading of the sentence: 'She sat on the chair after lunch'. A child who reads it as 'she sat on the table after lunch, has used context clues to decode chair incorrectly. However s/he has not distorted the meaning of the sentence in any serious way. In contrast, the child who reads the same sentence as, 'she sat on the tea after lunch has used knowledge of the beginning consonant sounds to come up with another word that distorts meaning significantly. So following questions are noteworthy in analysing a reader's miscues:

(a) How well does the child use phonic information during reading?
(b) How well does the child use syntactic information during reading?
(c) How well does the child use semantic information during reading?

So, analysis of a child's miscues provides the teacher with information on what to emphasise with that child: phoneme-grapheme relationships, use of context clues, or use of prediction based on what one knows about language. In this respect, miscue analysis is a valuable diagnostic tool.

Vision Loss

Sometimes, vision problem also influence the reading ability. Often it is the elementary school teacher who first recognises a possible vision problem. For instance bending the head too much while readings, holding the book near the eyes. Teacher should advise such children to visit eye surgeon.

Neurological Problems

Some children have learning problems arising from neurological dysfunctioning rather than from low IQ or poor motivation. The term Alexia is used to refer to a reading disability that may be related to the impairment of the central nervous system, such as a lesson in a particular region of the brain. In some cases a child with alexia cannot grasp a whole word and puts even the simplest words together or he can recognise the meaning of words but has problem in reading aloud. Students commit reading error due to Alexia.

Faulty Reading Habits

Some reading errors transfer from L_1 to L_2. Many of these early reading habits, when continue into later stages of reading, slows down the reading process. These are:

(a) Sub-vocationalisation

Sub-vocationalisation refers to forming the sounds of the words you are reading and even murmuring them aloud with beginning readers, this offers the support of the spoken language when they try to interpret the written form. beginners in L_1, reading (and in L_2 as well) are often encouraged to make use of it. But reading aloud or sub-vocationalisation is much slower than silent reading. Our eyes move faster than our tongue, so efficient readers do not sub-vocalise. If you sub-vocalise, you will tend to read word by word instead of a sense groups, which slows you down.

(b) Finger Pointing

Another faulty habit that slows down the reading process is finger pointing which children use to fix their concentration on the word they are deciphering. Finger pointing is particularly common when the writing system in the second or foreign language is not the same as the one use L_1. One way to help such children to get rid of this habit is to choose texts with type, if possible.

(c) Regressions

Another reading error is regressive eye movements i.e. the eyes move backwards to check previous words instead of moving steadily forward. Sometimes even a skilled reader may have to return to earlier parts of a text and reinterpret them in the light of what has followed. You can remove this error among your students by frequent practice.

Errors of Language Learning

The language teachers have always been interested in finding out why second language (L_2) learners make mistakes. They wish to correct such mistakes in order to make sure that the learners do not repeat their mistakes. However, it is a well-known fact that error correction would be meaningful if the teacher knows the cause or the reason for the error. *Contrastive analysis* and *error analysis* are the useful tools to understand the mistakes made by the students.

Contrastive Analysis and Error Analysis

When a learner starts learning the second language, has to develop a fresh set of habits, His/Her already learned set of habits relating to first language (L_1) interfere in the process. This phenomenon often referred to as 'interference' or 'transfer' which simply stated, means that second language learners tend to carry over certain features of their L_1 into the second language they are engaged in learning. When there is similarity between the features of the two languages, there is no learning problem, but when there is a dissimilarity, error arises. This analysis of the two languages is known as Contrastive Analysis. This view maintains that:

(a) Error represents a failure to learn a new set of habits;
(b) Error, if allowed to continue, will become set habits since language learning is habit formation; and
(c) Errors are caused by interference whereby features of L_1 are carried over or transferred into the L_2 by the learner.

Types of Faults

All learning involves making mistakes, and so does the second language learner. But these mistakes are not of the same type. There are, in fact, different types of faults according to *Pit Corder* (1971).

(i) *Errors*: Error is a grammatically incorrect form that indicates that the learner has not mastered the code of the second language. If the learner says, "He sleep" instead of "He sleeps". "My brother is going to her school" instead of "his school", it means the learner has not mastered or learnt the correct grammatical forms and the rules that govern the language. Such grammatical faults are called errors:
(ii) *Mistakes*: These are faults due to socially inappropriate forms. These are the forms that are grammatically correct but socially inappropriate. Such faults are called mistakes.
(iii) *Lapses*: These are faults that can be best described as slips of the tongue or pen. They are not a matter of great concern as all of us, at one time or the other, make silly slips due to carelessness, sloppiness or just inadvertently. However, one has to be on one's guard, especially if one is a teacher, in deciding when a lapse is not lapse at all, but an error. If a learner while writing a composition, spells the word 'deceive' as 'decieve' or the word 'husband' as 'husbend', the first such occurrence will have to be treated as a lapse, i.e., a slip of the pen perhaps. But if the same thing is repeated in the same or subsequent compositions by the

same learner, it would have to be treated as an error representing an incorrect or faulty learning of the spelling system of English.

Besides committing mistakes in their writing, the students cannot speak fluently and correctly in English. Their reading comprehension is poor and they cannot read with speed. They have poor listening comprehension as their vocabulary is inadequate. All these facts necessitate remedial work in English.

The fundamental principle of remedial work is that it should be based on an analysis of errors made by the students.

Some Major Sources of Errors

(a) L_1 Pattern used in L_2

The system that had been learnt in L_1 interfere in learning second language (L_2). It is known as mother tongue interference. This phenomenon simply means that L_2 learners tend to carry over certain features of their L_1 into the second language.

(b) Overgeneralisation

Those who believe that language learning is a thinking process rather than a set of habits believe, that the learner forms hypotheses about the language system that she/he is learning, and generalises them to form rules of the second language. Now errors occur when this learner ends up making wrong generalisations about the input in his/her environment. In this type of error the learner often rightly captures the 'larger' generalisation but does not take into account restrictions to the rule. For example: At the elementary level, both English children learning their mother tongue and L_2 learners of English produce forms, such as, goed, sitted, cutted, mouses, etc.

(c) Reduced System

Both overgeneralisation and the use of a reduced system seems to be attempts to simplify the target language system. The reducing of the system may be of two kinds:

- The more radical reduction is when some part of the target language system such as the tense system, the articles, the plural terms—is dispensed with, resulting in the loss of some meaningful contexts. This gives us such sentences as:

  I go to market and buy apple
  She sit there; he go.

  This sort of reduction is perhaps the result of a communication strategy on the part of L_2 learners. If she/he stops to think of rules, she/he loses fluency, and his/her listeners become impatient, so she/he opts for communication by means of content words.
- A less 'radical' type of reduction is when some rule is absent in the learner's system; this may not involve the loss of any

meaning contrasts. For example, the subject auxiliary inversion rule is absent in the interrogative system illustrated by—

Where you have left your books?
Why you are going to college today?

Here again, the reduction is the result of a communication strategy.

(d) False Hypothesis

Sometimes due to false clues, the learner arrives at a completely false hypothesis, e.g., too and very are used synonymously.

The weather is too fine today.
He wanted to marry her because she was too beautiful.

(e) Confusion of Structure

Many pattern drill interfere in conversion.

Teacher: He walks slowly.
Instruction: Change to continuous form.
Student: He is walks quickly.

(f) Inconsistent Errors

Children produce inconsistent errors at the time when they are trying to incorporate a new rule into their system.

Causes and Types of Error

Certain deficiencies in learning English may be due to:

- inadequacy in learnings
- interference interlingual (effect of bilingualism)
- interlingual and developmental (typical of systematic errors in English language)
- circumstantial factors, such as, breakdown of work, wrong work habits, lack of incentive, faulty method of teaching and unsuitable textbooks, sensory defects of vision and hearing and inadequate parental assistance.

Speech Errors

Errors under this category may arise out of:

- Mispronunciation due to predominance of dialectal influence.
- Stress on wrong alphabet.
- English speech rhythm violated by Indian syllable—timed beats.
- Faulty intonation pattern.
- Incorrect production of sounds — vowels, consonants and diphthongs.
- Difficulty in pronouncing certain words.
- Difficulty in pronouncing certain cluster of sounds.

Others

- Normal fluency getting affected.
- L_1 interference in speech.

- Structural errors in sentence patterns, in phrase and idioms and in cultural utterances.
- Habit of repeating words and phrases while speaking.
- Incomplete answers.
- Wrong answers.

Errors in Writing

Errors in writing can be detected in two sections:

(a) in form of writing.
(b) in content.

Let us make a note of the following aspects:

- Wrong letter formation.
- Structural errors, interlingual.
- Incomplete answer.
- Wrong answer.
- Punctuation error.
- Errors in spelling.
- Weak paragraphing.
- Reinforced structure omitted when it could be used.
- Variety lacking in sentence patterns.
- Variety missing in composition pattern, in writing letters, stories, dialogue, report, essay and so on.
- Weak and defective essays.

Such classification of errors can go on endlessly.

Common Mistakes

1. The majority of mistakes are due to an inability to translate direct into indirect speech correctly with the resultant mixing up of tenses, e.g.,
   (a) He is very lonely and requests the spirit of Delight to come to him. He says that no one will come to me because I am unhappy so please come to me.
   (b) He said that we will go.
2. Another mistake also noticeable in the first example is the use of the first person instead of third, in indirect speech.
   Example:
   (a) The poet said that he loves and wants what he sees but he cannot get it. He says that the spirit of Delight you come to me why have you left me.
   (b) He says that I will not go to school today.
3. Yet another mistake connected with the indirect speech is the use of question marks and examinations.
   (a) Rita rose excitedly from her bed. She rushed to the window and shouted that Oh! It is raining.
   (b) He asked God why should I suffer thus?
4. They tend to use adjectives for Nouns and vice-versa.

(a) There was much noisy in the class until the teacher came.
(b) To be silence is golden.

5. A few mistakes were the result of changing a word from present to past tense.
   (a) He broked the vase.
   (b) I have awoked the cook.
6. A more common mistake is forgetting to use the article before common nouns and occasionally placing them before proper nouns.
   (a) Street where I live is famous for attractive gardens.
   (b) We are going to visit the Bombay in these holidays.
   (c) He said that girl was his sister.
7. Misuse of prepositions also causes many incorrect sentences.
   (a) They laugh on me because I am fat and still enjoy eating.
   (b) Put it at the table where the dog may not get at it.
8. Misuse of 'their' and 'there' is probably due to more thoughtlessness, as is also 'are' instead of 'our' and vice versa.
   (a) There is our train.
   (b) Why don't they keep there dog tied up?
   (c) Our we having a holiday tomorrow.
   (d) We our are own masters till tomorrow.
9. Some words which particular girls get wrong are 'describes about' instead of 'describes' 'where else' instead of 'whereas' and wild guesses as to whether 'poem' or 'poetry' should be used.
   (a) He liked apples where else she wanted oranges.
   (b) The poet describes about the beauty of the forest.
   (c) The poetry we will do today is called 'Tewkebury Road'.
   (d) Poem sharpens our senses.
10. Some girls get mixed up about when to use the singular form and when the plural.
    (a) They shows a film daily.
    (b) She show off her dress.
    (c) We goes away to Kashmir in our summer vacation.

Let me tell you that the mistakes, especially with regard to 1, 2, 3, 6, 8 and 10 could be easily avoided if the rules were explained. In case of 4, 5, 7, 9, 10 correct form can be followed with practice of speech.

Remedial English

However, meticulously the second language teaching is planned and however carefully it is learnt, there remain some gaps which drive the learners of the second language to fall into errors. Under best of teachers, mishearing and misunderstanding do occur. The individual pupil is baffled as not to know how certain distortions have crept in his language learning.

Remedy presupposes occurrence that are deviations from the expected norm. Applied in the field of language, remedial programme may begin by:

- teaching afresh what has been taught earlier.
- suspending the part of learning the new items in preference to reinforced practice of forgotten parts introduced earlier.
- intensive drill or meaningful practice of the linguistic elements.
- application in new situations of the pasts learnt, that is, constant vigilance so as to prevent the recurrence of the earlier flaws.
- planning a fresh strategy to re-do the bits around which some doubts still persist.

Remedial Teaching Strategies

a) Individualized Teaching strategies.
b) Peer support programme.
c) Reward scheme
d) Handling Pupils' language Acquisition Problems.
e) Development of Generic skills.
f) Feedback to students, parents and teachers

a) *Individualized Educational Strategies:* it becomes essential to take care of learning needs of individual pupils. It has been established that the foundation of learning should be strong among all children. If we make individualized programme/strategy, it can be helpful in knowing and overcoming the learning difficulties of students and develop their potentials.

Individualized educational programme should include short term and long term teaching objectives, learning steps, activities and reviews to ensure that the programme is implemented effectively. Teaching can be done in small groups or individually, it all depends on its purpose and target group. Teaching can be done in small groups or for individual. Parents and pupils can all participate in ensuring of programme. Remedial teachers hold meetings regularly to evaluate the effectiveness of work and gather opinión for improvement.

b) *Peer Support Programme:* to enhance any educational programme, it is essential that the skill of cooperation and good interpersonal relations among pupils should be developed.

Remedial teachers may train up pupils who perform better in a certain subject to become 'little teachers' and make them responsible for helping school-mates with learning difficulties in group teaching and self-study sessions as well as outside the class.

It depends on the teacher's efficiency how she/he can develop the efficiency of the student and to make training programme more effective. Such a programme is more suitable for pupils of higher grade.

c) *Reward Scheme:* For the purpose of motivating the students, reward scheme can be very useful. It helps the students in framing objectives and plans and reinforcing their good performance. It does not matter, what reward you give, the important feature is to cultivate students' interest in learning, which can be created by a reward scheme, which further helps in getting satisfaction and brings achievement. Some of the facts are to be kept In mind by the teachers while selecting the reward.

When designing the rewards offered, remedial teachers should take note of the following:

- Set clear and specific targets (for example: requirement on the score of dictation and number of assignments submitted);
- Only those objectives are selected which are achievable.
- Rewards can be verbal or material.
- There should be variety in reward scheme as per pupils' interest.
- There should not be much delay in giving reward. They should be given instantly.
- A reward scheme should be reviewed and revised regularly.
- Inviting parents can be fruitful as it can improve the work of their children.

d) *Handling Pupils' Language Acquisition Problems:* Remedial teachers should observe the following when dealing with the language acquisition problems of pupils:

- Always observe the performance of pupils in the class and their behaviour in groups.
- Establish close relationship with pupils, develop mutual trust and listen carefully to what they say.
- Help pupils understand the effect of their behaviour on others as well as on themselves.
- Parents meetings are useful in order to know the pupils' environment and advise parents to create congenial environment for language learning.
- Teacher can help children to form good study habits. Help children to build self-confidence.
- Let children know their weak areas and learning difficulties.
- Teacher must guide learners to make a list of errors, and try to remove them one by one. All the errors can not be removed at one time.

e) Development of Generic Skills

- Teacher in a remedial class must help students to develop good learning habits and attitudes. Students should be helped to remain disciplined and responsible so that they complete the assignments neatly.
- A constructive attitude lays the foundation for life long self learning and it enhances effectiveness of pupils' learning.
- It is essential for pupils to master basic self-learning skills and abilities. Teacher must help them in setting realistic goals, learning objectives, study habits, time management skills, note taking and note making, reading skills and examination taking skills.

- As we live in the digital age, teachers must help and motivate students to make use of information technology. Students must know the importance of self learning habits as it can pay them in their future life.
- Students must be helped to draw the benefit from past experiences and make use of different methods and tools of learning. Teachers must inculcate in them the habits of going to the library and consulting dictionaries and thesauruses. They must be in the habit of thinking analytically and critically. This will enhance the ability of flexibility, creativity and originality.

f) Feedback to Students, Parents and Teachers

Teachers: In order to know the learning progress as well as strengths and weaknesses of pupils, teachers may design different teaching activities which will help pupils learn in an effective manner. Besides, it is also a means to measure the discrepancy between IRTP, pupils and ordinary pupils so that teachers may decide whether it is desirable for the pupils concerned to withdraw from IRTP.

The two most common assessment methods are listed as follows for teachers' reference.

(i) Formative Assessment: Teachers can understand and assess the learning abilities of pupils from their daily class work and homework as well as individual or group projects, such as model making drawing, information collection, measuring activities and the way they relate daily events to the topics they learnt in the class, so that they can revise the teaching content accordingly.

(ii) Summative Assessment: With reference to the progress of teaching, teachers may assess the performance of students by means of examination/tests about the main points in teaching where the levels of difficulty meet pupils' abilities. The weightage and marks on questions should be balanced. Different types of questions should be included. School may have different form and weightage of assessment.

Remedial teachers should keep a detailed personal record for each pupil under IRTP. They should assess the progress of pupils regularly and systematically. A comprehensive record provides information and serve as a reference.

The response of pupils in their classroom is important and should be included in the evaluation column and then follow up action or changes in the teaching strategies should be taken care of accordingly.

Liaison with Parents

To know the cause of the problem of children, a liaison between parents and teachers is very helpful. Parents can guide their children in completing their home work. Apart from homework, parents can help them in solving other problems.

Sometimes parents give undue stress to their children by having unrealistic expectations from them. In such cases teachers can help parents getting out of problems which are not genuine. Children have their own aims and abilities. Let them grow according to them.

In order to help pupils with learning difficulties, schools must have close liaison with parents. Apart from providing guidance to their children in their homework. Parents can handle pupils' problems either in the same way or in similar ways according to the requirement of the school and their home assignments.

On the contrary some parents may have too low expectations. Teachers must then keep in contact with parents to help them understand their children and to provide appropriate guidance to develop potentials of the pupils.

☞ Point to Remember

1. Individualized Educational programme are geared to the learning needs of individual pupils.
2. Peer support programme help pupils reinforce their knowledge and develop their communication and co-operation skills as well as good interpersonal relationship.
3. Reward schemes reinforce pupils for good performance.
4. The teacher must help the students to know the specific area of their learning difficulties.
5. Pupils should be helped to master basic self-learning skills and abilities.
6. In order to help pupils with learning difficulties, schools must have close liaison with parents.

25

Preparation of an Achievement Test

"Achievement test is one designed to measure knowledge, understanding or skills in a specified subject or a group of students." —*Freeman*

Meaning of Achievement Test

Teachers, parents and learners all want to know the end products of education. It is measured by a tool or device known as Achievement Test. Thus 'achievement test' is a test of learning ability or measures what a child has learnt in different subjects on the basis of intelligence and other qualities.

An 'achievement test' is meant for testing the achievement of a student in one area or the other. Without teaching something, we cannot test the achievement of the learner. The achievement test brings into light the following aspects:

(1) Efficiency of the student;
(2) Efficiency of the teacher;
(3) Speed of learning by the students;
(4) Capacity of learning by an individual student;
(5) Grasping ability of the student;
(6) Giving feedback to the teacher about method used;
(7) Teacher comes to know about learning gaps.

Types of Achievement Test

They are mainly of two types:

(a) Standardised Tests
(b) Teacher Made Tests

(a) *Standardised Tests*: The word 'standardisation' distinguishes the basic difference between standardised and informal objective tests.

Standardisation means the process of finding comparative norms when we standardise a test. Curriculum is analysed very carefully and items are selected.

Lee J. Cronback says, "A standardised test is one in which the procedure, apparatus and scoring are fixed so that precisely the same test can be given at different times and places.

(b) *Teacher Made Tests*: Sometimes, new type tests are prepared by teachers themselves. These tests are objective in nature.

Procedure of these tests is similar to standrized test to a great extent.

Achievement tests measure generally the learning outcomes or educational outcomes. They may be classified in two forms:

(1) The cognitive outcomes of education
(2) The non-cognitive outcomes of education
(1) The cognitive outcomes of education are further divided into six major categories:
- Knowledge
- Comprehension
- Application
- Analysis
- Synthesis
- Evaluation — *B.S. Bloom*

(2) Non-cognitive outcomes of education
- Flexibility in thinking
- Balance judgment
- Critical perception
- Educability
- Selectivity, synthesising ability
- Cultural awareness

Motivation, persistence, creativity etc. are also included

Use of Achievement Test

1. *Assignments of Grades*: Standardised achievement tests are more often used to assign course grades in special programmes in government, industry and course diversification.
2. *Promotion to Next Class*: They are helpful in promoting the students to next class.
3. *Classification of Individuals*: On the basis of test students can be classified into various special courses.
4. *Counselling and Remedial Teaching*: Psychologists take help of these tests in knowing the difficulties of the students.
   On the basis of achievement test scores remedial teaching programmes can be organised.
5. *Vocational Guidance*: On the basis of achievement test scores students can choose the future vocational course.
6. *Measuring the effectiveness of learning situations*: Poor performance score of the students can be an indicator of poor teaching.

Limitations of Achievement Tests

1. Excessive standardisation ignores the individual differences.
2. It is difficult to construct an achievement test which measures all the factors.
3. Critical thinking is also ignored.
4. Guess work is encouraged.

5. Personal factors are likely to affect the reliability of the tests.
6. Deciding the validity of the tests is also difficult.

Preparation of Test

(Has been discussed in the earlier chapter, viz., Evaluation)

Characteristics of a Good Test in English

(i) It conforms very closely to the declared objectives of the course.
(ii) It does justice to the candidates.
(iii) A good test lists only what has been taught.
(iv) The tests and examinations should be carefully designed and the examiner should be clear in mind what skill or particular item in question aims at testing one item should test only one skill.
(v) The question paper should not be very lengthy and neither too difficult nor too easy.
(vi) Language should be definite.
(vii) Answer should be fairly and easily scorable.
  - It should be a judicious combination of
  - Objective Type Questions
  - Short Answer Questions
  - Essay Type Questions

Steps in Test Conducting

1. Prepare a Design

The first step in preparing a test is to construct a design. A test is not merely a collection of assorted questions. For this, objectives has to be kept in view. Weightage to different objectives, different areas of content and different forms of questions are to be decided, alongwith the scheme of options and sections and these are the dimensions which are known as a design of a test.

(a) *Weightage to objectives*: To make a test valid it is necessary to analyse the objectives of the course and decide which objectives are to be tested and in what properties. For this marks are allotted to each objective to be tested according to its importance. In English language testing the three major objectives are knowledge of the elements of language, comprehension and expression. For example, for a test of 50 marks the following weightage may be decided.

Objective	*Percentage of Marks*	*Marks Allotted*
Knowledge	10%	5
Comprehension	40%	20
Expression	50%	25
Total	100%	50

(b) *Weightage to different areas of content*: It is necessary to analyse the syllabus and allot weightage to different areas of content. This is again done to ensure the validity of the test. A hypothetical example is given below for an English language test showing weightage to content units for a Class XI test.

Content Areas	*Percentage of Marks*	*Marks Allotted*
Reading skills	30%	15
Writing skills	30%	15
Textual content	40%	20
Total	100%	50

(c) *Weightage to different forms of questions*: After analysing the objectives and the content, it is to be seen how they are to be tested. A particular objective and content can be tested more appropriately by a particular form of questions. So, different forms of questions are to be included in the test for testing different objectives and content and the marks carried by each of them are decided. In this way reliability of the test will also remain.

Forms of Question	*No. of Questions*	*Marks Allotted*	*% of Marks*
Essay type	3	19	38%
Short answer type	9	23	46%
Objective type	8	8	16%
Total	20	50	100%

(d) *Scheme of sections*: The design of a question paper may also indicate the scheme of sections for the paper. The question paper can also be divided into sections areawise like one section for reading comprehension, another for writing tasks, third for grammar, and so on.

The design may indicate the pattern of options, i.e., the complete elimination of overall options or retention of internal options within limits. While providing options, it may be kept in view that options are comparable in terms of objectives to be tested, the form of questions and the difficulty level of the questions.

While planning the paper, difficulty level of the questions should vary so as to take care of all the students to discriminate between high achievers and low achievers. The suggested percentage for easy and difficult questions is 20 per cent whereas average questions can be 60 per cent. The difficulty level of test paper can be varied according to the level of the students. If the class has a large number of good students, then 25 to 30 per cent difficult questions can be given.

2. *Preparing a Blue Print*

After deciding on the design of the test, the blue print is prepared. The blue print is a three-dimensional chart which shows the placement of each question in respect of the objective and the content that it tests. It also indicates the marks carried by each question. It is useful to prepare a blue print so that the test maker knows which question will test which objective and which content unit and how many marks it would carry. Without a blue print only the weightage is decided for objectives, content areas and types of questions.

The blue print concretises the design in operational terms and all the dimensions of a question (*i.e.* its objectives, its form, the content area it would cover and the marks allotted to it) become clear to the test maker.

Suggested Steps for Preparing a Blue Print

1. Transfer the decisions regarding weightage to objectives—knowledge, comprehension and expression on the given proforma.
2. Transfer the weightage already decided for different content units. For this, list the content units under the content areas in the column given at the left hand and the marks under the column of total given at the right hand side.
3. Place the essay type questions first in the blue print. Place them under the objectives which you want to test through these questions. The marks of the questions may be shown in the column under the objectives and the number of questions may be given in the brackets.
4. If in a question, marks are to be split between two objectives indicate it with asterisks and a dotted outline as shown in the example.
5. After placing the essay type questions, place the short answer type questions under the objectives and beside the content unit that you want to test through them.
6. Place the very short answer type questions in a similar way.
7. Place the multiple-choice questions in the same way—marks outside the bracket, number of questions, inside the bracket.
8. Calculate the sub-totals of all the questions under all the objectives.
9. Calculate the totals. Your total should tally with the weightage of objectives and content units that you had already marked on the blue print.
10. Fill in the summary of types of questions, scheme of sections and scheme of options.

Sample Blue Print

Subject: English — M.M.: 50
Class: XI — Time: 2 hours

Objectives/ Content Area	*Knowledge*				*Comprehension*				*Expression*			*Total*
	E	*SA*	*VSA*	*O*	*E*	*SA*	*VSA*	*O*	*E*	*SA*	*VSA*	
Reading Skills							4(4)					
Passage I						2(2)*				2(-)*		
Passage II						2(1)* 1(1)*				2(-)* 2(-)*		15(8)
Writing Skills												
Letter writing	2(1)*								3(-)*			
Notice writing		1(1)*								3(-)*		
Report writing	1(1)*								5(-)*			15
Textual Content												
Long Answer Questions					4(1)*					4(-)*		
Short Answer Questions		1(1)*			2(2)*						2(-)* 1(-)*	20
Extract						1(1)*	4(4)				1(-)*	
Sub-Total	3(2)	2(2)	—	—	4(1)	8(7)	8(8)		12(-)	13(-)		
Total	5(4)				20(16)				25(-)			50(20)

Note:Figures within brackets indicate the number of questions and figures outside the brackets indicate marks

* Denotes that marks have been combined to form one question.

Summary

Types of Questions	*No. of Questions*	*Marks*
Essay (E)	3	19
Short Answer (SA)	9	23
Very Short Answer (VSA)	8	8
	20	50

Scheme of Sections:	Three Sections
Section A:	Reading Skills
Section B:	Writing Skills
Section C:	Text Books
Scheme of Options:	Options will be given in essay type questions.

3. *Preparing Questions Based on the Blue Print*

After the blue print is ready, questions are to be prepared according to the dimensions defined in the blue print. For example, if there are essay type questions to be prepared to test the writing skills, one letter and one report and also a short answer questions on writing a notice, the test constructor should prepare these three questions along with their options which may be comparable in terms of objectives to be tested, content area, forms of questions and the difficulty level. While preparing questions it must be kept in view that the question—

(a) is based on the specific objective of teaching as indicated in the blue print.
(b) relates to the specific content area as per the blue print.
(c) is written in the form as required by the blue print and satisfies all the rules for framing that form of questions.
(d) is at the desired level of difficulty.
(e) is written in clear, correct and precise language which is well within the comprehension of pupils.
(f) clearly indicates the scope and length of the answer.

4. Assembling the Question Paper

After the questions are prepared they are to be assembled in a question paper form. For this instructions are to be written. General instructions for paper may be given on top whereas instructions for specific questions may be given just before the questions.

The order of questions is also to be decided while assembling the question paper. Sometimes it is according to the forms of questions, i.e., objective type questions may be put first, then very short answer, short answer and essay type questions or it may be according to the content as in the case of a language question paper where we may have structure question first then question of unseen passage and then composition questions.

The assembling and editing of the question paper is important from the point of view of administration. For example, if the question is divided into two sections, one of which is to be collected within a specific time limit, clear instruction to do so should be mentioned and also the arrangement of questions should be such that both the section are easily demarcated.

5. Preparing the Scoring Key and the Marking Scheme

Scoring key is to be prepared for objective type questions and the marking scheme for other questions.

The scoring key gives the alphabet of the correct answer and the marks carried by each questions. The marking scheme gives the expected outline answer and the value points for each aspect of the answer. Detailed instruction for marking are also worked out, e.g., in making compositions etc. it is specified as to how many marks are to be deducted for spelling mistakes or structural mistakes, or if the composition is to be graded how it is to be done and on what basis.

The detailed marking scheme is necessary to ensure consistency and uniformity in scoring by different examiners. In other words it ensures reliability of scoring.

6. Preparing Questionwise Analysis

After the question paper and marking scheme is finished, it is desirable to prepare a questionwise analysis. The analysis helps in tallying the question in the test with the blue print. It also enables us to know the strength and weaknesses of the test better, e.g., through the analysis we can know how many topics have been covered in the syllabus, what is the difficulty level of each question and what specifications are being tested by each question. The analysis is done on following points:

(i) Number of the question
(ii) Objective tested by the question
(iii) Specification on which the question is based
(iv) Topic covered
(v) Form of the question
(vi) Marks allotted
(vii) Approximate time required for answering
(viii) Estimated difficulty level

☞Points to Remember

1. Achievement test measures the learning outcomes or educational out comes.
2. Achievement test have various uses like: promotion to the next class, Assignment of grades, classification of individual and many more.
3. While constructing a test, various characteristics must be considered.
4. How much correct and effective test/question paper you have prepared, shows your teaching efficiency and competency.

26

Lesson Planning

"Careful reflections on past experiences result in teacher growth and more effective planning and teaching." —*Donald Cruickshank*

Planning is undoubtedly an important aspect in all the spheres of life. If we talk about teaching, then all depends on the efficiency and intelligence of the teacher how she/he plans. The teacher should know beforehand what to teach and how to teach. The teacher should have clarity about objectives then the planning will be effective. Thus, lesson planning is a plan of actions which includes the objectives, strategies, material and methods of teaching.

Need of Lesson Planning

(1) It ensures balance in language skills: listening, speaking, reading and writing.
(2) It helps one to be organised and systematic.
(3) It helps in achieving the desired aims and objectives.
(4) It becomes a permanent record.
(5) Continuity can be maintained.
(6) Time of the teacher as well as students is saved.
(7) Teacher can be sure and confident.

Herbertian Steps of Planning

(1) Preparation or introduction
(2) Presentation
(3) Generalisation
(4) Application
(5) Recapitulation

Three Phases of Planning

(1) *Pre-Teaching Planning*: Before coming to the class she/he thinks and plans about what and how aspects like, which method and A.V. aids will be helpful.
(2) *Planning During Teaching*: During teaching in the classroom she/he plans the teaching activities, chalkboard work and using A.V. aids etc.
(3) *Post-Teaching Planning*: After classroom teaching she/he analysis whether the objectives have been achieved.

Characteristics of a Good Lesson Plan

A good lesson plan is the key to success. It has the following characteristics:

(1) It clarifies the general aims and behavioural objectives.
(2) Selection of teaching aids is proper.

(3) It tells about reference books.
(4) It is free from unnecessary repetition.
(5) Students' involvement is always there.

As a teacher you should know that there is no one set lesson format which you can use for all lessons. However, in this chapter we include for you two sets of format for each lesson which you may like to use when you start planning your lessons.

PT's Name	:	**Roll No.**	:
Subject	: English	**Class**	: IX
Topic	: Grammar (Kinds of adjectives)	**Section**	: A
Duration	: 45 Minutes		

General Aims

1. To enable the students to write good English.
2. To enhance students' comprehension of English grammar.
3. To create students' interest in English.
4. To improve their vocabulary.

Behavioural Objectives

1. Students will come to know about the seven kinds of adjectives.
2. Students will be able to identify the kind of adjective and its usage in their daily life.

General Teaching Aids

A well-equipped classroom, pieces of chalk, duster, chalkboard, pointer, etc.

Instructional Teaching Aids

A chart showing the different kinds of adjectives.

Previous Knowledge Assumed

Students are well aware of simple vocabulary and adjectives.

Introduction

In order to introduce the topic pupil-teacher will ask the following questions:

Q. Identify the adjectives in the following sentences:

(i) The rose is red in colour.(ii) Seema is a sweet girl.
(iii) I have five pencils. (iv) Give me a small piece of paper.

Pupil-teacher will now ask the students to tell the kinds of the adjectives identified.

Announcement of the Topic

Finding the students unable to answer pupil teacher will announce we shall study about the different kinds of adjectives.

Presentation

Pupil-teacher will develop the lesson with the active involvement of students.

	Teaching Points	*Pupil-Teacher's Activities*	*Pupils' Activities*	*Chalkboard Work*
	Adjectives	1. She has three bags. 2. Sita is an intelligent girl *Identify the adjectives*. Give another example of adjectives:	Three Intelligent The rose is red	She has *three* bags. She is an *intelligent* girl. The rose is *red*
1.	Adjectives of Quality	Pupil-teacher writes on the chalkboard: Delhi is a big city. Which kind of adjective is denoted in this sentence? "Adjective of quality show the kind of a quality of a person or thing". Give another example.	 Adjective of Quality Yamuna is a sacred river.	 Delhi is a *big* city Quality Yamuna is a *sacred* river.
2.	Adjective of Number	Pupil-teacher writes on the chalkboard: The hand has five fingers. What is five denoting? Which kind of adjective is denoted in this sentence? Adjective of number show how many person or things are meant or in what order a person or thing stands. Give another example.	 Number Adjective of Number Give me seven mangoes.	 The hand has *five* fingers. Give me *seven* mangoes.
3.	Demonstrative Adjectives	Pupil-teacher writes on the chalkboard: This boy is stronger. What is the word 'this' denoting? Which kind of adjective is denoted in this sentence? Demonstrative adjectives point out which person or thing is meant. Give another example.	 This is pointing which boy. No response I hate such things.	 This boy is stronger. Demonstrative adjectives. I hate *such* things.
4.	Adjectives of Quantity	Pupil-teacher writes on the chalkboard: I ate some rice. What is the word 'some' denoting? Which kind of adjective is denoted in this sentence? Adjectives of quantity show how much of a thing is meant. Give another example.	 'Some' is denoting quantity of rice. Adjectives of quantity. You have no sense.	 I ate *some* rice. Adjectives of quantity. You have *no* sense.

(*Contd.*)

	Teaching Points	Pupil-Teacher's Activities	Pupils' Activities	Chalkboard Work
5.	Interrogative Adjectives	Pupil-teacher writes on the chalkboard: Which way shall we go? What is the word 'which' denoting? Which kind of adjective is denoted in this sentence? What, which, whose and when used with nouns to ask questions are called interrogative adjectives. Give another example.	 'Which' is denoting question Interrogative adjectives. Pupils listen attentively. Whose book is this?	 Which way shall we go? Interrogative adjectives. *Whose* book is this?
6.	Emphasising Adjectives	Pupil-teacher writes on the chalkboard Mind your own business. Which kind of adjective is denoted in this sentence? The word 'own' and 'very' are sometimes used as emphasising adjectives when they are used to emphasise something. Give another example.	 No response Pupils listen attentively Man is his own master.	 Mind your *own* business. Man is his *own* master.
7.	Exclamatory Adjectives	Pupil-teacher writes on the chalkboard: What an idea! Which kind of adjective is denoted in this sentence? The word 'what' is sometimes used as an exclamatory adjective. Give another example.	 Exclamatory adjective Pupils listen attentively. What a genius!	 *What* an idea! Exclamatory adjectives *What* a genius!

Recapitulation

In order to recapitulate the lesson taught and also to evaluate knowledge gained by them, pupil teachers will ask the following questions from the students:

1. What are demonstrative adjectives?
2. Give three examples of adjective of number.

Home Work

Write two examples of each type of adjective.

Supervisor's Remarks:

PT's Name : **Roll No.:**

Subject : English **Class** : IX
Topic : Poem "Open thy Eyes and See thy God" **Section** : A
Duration : 45 Minutes **Date** :

General Aims

1. To add new words to vocabulary of students.
2. To increase their understanding of spoken English and expression.
3. To enable them to speak English fluently.

Behavioural Objectives

1. Students will be able to understand the main idea of content and the flow of thoughts.
2. Students will be able to understand the explaining link by corelating the theme with their own life.

General Teaching Aids

A well-equipped classroom, pieces of chalk, duster, chalkboard, pointer, etc.

Instructional Teaching Aids

A chart showing picture of people working along with the poem.

Previous Knowledge Assumed

It is assumed that students know that different men perform different activities to earn their livelihood. Students also have some vocabulary of their own.

Introduction

In order to introduce the lesson pupil-teacher will ask the following questions from the students:

What do we do in temples?
What do tillers and pathmakers do?
How are the lives of pathmaker and priest different?

Announcement of the Topic

Finding the students unable to answer, pupil-teacher will announce, we shall study a poem with a theme 'Work is worship' and the title of the poem is "Open the eyes and see thy God".

Paragraph:

Leave this chanting and singing and telling of beads!

Whom dost thou worship in this lonely dark corner of a temple with doors all shut? Open thine eyes and see thy God is not before thee!

Thought Content

The main idea behind the poem is that we visit places of worship to pray to the God but God is not there, instead he is there where the men are working hard.

Presentation

Poem will be developed with the active participation of the students. Explanation method will be used. Relevant grammar position will be written on Chalkboard.

Teaching Points	*Pupil-Teacher's Activities*	*Pupils' Activities*	*Chalkboard Work*
Step 1 First Model Reading	Leaving this chanting and singing and telling of beads! Whom dost thou worship in this lonely dark corner of a temple with doors all shut? Open thine eyes and see thy God is not before thee! Pupil-teacher will read with proper voice modulation.	Pupils will listen to the pupil-teacher with their books closed.	
Step 2 Second Model Reading	Pupil-teacher will do the second model reading of the poem. This time with the books of the students open	Pupils will listen to the pupil-teacher and look into their textbooks.	
Step 3 Explanation	Chanting of holy words and rolling of beads is of no use. Why are you praying in the lonely and dark corner of the temple whose doors are all shut? Whom are you worshipping? The poet says, "Open your eyes and just see your God is not here".	Pupils will listen attentively and try to understand.	Chanting—singing dost—does thine—your thee—you

(Contd.)

Step 4 Loud Reading	Pupil-teacher asks few students to recite the poem loudly with proper style one by one. Difficult words and their pronunciation will be pointed out and corrected.	Pupils asked will read the poem while rest will listen attentively.

Recapitulation

In order to recapitulate the lesson taught and also to evaluate knowledge gained by them, pupil teacher will ask the following questions from the students:

What does the poet want us to leave and why?
'Thy God is not before thee' where can he be found?
Where are people worshipping?

Homework

What does the poem teach us?

Supervisor's Remarks:

PT's Name : **Roll No. :**
Subject : English **Class** : IX
Topic : Letter (Personal) **Section** : A
Duration : 45 Minutes **Date** :

General Aims

1. To enable the students to write correct English.
2. To enable the students to speak correctly and fluently.
3. To develop listening skills in the students.
4. To develop vocabulary of the students.

Behavioural Objectives

1. The students will be able to understand the format of the letter.
2. They will be able to write letter to their friends or relatives properly.

General Teaching Aids

A well-equipped classroom, pieces of chalk, duster, chalkboard, pointer, etc.

Instructional Teaching Aids

A layout of a letter will be used to show the format of the letter. An OHP sheet will be used to show the different parts of the letter.

Previous Knowledge Assumed

It is assumed that students have some knowledge of communicating in a verbal or written manner.

Introduction

In order to introduce the topic, the pupil-teacher will ask the following questions:

1. In ancient times how did people receive and send their messages?
2. Give the format of a personal letter?

Announcement of the Topic

Finding the pupils unable to answer, pupil-teacher will announce the topic that students, today we will learn about different parts of a letter.

Presentation

The topic will be developed with the active cooperation of the students. The main points will be written on the chalkboard. The pupil-teacher will use aids from time to time and question-answer method will be used to motivate the students and to make the lesson interesting.

Teaching Points	*Pupil-Teacher's Activities*	*Pupils' Activities*	*Chalkboard Work*
Kinds of Letter 3	Pupil-teacher explains that there are generally three kinds of letters: 1. Personal letters or private letters 2. Business letters 3. Official letters	Pupils will listen attentively	3 kinds of letters 1. Personal 2. Business 3. Official
Other types of letters	Now pupil-teacher explains that there are other types of letters like: 1. Thanking and making request 2. Acceptance and rejection of offers	They are following the teacher.	Other types of letters: 1. Thanking & making request 2. Acceptance & rejection of offers
Personal Letter Parts	Pupil-teacher explains that a personal letter consists of six parts: 1. The Heading 2. The Salutation 3. Body of the Letter 4. Subscription 5. Signature 6. Super subscription or outside address	Pupils will listen carefully	Parts of a letter 1. Heading 2. Salutation 3. Body 4. Subscription 5. Signature 6. Super subscrip-tion
1. Heading	Pupil-teacher tells that heading consists of writer's address and date and it is written on the left hand side of the letter	Pupils will follow the teacher and try to grasp the meaning	Heading consists of writer's address & date
	Pupil-teacher explains that personal letters are written to relatives, to friends and to acquaintances.		Personal letters are written to friends, relatives & acquaintances.

(*Contd.*)

Teaching Points	*Pupil-Teacher's Activities*	*Pupils' Activities*	*Chalkboard Work*
2. Salutation	Pupil-teacher tells that salutation is the greeting to the person to whom letter is written as Respected Sir, Dear father, etc.	They will listen and try to understand	Salutation is like: Respected Sir, Dear father
3. Body of the letter has 3 parts	Pupil-teacher explains that body of the letter is main part of the letter consists of	Pupils will listen attentively	Body of the letter has 3 parts
(a) Introduction	(a) Introduction	and answer the question asked	(a) Introduction
(b) Message	(b) Message e.g. I am overjoyed to hear the news of your success in the exam.		(b) Message
(c) Conclusion	(c) Conclusion should be ended politely e.g. with best wishes		(c) Conclusion
	Q. Give another example of conclusion	With kind regards	With kind regards
4. Subscription	Pupil-teacher explains that subscription is written according to the salutation after leaving one space e.g. yours' obediently.		
	Q. How will you write subscription to your friend?	Yours' sincerely	Yours' sincerely
5. Signature	Pupil-teacher tells that signature should be done below the subscription and full name is not mentioned in the signature	They will follow the teacher	
6. Address	Pupil-teacher explains that after leaving some space it is written on left side of the envelope e.g. Dr. Ram Singh, H. No. 10, Lodi Lane, Bangalore-21		Address is written on left side of envelope

Recapitulation

In order to recapitulate the pupil-teacher will ask the following questions from the students:

1. How many types of letters are there?
2. To whom are the personal letters written?
3. What are the various parts of a letter?
4. Give the important components of body of a letter?

Homework

Write a letter to your friend inviting him at your birthday party?

Supervisor's Remarks:

PT's Name	:	**Roll No.**	:
Subject	: English	**Class**	: IX
Topic	: Prose (Good Bricks)	**Section**	: A
Duration	: 45 Minutes	**Date**	:

General Aims

1. To enable the students to write good English.
2. To create students' interest in English.
3. To improve the vocabulary of the students.
4. To develop listening skills in students.

Behavioural Objectives

1. Students will learn the qualities which would make them nation builders.
2. Students will become sincere towards their career and life.
3. Students will develop a healthy attitude towards the feminine sex.

General Teaching Aids

A well-equipped classroom, pieces of chalk, duster, chalkboard, pointer, etc.

Instructional Teaching Aids

Flash cards showing some good qualities expected from students.

Previous Knowledge Assumed

Students are well aware of the qualities which are expected from good students, who are in future going to become nation builders.

Introduction

In order to introduce the lesson, pupil-teacher will ask the following questions from the students:

1. Name some qualities which are expected from the students?
2. Who are known to be the nation builders?
3. How can you become good nation builders?
4. What does C. Rajgopalachari suggest to students?

Announcement of the Topic

Finding the students unable to answer, pupil-teacher will announce, we shall study what C. Rajgopalachari suggests to the students.

Paragraph

I wish I had the eloquence which your Vice-Chancellor commanded. I wish I had the courage which your representative sister commanded. I do not believe that when I was so young as that girl, I could have faced such a vast gathering of exhilarated, potentially mischievous, material as the one ranged before me. I am amazed at the courage of your sister, my dear boys.

Thought Content

In the present paragraph C. Rajgopalachari is appreciating the courage of a female student who spoke in front of a large crowd. In a sense he is trying to emphasise the qualities and goodness which a female can possess.

Presentation

The topic will be developed with the active participation of the students. Explanation and question answer method will be used.

Teaching Points	*Pupil-Teacher's Activities*	*Pupils' Activities*	*Chalkboard Work*
Step 1 Model Reading	Pupil teacher will give a model reading of the text, she will read the text with proper stress and pause	Students will look into their books and read the lesson simultaneously. They will try to grasp the style of reading the text.	
Step 2 Explanation	C. Rajagopalachari is amazed at the skill of speaking of a girl and he wishes that he also had such an ability which the little girl commanded. He says that he did not have such courage when he was young so as to address such a large number of people. He asks from the boys of that class that does any one of them possess so much guts as this little girl, whom she addresses as their sister. Now pupil-teacher will write the meaning of difficult words on the chalk-board and pupil-teacher will ask some questions based on the explanation:	Pupils listen to the teacher attentively and try to understand.	Eloquence—Style of speaking Exhilarated—Cheerful and excited Congregate—Gather together
		Pupils' will answer the questions.	
	1. Who is amazed at the skill of speaking of a girl?	Ans. C. Rajagopalachari is amazed at the skill of speaking of a girl.	C. Rajagopalachari

(*Contd.*)

Teaching Points	*Pupil-Teacher's Activities*	*Pupils' Activities*	*Chalkboard Work*
	2. Who is addressed as their sister?	Ans. The little girl is addressed as their sister.	The little girl.
	3. Why C. Rajagopala-chari was not able to address large number of people when he was young?	Ans. C. Rajagopala-chari was not able to address large number of people when he was young because he did not have such courage.	Because he did not have such courage.
Step 3 Loud Reading	Pupil-teacher will ask few students to do the loud reading of the text one by one, in the same way as she did earlier and on the spot correction will be done.	Those few students will read the text, rest will listen to them.	
Step 4 Silent Reading	Pupil-teacher will now ask all the students to read the text silently & ask any difficulty they face while doing so.	Students will do the silent reading and asking few Q.	

Recapitulation

In order to recapitulate the lesson taught and also to evaluate knowledge gained by them, pupil-teacher will ask the following questions from the students:

1. How has freedom become responsibility for our country?
2. What does the author compare the young people of today to? Why?
3. What are the qualities of a true and worthy leader?

Homework

Write in about 100 words—"We shall in no matter swerve from the paths of rectitude". Explain.

Supervisor's Remarks:

PT's Name : **Roll No.:**

Subject : English **Class** : IX
Topic : Story "The Greedy Dog" **Section** : A
Duration : 45 Minutes **Date** :

General Aims

1. To enable the students to speak correct English.
2. To improve the knowledge of vocabulary.
3. To improve the power of expression and understanding English.
4. To create interest in English language.

Behavioural Objectives

1. Students will be able to understand the moral—The greed is a curse.
2. The students are able to recognise and recall the story and the sentences used in it.
3. The students get listening practice.
4. The students are able to apply moral of the story in their day-to-day life.

General Teaching Aids

An ordinary well-equipped classroom, pieces of chalk, duster, chalkboard, pointer, etc.

Instructional Teaching Aids

Chart divided in four parts showing pictures related to the story.

Previous Knowledge Assumed

Students have their own vocabulary and they are in a position to understand spoken English and write simple sentences.

Introduction

In order to introduce the topic, pupil-teacher will ask the following questions:

1. Students, name some animals you have seen moving around.
2. Name some stories you have heard about these animals.
3. Name some stories related to dogs.

Announcement of the Topic

Finding the students able to answer simple questions, pupil-teacher will announce the topic by saying, "Well students, today I will discuss a story of "The Greedy Dog", with you.

Presentation

The story will be developed with the active cooperation of the students. Question Answer method and discussion method will be used.

Teaching Points	*Pupil-Teacher's Activities*	*Pupils' Activities*	*Chalkboard Work*
Once .... bone.	The pupil-teacher will display the chart showing the picture of different stages and oral development of story. She will be speaking sentences and asking questions by pointing towards various aspects of the story. She will also write the outline of the story on chalkboard side by side showing first picture:	Students showing interest.	The Greedy Dog.
	1. What do you see in the first picture?	Ans. A dog is there	A dog
	2. Where he is standing?	Ans. Near a butcher shop.	Butcher shop
	3. What do you see in second picture?	Ans. A dog holding a piece of bone in his mouth.	piece of bone in his mouth.
	4. What else do you see in this picture?	Ans. Dog is running beside the bank of river.	
	5. What do you see in third picture?	Ans. Dog is looking into the water.	
	6. What does he saw in the water?	Ans. His overshadow is seen.	His overshadow.
	7. What he is doing in the next picture?	Ans. He is barking at his own shadow.	Barking.
	8. What do you see in the last picture?	Ans. A dog without any bone in his mouth.	Dog without bone.
	9. What do you learn from this story?	Ans. Greed is a curse.	Greed is a curse.

Narration

Once there was a greedy dog. One day he found a piece of bone near the shop of butcher. He took it in his mouth and went away. On the way there was a river and over bridge on it. When he was crossing it he saw his overshadow in the water and thought that it is another dog having bigger bone in his mouth. In order to snatch his bone he barked at his overshadow. His piece of bone fell down into the water and sank. He felt sorry for the greediness.

Moral: Greed is a curse.

Recapitulation

In order to test whether the students could understand the story pupil-teacher will ask few questions:

1. Where did the dog find a piece of bone?
2. What was there in his way?
3. Why he barked on his overshadow?
4. What is the moral of the story?

Homework

Students will be assigned to learn the story at the home.

Supervisor's Remarks:

ANOTHER PATTERN OF LESSION PLANS

PT's Name :		**Class** :	IX
Subject :	English	**Time** :	45 Minutes
Topic :	Letter	**Date** :	

General Objectives

(a) To enable students to understand English when spoken.
(b) To enable students to organise their ideas properly and to write sentences in sequence.
(c) To develop expression power of the pupils.
(d) To develop the ability and skills among students to speak and write correct English language.
(e) To increase interest of students in English language.
(f) To enable students to use the rules of grammar in speaking and writing English.

Specific Objectives

(a) To enable students to write formal letters.
(b) To enable students to explain different parts of letters.
(c) To enable students to interpret formal letter in correct format.

Teaching Aids

1. Pointer, Roller Board, Chalk, Duster.
2. Model showing format of letter.
3. Flashcards showing different parts of letter.

Previous Knowledge

Students are expected to have knowledge about framing sentences and organise their ideas and express it.

Introduction

1. Do you have friends?
2. How do you communicate with them?
3. What are other means of communication?
4. What is pen friend?

Announcement of the Topic

Well students today we shall study about formal letter.

Teaching Points	Behavioural Objective	Pupil-Teacher Activities
Letter	They will be able to recall about letters.	What is letter? A letter is one of the best modes of conveying your message to someone far off. In the letters one can express one's thoughts and ideas freely.
Types of Letter	They will be able to list types of letter.	Letters are of two types: 1. *Informal Letters*—are personal letters written to relatives, friends. 2. *Formal Letters*—are letters written to authorities, newspapers, editors, executives and business firms.
Format of formal letter	They will be able to explain different parts of letter Chalkboard work	What is format? 1. *Sender's Address*—It is address of person who sends the letter. 2. *Date*—10 January, 2003. 3. *Address of Addressee*—It is address of person you are writing to What is written in subject? 4. *Subject*—It is heading of letter and written in only formal letters. 5. *Salutation*—Sir/Madam What is written in body of letter? 6. *Body of letter*—This is the main part of the letter. 7. *Subscription*—Yours faithfully. 8. *Signature*—Signed by thc writer. 9. *Name*—Name of the sender.
You are Suresh. The postman of your area does not deliver your letters properly. Write a letter to the Postmaster complaining against the Postman.	They will be able to write letter in correct format.	10, Asoka Road New Delhi 22 December, 2007 The Postmaster, Parliament Street, New Delhi Subject: Complaint against Postman. I wish to bring to your kind notice that my letters are not being delivered to me properly. I have put up a letterbox at the gate of my house. Still I found my letters thrown in the porch. Some times, postman hands them over to wrong persons. Shri Prem Nath is the Postman of our locality. I have requested him to put my letters into letterbox. But, all my requests have fallen on deaf ears. My important letter was due on last Saturday, but I have received it just today. It has caused a big loss to me. The magazines which I receive by post are not delivered in time.

(*Contd.*)

Teaching Points	Behavioural Objective	Pupil-Teacher Activities
		I would, therefore, request you to look into the matter personally. I shall feel highly obliged to you. Thanking you, Yours faithfully, Suresh

Recapitulation

1. What is letter?
2. How many types of letters are there?
3. What is formal letter?
4. What are different parts of letters?
5. What is written in subscription?

Home Assignment

You are Sonu living at L-18, Sarojini Nagar, New Delhi. Write a letter to the Director of Education requesting him to introduce compulsory computer education in schools.

PT's Name : **Class :** IX
Subject : English **Time :** 35 Minutes
Topic : Prose (Money) **Date :**

General Objectives

(a) To enable the pupil to speak and write in English.
(b) To acquaint them with conversion of sentences.
(c) To make pupil capable in expressing their ideas in correct English.
(d) To enable the pupil to organise their ideas properly and write in sequence.
(e) To develop their power of logical thinking.

Specific Objectives

(a) To acquaint the pupil with 'money' word.
(b) To acquaint the pupil about the invention of money.
(c) The students will be able to understand about better system.
(d) The students will be able to list different types/forms of money.
(e) The students will be able to identify the credit cards, cheques, bank notes.
(f) The students will be able to answer the different names of currencies of different countries.

Teaching Aids

(a) Blackboard
(b) Chalks
(c) Duster
(d) Flashcard showing currencies notes, credit cards, cheques, currency coins.

Previous Knowledge

The students are expected to know about—

(a) Money
(b) Need of money
(c) Name of Indian currency

Introduction

Q. 1 How many of you do get any pocket money?
Ans: Students who get pocket money will raise their hands.
Q. 2 How often do you get it?
Ans: Students Response—Every month, every week or daily.
Q. 3 On what do you spend it?
Ans: I spend on chocolates, snacks or save it.
Q. 4 In which form we have money?
Ans: We have money in coins or notes forms.
Q. 5 Do you know who prints the rupees notes that we use?
Ans: Bank. (They might also not answer this questions)
Q. 6 How was money invented?

Or

Where does money come from?
Ans: No Response

Announcement of the topic

Today, we shall study about money and invention of money and need of money.

Teaching Methods

Presentations

Teaching Points	*Behavioural Objective*	*Pupil-Teacher Activities*
		Model Reading
Develop their pronunciation skills	To impart the knowledge among the students	The teacher will read out passage and she will put proper attention in proper phrasing, pronunciation and innovation.
Pupil Activities	Teaching Aids/Chalkboard Summary	Evaluation
The students will listen the teacher reading and concentrate it.	Where does money come from?	

(*Contd.*)

Teaching Points	*Behavioural Objective*	*Pupil-Teacher Activities*
Presentation Skill of Speech	Enhancement of pronunciation	Money…. trust them. Enhancement of pronunciation The teacher will ask the students to read the chapter.
Removal of language difficulty	To enrich active and passive vocabulary to the pupil.	The teacher will pronounce the difficult words and write meaning of those on blackboard. Difficult Words Exchange: To transfer or share of goods, things to someone. Owned: Belonging
Pupil Activities	Teaching Aids/ Chalkboard Summary	Evaluation
Students will listen attentively and read the text carefully. Loud Reading Turn-wise, students will read the chapter loudly. Students will write difficult words in their notebook correctly.		
		Shoemaker: The person who makes shoes. Toolmaker: The person who makes tools.
Comprehension	To enrich their reasoning ability	The teacher will ask the students to read out the passage silently.
Explanation	Students will be able to understand the meaning of the passage.	The teacher will explain the passage to the students thoroughly by giving examples.
Evaluation	Development of knowledge gaining capacity.	The teacher will ask some questions on the basis of what she has already taught.
Students will read the passage silently. Students will listen carefully and attentively. Students will try to answer the questions on the basis of their ability.	Question and Answer	
Thought Analysis	To develop their reasoning ability	Q. How people used to fulfil their needs when there was no money? Q. Why there was a need of money?

(*Contd.*)

Teaching Points	Behavioural Objective	Pupil-Teacher Activities
		Q. What were the different forms of money? Q. Which type of money speed up trade?
Pupil Activities	Teaching Aids/Chalkboard Summary	Evaluation
Pupil used to exchange something they owned for something they needed.	It is used to exchange something they owned for something they needed.	
Because, sometimes people doesn't able to exchange something they owned for something they needed.		
Ans. Shells, beads and salt.	Shells, beads & salt.	
Ans. Coins & Bank notes	Coins & bank notes	Q Why there was a need of money?

Recapitulation

Q. Write "T" for True and "F" for False?

(a) With money you can buy whatever you need. ( )
(b) Coins and bank notes are better than shells and beads. ( )
(c) Salt and shells all easy to carry. ( )
(d) The first coins used were made of leather. ( )
(e) People trust bank notes. ( )

Home Assignments

Q. 1 When the first coins were used first time?
Q. 2 When the first paper money was used?
Q. 3 Which banks were printing bank notes and promised to pay their owner in gold or silver?

Remarks

PT's Name : **Class :** IX
Subject : English **Time :** 35 Minutes
Topic : Poem (on killing a tree) **Date :**

General Objectives

(a) To enable the students to appreciate the beauty rhyme and style of the poem.

(b) To enable the pupil to read aloud the poem with proper rhythm and intonation.
(c) To enable the students to enjoy recitation, individual or chorus of the poem.
(d) To develop their aesthetic sense.
(e) To make students understand the thought and imagination contained in the poem.

Specific Objectives

(a) To give the students a general view that it is not easy to kill a tree.
(b) To enable the pupil to recall that the barks of the tree gets wounded but in meantime the new things will grow.
(c) To enable the pupil to understand that to kill a tree, it has to be uprooted completely.
(d) To enable the students to know about the feelings of a tree when it is bleeding profusely after it is being hacked.

Teaching Aids

A chart showing 'A tree in full bloom'. A chart showing 'A tree being chopped'.

Previous Knowledge

Students are expected to know the importance of trees.

Introduction

Teacher will ask certain questions based on the pictures to introduce the poem.

Q. 1 *Teacher*: What do you observe in the first picture?
Ans: *Student*: We see a huge tree with its branches swinging with the breeze.
Q. 2 *Teacher*: What do you see in the second picture?
Ans: *Student*: The same happy tree is being chopped and it is weeping.

Announcement of the Topic

Today, we shall study the poem 'On killing a tree' written by Giene Patel.

Teaching Methods

Question Answer and Explanation Method

Presentation

Teaching Point	*Behavioural Outcomes*	*Pupil-Teacher Activities*	*Pupils' Activities*	*Chalkboard Work*	*Evaluation*
Recitation of the poem by students	Students will be able to recite the poem "On killing a tree".	Recitation of the poem by students "On killing a tree". The teacher is reciting the poem.	Students recite the poem in a chorus.		

(*Contd.*)

Teaching Point	*Behavioural Outcomes*	*Pupil-Teacher Activities*	*Pupils' Activities*	*Chalkboard Work*	*Evaluation*
Learning of the poem	Pupil try to learn the poem "On killing a tree".	Teacher recites the poem and ask the students to recite the poem along with her.	The students recite the poem along with their teacher.		What is the meaning of bleeding bark?
Testing of comprehension	Students will be able to answer the questions given by the teacher.	Why a single jole of knife cannot kill a tree? What is the meaning of bleeding bark?	The tree has grown to its full size and has become strong, thick and stout over the years. The tree is bleeding because it has been hacked and chopped	Q. Why a single jole of knife cannot kill a tree? Q. What is meaning of bleeding bark?	
Introduction of the poem	Student will be able to understand the introduction of the poem	Teacher will introduce the poem "On killing a tree" to the class.	Students listen carefully keeping their books closed.	"On killing a tree". The bark is bleeding.	
Explanation of the poem.	Students will be able to recall the important lines of the poem	The important lines are being explained. 1. A simple jole of the knife kill a tree. 2. The roots are to be pulled out—out of the anchoring earth.	Students note down the important lines and underlining them.	'A single jole of knife'.	What do you understand by the roots pulled out.
Key words and images	Students will be able to write down the important words.	Teacher will try to explain the meaning of different words, word meaning. Hack-Cut by blows Miniature-Tiny Anchoring—Supporting Snapped out—Pulled out by jerk	The students will note in their copies & try to grasp the meaning of the words and phrases.	Word meaning Hack-Cut by blows Miniature-Tiny Anchoring—Supporting Bleeding bark—Wounded	

Recapitulation

The teacher will ask some questions to evaluate whether the students have understood or not.

1. How has a tree grown to its full size?
2. What is the meaning of anchoring earth?
3. What does the poet mean by "The strength of the tree exposed"?

Home Assignment

Write down the meaning of these words and make sentences from these words:

1. Snapped out
2. Sprouting
3. Miniature
4. Heal

PT's Name : **Class :** IX

Subject : English (Grammar) **Time :** 35 Minutes

Topic : Preposition **Date :**

General Objectives

(a) Students will be able to understand the rule of grammar.
(b) To make learning of English grammar easy and interesting.
(c) Students will be able to speak and write correct English.
(d) Students will be able to understand English when spoken.
(e) Students will be able to convert sentences in another form without changing the sense of the sentence.

Specific Objectives

Knowledge — Recall the use of on and under in the written language.
— Recall the use of among and between and among in written language.

Understanding — Understand the knowledge of on and under.
— Students will be able to identify the use of among and between.

Application — Students will be able to apply the use of on and under correctly.
— Students will be able to apply the use of among and between correctly.

Teaching Aids

Blackboard, chalk, duster, chart and some objects.

Previous Knowledge

Students are able to frame simple sentences.

Introduction

Pupil-teacher will ask the following questions:

Q. 1 What is this? (Showing book)
Ans: *Pupil*: This is book.
Q. 2 Where is the book?
Ans: Pupil: The book is on the table.

Q. 3 Where is the pen? (Placing the pen between two chalks)
Ans: *Pupil*: Pen is between the chalks.
Then teacher ask the students what is on, under between and among?
Ans: No answer.

Announcement of the Topic

Well, students today, we shall study about the preposition.

Teaching Method

Presentation

Teaching Point	*Behavioural Outcome*	*Pupil-Teacher Activities*	*Pupils' Activities*	*Chalkboard Work*	*Evaluation*
Use of 'On'	Students will be able to make use of 'On'.	By showing a pencil, P-T ask what is this?	Pencil		
		What is this? (Pointing out on the table)	Table		Where is the pencil?
		After placing the pencil on the table, P-T asks where is the pencil?	Pencil is on the table.		
Meaning of 'On'		P-T will explain the use of 'On'—Preposition 'On' is used when one thing is placed upon another thing.		ON 'On' is used when one thing is placed upon another thing.	Where is the pencil?
Use of 'Under'	Students will be able to make use of 'Under'.	What is this? (By showing a glass)	Glass		
		What is this? (By showing a chair)	Chair		
		Putting the glass under the chair, P-T ask where is the glass? Explain the use of 'Under'—Preposition 'under' is used when one thing is placed below another thing.	The glass is under the chair	UNDER 'Under' is used when one thing is placed below another thing.	Where is the book?
Explain the examples.	Students will be able to understand the examples	(a) The duster is on the table. (b) The pen is on the table. (c) The book is under the desk. (d) The pencil is under the book.	Students listen carefully and given the answer		Where is the chalkboard ?
		Q. Where is toy?	The toy is on the table.		

(*Contd.*)

Teaching Point	*Behavioural Outcome*	*Pupil-Teacher Activities*	*Pupils' Activities*	*Chalkboard Work*	*Evaluation*
Use of 'Between'	Students will be able to know about 'Between'	P-T will place a flower between the two leaves and say— This is a flower. These are leaves. The flower is between the leaves. Explanation of 'Between' Between is used when one thing is placed in the middle of two things.	Listen carefully	BETWEEN 'Between' is used when one thing is placed in the middle of two things.	
Example	Students will be able to understand the examples	1. The flower is in between the pens. 2. The pencil is between the pens. 3. The pencil is between the chalks. Q. Where is Meena?	Listen carefully and note it down Meena is sitting between Sunita and Reena.		
Use of 'Among'		Among is used when one thing is placed in the middle of more than two things.		AMONG Among is used when one thing is placed in the middle of more than two things.	
Example	Students will be able to understand the use of 'among'	1. The pencil is among the leaves 2. The chalk is among the pens. 3. The pen is among the chalks.	Listen attentively		Where is the flower? Where is the book?

Recapitulation

(a) Where is the book? (By placing it under the desk)
(b) Where is the pen? (By placing it under the table)
(c) Meena is standing .... Sita and Geeta.
(d) Distribute the sweets .... the students.

Home Work

Write 10-10 sentences of on, under, among and between.

SAMPLE OF ACHIEVEMENT TESTS

Here below are given a few sample of achievement tests prepared for the different examinations conducted by different boards/institutions or other examining bodies.

Sample 1 (Haryana Board) **Class X**

Section A (Language)

SAMPLE PAPER

(Haryana Board)
Class X: English (Course A)

Section A

1. Attempt all parts of this question:

(a) Use the proper form of non-finites in the following sentences. (Do any three)
   (i) Are you interested in ___________ (point)?
   (ii) Dancing is difficult ___________ (learn).
   (iii) We enjoyed ___________ (boat) in the lake.
   (iv) I saw the ball ___________ (roll) into the well. 3

(b) Rewrite the following sentences beginning with 'it'. Do any two:
   (i) To touch a live wire is dangerous.
   (ii) Living without water is impossible.
   (iii) Missing this chance would be a pity. 2

(c) Fill in the blanks with suitable sentence connectors. Do any three.
   (i) Sita is playing ___________ her sister is studying.
   (ii) No sooner did we step out of the house________ it began to rain.
   (iii) I shall help you ___________ you are my friend.
   (iv) You will not succeed ___________ you work hard. 3

(d) Combine the following pairs of sentences using the first sentence as a noun clause. Do any three.
   (i) Where has he disappeared? Nobody knows.
   (ii) What is your opinion about this?
   (iii) When did we meet last? I do not remember.
   (iv) How can I do so much work? I do not understand. 3

(e) Use the correct form of the verb given in brackets. Do any two.
   (i) His father …….. (die) in 1990.
   (ii) We …….. (finish) our work before the guests arrived.
   (iii) As soon as someone …….. (knock) at the door, the dog began to bark. 2

(f) Fill in the blanks out of the following modals. Do any three.
Could, might, should, may, must
   (i) He worked hard so that he …….. pass.
   (ii) You …….. consult some good doctor.
   (iii) Though he tried hard yet he …….. not succeed.
   (iv) You …….. come whenever you like. 4

(g) Change the following sentences into indirect speech. Do any four.
   (i) The teacher said, "Have you done your home work?"
   (ii) The mother said to the daughter, "Why do you get up late?"
   (iii) The inspector asked, "what is the population of this city?"

(iv) The Doctor said to the patient, "Are you feeling better now?"
(v) I asked him, "How long have you been living here?" 4

2. Write a letter to the Health officer of your town complaining about the sanitary conditions of your locality. 10
3. Write a paragraph of 100 words on any one of the following:
   A scene at the Railway station
   Need of family planning
   An ideal student
   A cricket match you witnessed 10
4. Read the passage given below and answer the questions:
   Most of the people who appear most often in history books are great conquerors and generals. Strangely enough the people who really helped civilisation forward are often never mentioned at all. We do not know who made the first boat or calculated the length of the year. But we know all about killers and destroyers. We raise statues for them simply because they fought bravely. But even animals fight. So real civilised people have been those who have brought peace and happiness to mankind. They have been prophets, saints, doctors, inventors and discoverers. They have been truly great, since instead of inflicting pain and hardships on humanity, they have healed their wounds. Instead of killing they have saved human lives. They really deserve our admiration and respect.
   (i) What sort of people generally appear in history books?
   (ii) What kind of people really helped civilisation forward?
   (iii) For whom do we raise statues?
   (iv) What is common between men and animals?
   (v) Who have helped mankind?
   (vi) Who deserve our admiration and respect?
   (vii) Find words from the passage having the same meanings as:
   (a) Find out working with the numbers. (b) Mankind

Section B

5. Read the passage given below and answer the questions that follow. Attempt any two passages.

(a) Throughout India, edicts carved on rocks and iron pillars are reminders that 22 centuries ago, Emperor Ashoka defined the king's duty as not merely to protect citizens and punish wrong doers but also to preserve animal life and forest trees. Ashoka was the first and perhaps the only monarch until very recently to forbid the killing of a large number of species of animals for sport or food. He went further, regretting the carnage of the military conquests and enjoining upon his successors to find their only pleasure in the peace that comes through righteousness".
   (i) What were the two duties of the king according to Ashoka?
   (ii) What do you understand by: (a) preserve, (b) righteousness.
   (iii) What did Ashoka ban?
   (iv) What did Ashoka advise his successors? 4

(b) For there are few things more catching than bad temper and bad manners we infect the world with our ill-humours. Bad manners probably do more to poison the stream of the general life than all the crimes in the calendar. But no court could administer a law which governed our social civilities, our speech, the tilt of our eyebrows and all our moods and manners.
   (i) How do bad manners harm our life?
   (ii) What do you mean by: (a) infect (b) civilities?

(c) A few minutes after the forest guard turned up to lead woe to the machaan. The killer was nearly a mile from the bungalow, and the sun was about to set when we got to it. As I climbed into the machaan, I tried to measure its height from the ground. I had read that a tiger could jump to eighteen feet. Just to make sure, I asked the Forest Guard, "what height is this?" "about fifteen feet", he said.
   (i) What for did the Forest Guard turn up?
   (ii) What do you understand by (a) Machaan, (b) Measure?
   (iii) How far was the killer from the Bungalow?
   (iv) What had the author read?

6. Answer in about 100 words. Describe the little brother's journey to Holland.
   Or
   Attempt a character sketch of the tailor.

7. Answer any four of the following in about 30 words:
   (i) How did Griffin spend his night in the London store?
   (Footprints without Feet)
   (ii) What did Lencho write in his letter to God?
   (A letter to God)
   (iii) Nehru wanted a major portion of his ashes to be scattered over the fields, why?
   (The Ganga)
   (iv) What did Dessa do after beating Moti Guj?
   (Gurj-mufineer)
   (v) Why did the Bishop keep the doors of his house open?
   (The Bishop's Candlesticks) 8

8. Answer any three of the following in one sentence each:
   (i) Whose house did Griffin set on fire?
   (Foot prints without Feet)
   (ii) Where did Nehru spend his childhood?
   (The Ganga)
   (iii) How long was the convict in prison?
   (The Bishop's Candlesticks)
   (iv) Who was Swami Hari Dass and where did he live?
   (Our Indian Music)

Section C

9. Read the extract given below and answer the questions that follow:

   The storm came on before its time:

She wandered up and down:
And many a hill did Lucy climb;
But never reached the town.

(i) Name the poem and the poet.
(ii) When did the storm come?
(iii) What did Lucy do during the storm?
(iv) Where could she not reach?

Or

If there were dreams to sell Merry and sad to tell,
And the Crier rang the bell,
What would you buy?
A college lane and still,
with bowers nigh,
Shadowy, my woes to still,
Until I die.

(i) Name the poem and the poet.
(ii) What did the Crier's do?
(iii) Where does the poet want to live?
(iv) What are the two kinds of dreams?

10. Answer in about 100 words:
Describe the miseries of the Slave's life as depicted in the poem "The Slave's Dream".

Or

How does the poet use the examples of an oak and a lily to give his idea of the perfect life?

Section D

11. Answer in about 100 words:
Attempt a character sketch of Gontheor. (The End of the Rope)

Or

Narrate how Simon lebrument cheated the simple feanne cordier of her dowry? (The Dowry) 6

12. Answer any three in 30 words:
(i) How was the circus manager worried? (A High Drive)
(ii) The little girl was happy to get the blue ball but her happiness was short lived. Why, that happened? (Not just oranges)
(iii) Why did Marian not like to play with other children? (I can play schools)
(iv) How did the lawyer look after fifteen years of solitary imprisonment? (The Bet) 3

13. Answer any three of the following in one sentence:
(i) How long did Mr. Das remain in the hospital? (The Coward's Way)
(ii) Where were the fat woman and her husband going? (War)
(iii) What happened to Mrs. Malachor's flower vase? (Not just oranges)
(iv) What was the cause of Gesseler's death? (Quality) 3

Glossary

Active Vocabulary: Words that are taught so intensively that students can understand and say them and, later, read and write them.

Articulation: The production of sounds by the meeting of the vocal organs.

Communication: (i) The transmission and reception of meaningful information. (ii) The ability to understand, to speak and to respond to the signals to another individual.

Context: A socio-cultural situation, the surrounding words in an utterance that give a word or structure, its particular meaning.

Culture: The pattern of the customs, traditions, social habits, values, beliefs, and language of any society of human beings.

Curriculum. The knowledge, information, skills habits, attitudes, activities, and materials that are included in the teaching of any subject.

Derivational: Pertaining to the prefixes suffixes and infixes, that change the meanings and function of word, e.g. trust, mistrust, bright, brighten.

Determiner: A word like "the", "a", "same", "each", "all", which is placed before the noun and which limits or modifies it.

Dipthong: Two vowel sounds combined to form one sound, e.g. "i" in "ice" (a + i)

Equivalent: A word or expression in one language that conveys a similar meaning in another language. Equivalents should not be confused with word by word translations.

Function Word: One having little or no meaning by itself because it does not refer to an object or action in the world of reality. Function words are considered one of the four major meaning signals of English since they indicate relationships of content words to each other. Prepositions, auxiliaries, conjunctions are examples of such words.

Generalisation: A statement describing the form, function, position and meaning of the recurring feature or element of any language item or cultural concept; a 'rule'.

Inflection: The addition of an ending to express a grammatical relationship; e.g. ed added to 'walk' to indicate past tense.

Integration: (i) the process of bringing together materials and skills that are related and that can be used concomitantly as in the language arts, (ii) the feeling on the part of an individual that he participates and functions in another society while retaining his own sense of identity.

Internalise: To make some learning part of oneself, to achieve full control of.

IPA: The International Phonetic Alphabet.

Item: An element of language, e.g. a phoneme, a morpheme, a word, a structure.

Labial: Pertaining to lips.

Language Laboratory: A room or part of a room equipped with one or more tape recorders, microphones, listening and playback equipments with which pupils can listen to and imitate tapes and engage in varied practice activities for the purpose of reinforcing language skills.

Lexical: Pertaining to the vocabulary of a language (the content and function words)

Model: The 'perfect' native production of a sound, word or expression by a learner or a tape for imitation and repetition by the students.

Morpheme: A minimal unit of meaningful speech; e.g. a word , "boy", an inflection "s", as in boys a suffix, "ish" as in boyish.

Morphology: The study of grammatical changes in the forms of a word, e.g. boy, boys, boy's, boys', sure, ensure.

Native Speaker: A person who has native or near native command of a language because he has either born into that language community or has learned the language well enough to master it.

Passive Vocabulary: Words which the learner can understand when spoken or recognise when read but which he cannot produce in speaking or in writing.

Pattern: An arrangement of sounds, letters or words that recurs systematically in a language that is systematically in a language that is meaningful; the framework or design of an utterance; e.g. noun-verb (birds fly).

Pattern Practice: Drills, activities and exercises that help giving students control of patterns of language (word order, word form, function words, intonation).

Phoneme: The smallest unit of sound in a language that distinguishes one word from another. For example 'p' and 'b' are phonemes because they make a meaning difference, in words like 'pit' and 'bit', 'peat' and 'beat' or 'pear' and 'bear'.

Phonemics: The study of meaningful units of speech.

Phonetics: The study of the sounds of speech and the way in which the sounds are produced.

Phonology: The study of the sounds, intonation, rhythm, stress and pauses in the language.

Pitch: Contrast in the relative height of the tone of voice. Pitch is an important component of intonation.

Slot: The position of a word or phrase in an utterance or sentence that can be occupied by words or phrases of the same class or type: for example, "the", "a", "some", "each" can fit into the same slot.

Stress: The prominence of syllables or words in speech. The stressed syllable in English is longer and louder than others.

Structure: (i) the grammar of a language (ii) the recurring patterns of a language as they occur in forms and arrangement of words.

Syntax: The arrangement of words in utterances and sentences, "I always go there", "I go there in the afternoons" words like "always" generally, and never are placed before the main verb whereas true phrases are placed at the end of a sentences.

Utterance: A word, expression or sentence that conveys full meaning to a listener for example 'no' is an utterance.

Unit: (i) A large sub-division of a subject, (ii) A number of lessons or activities built around one topic, (iii) One item of speech.

Voiced Sound: One produced with the vocal cords vibrating e.g. 'Z" or 'b'.

Voiceless Sound: A sound made while the vocal cords are not vibrating, e.g. "s", or "p".

Bibliography

Acharya, S.M., *Pedagogy of English Language*, Laxmi Book Depot, Haryana.

Agnihotri, R.K. and Khanna, A.L., *Problematising English in India*, New Delhi, Sage Publications (1977).

Anderson, A. and Lynch T., *Listening*, Oxford, Oxford University Press.

Bhandari, C.S., (1961), *Teaching of English*, (1988).

Bhatia, K.T., Teaching of English in Indian, Prakash Publishers (1988).

Billows, F.L., *The Techniques of Language Teaching*, Logomans, London (1961).

Bose, K. Shanika, *Teaching of English: A Modern Approach*, Doaba House (1979).

Bright, J.A. and Mc. Gregor, G.P. Teaching English.

Burstall, C., Factors Affecting Foreign Language Learning Consideration of Some Recent Research Findings, Language Teaching and Linguistics, Abstracts (1975).

Bygate, M., *Speaking*, Oxford, Oxford University Press (1987).

Calkins, Lucy M., *The Art of Teaching Writing*; Heinmann Educational Books (1986).

Dunkel, Harold, *Second language learning* Grain and Company (1952).

Elbow Peter: Writing with Power Techniques for Mastering the Writing Process (1981).

Fred Inglish. *The Englishness of English Teaching*, The University of Sheffield, Western Printing Services Ltd., Bristol, (1969).

Freeman S., *Written Communication English*, Madras Orient Language (1977).

French F.G., *The Teaching of English Abroad*, London Oxford University Press (1950).

Games for Language Learning, Cambridge, Cambridge University Press.

Gardner R.C. and Lambert, W.E., *Attitudes and Motivation in Second Language Learning*, Mas Newberry House, Rowley (1972).

Gokak, V.K., *Future of English in India*, Asia Bombay (1964).

Govil Punita, *Teaching of English*, HP Bhargava Book House, Agra (2006).

Gray, W.S., *Teaching of Reading and Writing* UNESCO (11 ed) (1969).

Green Thoma, F., *The activities of teaching*, McGraw Hill Book Company, London.

Harold, B.A. Allen, *Teaching English as a Second Language*, Tata McGraw Hill Publishing Co. Ltd, New York, Bombay (1965).

Heaton, J.B., *Writing English Tests*, Longman (1988).

Higher Education: The Psycho-Social Context towards understanding the processes of teaching and learning in higher education, MES 103 IGNOU Delhi (2001).

Hornby A.S. and Others, *The Advanced Learners Dictionary of Current English,* Oxford University Press (1968).

IDB ICT Education Blog UNESCO Bangkok ICT and Education.

Jaggi, Simi, *Pedagogy of English Language,* Amit Prakashan, Jalandar.

Jain, R.K., *Essentials of English Teaching,* Vinod Pustak Mandir, Agra (1992).

Jesperson, Otto, *Language: Its Native Development and Origin,* Alien and Unwin, London (1928).

K. Shanika Bose, Teaching of English: A Modern Approach, Doaba House (1979).

Kemp *et al.,* Designing Effective Instruction, Macmillan College Publishing Company (1994).

Krashen, S.D., *Second language acquisition and Second Language learning,* Oxford Pergamon (1981).

Lado, Robert (1964), *Language Teaching—A Scientific Approach,* McGraw Hill, New York.

Listening comprehension and Speaking teaching of English ES 344 IGNOU (2000).

Littlewood, W., *Communicative Language Teaching—An Introduction,* Cambridge, Cambridge University Press (1981).

Makey Sandra L., *Teaching Grammar,* Oxford, Pergaman Institute of English (1985).

Mehta, Prem, *Teaching of English Language,* Doaba House, Delhi (2015).

Menon and Patel, *The Teaching of English as a Foreign Language* (1957).

MESE Teaching of English : Teaching speaking and listening booklet 5 IGNOU (2004).

MESE 005, Teaching of English: Teaching writing and grammar, Booklet 4 IGNOU (2004).

Newman, Dr. Judith, *The Craft of Children's Writing,* Scholastic Professional Books (1984).

P. Gurrey: *Teaching English as a foreign language,* Longman's Green and Co. Ltd. (1955).

Penfield, W.G., and Roberts L., *Speech and Brain Mechanisms,* Princeton, Princeton University Press (1959).

Ratawal, S.P., *Teaching English Language,* Cyber Tech Publications, New Delhi (2006).

Richards, L.A., *Basic English and its uses,* W.W. Norton and Co. Inc., New York (1963).

Rixon S., *Developing Listening Skills,* Essential Language Teaching Series, Macmillan (1986).

Satish C. Chadha, *Art and Science of Teaching English* (2003).

Sharma, R.A., *Fundamentals of teaching English,* R. Lall Book Depot, Merrut (1999).

Sinha, A.K., *Empowering Communication Skills*, Shipra Publications, Delhi (2016).

Srivastava, B.D., *Structural Approach to the Technique of English* (1966).

Srivastava, H.S., *Curriculum and Methods of Teaching*, Shipra Publications, Delhi (2010, Second Revised Edition).

Teaching learning in the classroom (2), Teaching of English MESE IGNOU (2004).

Teaching of English as a Second Language CTE. Course 2-The Structure of English, Block I English and Its Varieties, IGNOU (1995).

Teaching of English ES 344 booklet 1 to 4 IGNOU Delhi (2004).

Teaching of English: Reading Comprehension ES 344 IGNOU (2004).

Teaching of English: Teaching Speaking and Listening MESE 005 IGNOU (2004).

Technknowlogia, January-March 2003 @ Knowledge Enterprise, Inc., Education the World Bank.

Tomkinson, *The Teaching of English in India*, Oriental Longmans, Bombay (1967).

Underhill, N., *Testing Spoken Language: A Handbook for Oral Testing Technique*, Cambridge, Cambridge University Press (1987).

Ur. Penny, *Grammar Practice Activities*, Cambridge, Cambridge University Press (1988).

Vashishtha, Rajesh, *Proficiency in English*, Laxmi Book Depot, Haryana.

Wadhwa, S.S. and Shaida A.K.: *Teaching of English*, ABC Publications, Chandigarh (1971).

Wallace J. Michael, Study Skills in English, Cambridge, Cambridge University Press (1980).

West Michael, *Teaching English in Difficult Circumstances*, Longman (1941).

Wilkins D.A., Second language teaching and learning Edward Arnold (Reprint), London (1982).

Wright Andrew, Betteridge David and Buckby Michael (1984).

www.oiirj.org.ISSN224-9898

www.teachingenglish.org.uk/deduvtiveapproach

Revision Questions

1. NATURE OF LANGUAGE

Essay Type Questions

1. Discuss the concept of language.
2. Define language. Mention the nature of language.
3. What are the varieties of language?

2. IMPORTANCE OF LANGUAGE

Essay Type Questions

1. "English should be taught for utilitarian rather than cultural purposes". What are these utilitarian purposes and why should they be considered more important than other purposes?
2. "English is our major window on the modern world". Discuss the importance of English in today's India.
3. What is the role of English in a developing country like India in the present circumstances?
4. "English is a language of international commercial purpose; it is the language of diplomacy and it contains many a rich treasure". Discuss.
5. "English has been playing, is playing and will continue to play a significant role in India's national life". Discuss.

Short Answer Type Questions

Write short notes on:

6. English as a library language.
7. Future of English language.
8. English in our social life.
9. English as a language of trade and industry.

3. FUNCTIONS OF LANGUAGE

Essay Type Questions

1. What do you mean by directive function of language?
2. What are the different functions of a language? Explain.
3. Write a note on 'Expressive function' of a language.

4. LINGUISTIC PRINCIPLES

Essay Type Questions

1. Discuss in detail the principles of language learning.
2. How far linguistic principles help a language teacher? Discuss.
3. What do you mean by maxims of teaching? Discuss briefly the various maxims of teaching by giving suitable examples.

5. AIMS AND OBJECTIVES OF TEACHING ENGLISH

Essay Type Questions

1. What is the need of fixing aims and objectives of teaching English?
2. Discuss the aims and objectives of teaching English.
3. Differentiate between the aims of teaching English at Junior and Secondary level.

Short Answer Type Questions

Which aim is significant for a class of beginners?

1. Reading as aim of teaching English.
2. Listening as aim of teaching English.
3. Speaking as aim of teaching English.
4. Writing as aim of teaching English.

6. STATING OBJECTIVES IN BEHAVIOURAL TERMS

Essay Type Questions

1. What do you understand by 'Objectives in Behavioural Terms'? Discuss the steps involved in writing such objectives.
2. Discuss briefly the three aspects of an individual's behaviour.
3. How is RCEM approach better than Robert Mager and Robert Miller's approach? What are the constituents of RCEM approach?
4. Take up any topic of your choice at secondary level and write the objectives in behavioural terms.

7. PSYCHOLOGY OF FOREIGN LANGUAGE LEARNING

Essay Type Questions

1. What are the Psychological bases of Language Learning ? explain.
2. Discuss the social bases of Language Learning.
3. What are the Philpsophical bases of Language Learning?

8. TEACHING OF PROSE

Essay Type Questions

1. What are the different steps of teaching prose? Mention its advantages and disadvantages?
2. What is the importance of silent and loud reading?
3. Select a topic of your own choice and prepare a detailed lesson on teaching prose lesson.
4. Bring out the difference between intensive reading and extensive reading.

Short Answer Type Questions

1. How far do you agree that reading aloud is better than silent reading?
2. How does the habit of silent reading lead pupil to the library?
3. Suggest ways to cultivate the habit of reading among your students.

9. TEACHING OF POETRY

Essay Type Questions

1. What do you think is the aim of teaching poetry? How can it be obtained?
2. How far do you agree with the statement "Poetry cannot be taught"? Explain.
3. What is the difference between teaching prose and poetry? Prepare a lesson plan for teaching poem to VIII class.
4. What are the drawbacks in teaching poetry in India? How can these be overcome?

Short Answer Type Questions

1. What are the aims of teaching poetry?
2. How can oral lessons be helpful to the students, in the teaching of poetry?

10. TEACHING OF COMPOSITION

Essay Type Questions

1. Discuss the various stages in teaching composition to the learners of English as a foreign language.
2. Guided composition leads to free composition. How far do you agree with the statement? Justify your answer.
3. "Most of the students at school write poor compositions in English". Discuss. What are your suggestions for improving the composition work of your pupils, especially at the senior stage?
4. Indicate the technique of writing paragraph. Enumerate the forms of composition.
5. What is meant by free composition? Illustrate how will you teach a free composition on any topic of your choice.

11. TEACHING OF GRAMMAR

Essay Type Questions

1. What is the place of grammar in teaching and learning English language?
2. What are the objectives of teaching grammar and its place in school curriculum?
3. Discuss the various approaches of teaching Grammar?
4. What do you understand by teaching of functional grammar? Discuss.
5. Suggest some ways to teach grammar effectively.

Short Answer Type Questions

1. Principles of teaching grammar
2. Define grammar
3. Types of grammar

12. PEDAGOGICAL ANALYSIS: BASED ON UNIT ANALYSIS

Essay Type Questions

1. Discuss pedagogical analysis based on unit analysis by giving suitable examples.
2. Write short notes on: Learning experiences and objectives.
3. Discuss the steps involved in the presentation and utilisation of a unit test.

Short Answer Type Questions

1. Write the objectives of teaching any Unit.
2. Write note on evaluation of a Unit.

13. MICROTEACHING SKILLS

Essay Type Questions

1. What is Micro-teaching? How will you prepare a Micro-lesson for 7th class based on the questioning skill?
2. What is the need of explaining skill in teaching English? Prepare a Micro lesson plan based on 'Skill of explaining' choosing a topic of your own choice.
3. Explain the meaning of stimulus variation? Prepare a lesson plan on Demonstrative Pronouns for class 8th.
4. What is the importance of illustration skill? Prepare a lesson plan on the 'topic' tense using this skill.

Short Anwer Type Questions

5. Explain observation schedule.
6. What are the characteristics of good question?

14(A). MAJOR METHODS OF TEACHING

Essay Type Questions

1. Explain the main principles of translation method of teaching English. What are the merits and demerits of this method.
2. Translation method is the best as governed by the maxim, "Proceed from known to unknown". Discuss this statement giving reasons. Why do you agree or disagree with it?

Short Answer Type Questions

1. Define a method.
2. What are the objectives and characteristics of Translation Method?

14 (B).

Essay Type Questions

1. What is the meaning of Direct Method? What are its merits and demerits?
2. What do you understand by Direct Method? What are its principles?
3. Direct Method of teaching a foreign language is popular in other countries but not in India. Why?

Short Answer Type Questions

1. What are the aims of Direct Method?
2. Explain the process of teaching.

14 (C).

Essay Type Questions

1. What is the meaning of Bilingual Method? What are its principles?
2. Which method of teaching English is best and why?
3. Explain the merits of Bilingual Method? How far it is an improvement over translation method?

Short Answer Type Questions

1. Meaning of Bilingual Method.
2. Utility of Bilingual Method.

14 (D). AUDIO LINGUAL METHOD

Essay Type Questions

1. Discuss the main features of Audio Lingual method in detail.

15 (A). APPROACHES OF TEACHING ENGLISH

Essay Type Questions

1. What is structural approach? How can a teacher provide practice of structures to the students?
2. What is a structure? What are the objectives of structural approach?
3. What are the principles for the selection and gradation of structures of patterns in teaching English?

4. "In learning a foreign language mastery of structures is more important than mere acquisition of vocabulary." Discuss.
5. What is structural approach to the teaching of English? What are its characteristics, features, merits and demerits?
6. What is the structural approach to teaching of English? How is, it an improvement upon the 'Direct Method' of teaching English?
7. Describe the meanings of structures and structural patterns. How should these be selected and graded to improve the teaching of English?

Short Answer Type Questions

8. (a) What do you mean by a structure? Give four examples.
   (b) Write a note on 'selection of structures'.
9. How are structures graded?
10. Prepare a suitable substitution table for practising past perfect continuous tense.
11. Write short notes on: (a) Method, (b) Structure, (c) Technique.

15 (B).

1. What is the meaning of Situational Approach?
2. What are the merits and demerits of Situational Approach?

15 (C).

Essay Type Questions

1. What is Communicative Approach to the teaching and learning of a language specially English?
2. What are the pre-requisites of Linguistic Communicative Approach? Discuss briefly.
3. What is Communicative Approach to language teaching? Discuss its advantages and limitations.
4. Discuss the main points which are put into practice while adopting communicative language teaching approach. What should be the role of the teacher?

Short Answer Type Questions

1. Write a short note on 'Linguistic Communicative Approach'.
2. Write a short note on Language learning and social setting'.

15 (D).

Write Short Notes on:

1. What is aim of teaching by Project Method.
2. How would you teach your students by Project method at junior level and senior level.

15(E).

Essay Type Questions

1. Differentiate between Inductive and Deductive approach of teaching English language.
2. Inductive Approach is natural. How far do you agree? Discuss it.

Short Answer Type Question

1. In Inductive approach examples are given first then the rules, but in Deductive approach rules come first then the examples.

2. In Inductive approach is student centred, whereas the Deductive approach is teacher centred.
3. In Inductive approach Grammar is learnt subconsciously, but in Deductive approach Grammar is learnt consciously.

15(F).

Essay Type Questions

1. Discuss the process of Whole Language Approach

Short Answer Type Question

1. What is the meaning of Whole Language Approach in learning English?

15(G).

Essay Type Questions

1. What do you mean by Constructive Approach to learning English? Explain.

Short Answer Type Questions

1. Name any three principles of Constructive Learning.
2. What is the role of learning in Constructive Approach?

15(H).

Essay Type Questions

1. Which are the principles of Multilingualism in the class-room? Discuss in detail.

Short Answer Type Question

1. What is the meaning of Multilingualism?
2. What are the merits of Multilingual Approach in learning English language?

16 (A). DEVELOPMENT OF LINGUISTIC SKILLS

Essay Type Questions

1. What is the role of listening in the process of learning English?
2. What is the importance of oral work in a classroom? How will you carry on oral work successfully while teaching English?
3. A good listener is a good speaker. How far do you agree with the statement? Discuss.
4. How will you develop linguistic skills in respect of listening and speaking English?
5. What is a drill? Is it different from cramming? Discuss the advantages of giving drill in teaching-learning of English.

Short Answer Type Questions

1. Discuss the problems in the development of listening skills.
2. How can the oral work be made a great success? Suggest.
3. What are the advantages of giving drill?

16 (B).

Essay Type Questions

1. "The speech is the language". Comment on it.
2. What is the role of the teacher in developing speaking skill?
3. What are the causes of poor pronunciation? Give some suggestions.
4. What are the methods of teaching pronunciation? Suggest some activities to improve pronunciation.

5. What are vowels and consonants? Explain.

Short Notes

1. What do you understand by intonation?
2. What is the importance of stress and rhythm?

16 (C)

Essay Type Questions

1. What do you mean by reading? What are the various methods of reading?
2. What are the various stages in reading English? Elucidate.
3. What are the aims of teaching reading? When should it be started?
4. Discuss the various teaching skills required for developing reading skills.
5. In what way is teaching of intensive reading different from extensive reading? Give examples in support of your answer.
6. What is the meaning and importance of reading? Give the nature of reading process and also discuss the different stages in the teaching-reading in English.
7. What is reading? What are the various methods of teaching reading to the beginners of English? Describe in detail the methods you would like to follow.

Short Answer Type Questions

1. Discuss the objectives of teaching reading.
2. Discuss the causes of retardation in reading English.
3. How will you promote reading habits in school children?
4. Write a note on silent reading.
5. Write a note on loud reading.
6. List out 8 co-curricular activities for developing reading skills in your students.

16 (D).

Essay Type Questions

1. What is the importance of good handwriting? What are the characteristics of a good handwriting?
2. What are the causes of bad handwriting? How can you help beginners to write beautifully?
3. When should writing be introduced? What are the initial difficulties in the way of teaching writing? How will you overcome them?
4. "Spelling is caught rather than taught". Comment.
5. "English spellings are often unreliable". Comment. What steps will you take to ensure that your students spell correctly.
6. What are the different types of writing scripts? Which script would you make your students to follow in the beginning and why?

Short Answer Type Questions

1. What are the characteristics of good handwriting.
2. Write a short note on 'causes of bad handwriting'.
3. Suggest two ways for the improvement of handwriting of school going children.
4. Role of teacher in expansion of vocabulary.

16(E)

Essay Type questions

1. What are the Gathering Skills? Discuss.
2. Discuss storing Skills in detail.
3. Explain Retrieval Skills.

Short answer type questions

1. Write short notes on the use of
   1. Dictionary
   2. Encyclopaedia
   3. Thesaurus

17. INSTRUCTIONAL MATERIAL

Essay Type Questions

1. Define the term audio-visual aids. Explain its aims and importance in teaching a foreign language.
2. What audio-visual aids would you prepare or obtain to make your lesson on any one of the following interesting and effective? How would you use those aids?
   (a) An essay on 'A Railway Station' to IX Class.
   (b) A Greedy Dog (A Story) to VIII Class.
   (c) Use of 'to' and 'from' to VIII Class.
   (d) Change the narration to IX Class.
3. Discuss how the chalkboard can be used effectively in the English classroom.
4. Explain how can the different teaching aids be used for the improvement of the following:
   (a) Handwriting
   (b) Pronunciation
   (c) Spelling
5. Discuss the utility of the following instructional aids in the teaching of English:
   (a) Radio. (b) Overhead Projector. (c) Tape recorder
6. Discuss the meaning and functions of language laboratory.
7. What is the role of television in supplementing classroom teaching? What are the advantages of TV in English teaching?
8. What are charts? Discuss their nature and types. What are the qualities of good charts? How do charts help in teaching English?
9. Suppose you want to teach two lessons to 8th Class students—one on prose and another on poetry. Which instructional aids will you like to use and how will you use them effectively? Write fully by giving suitable examples.
10. Pictures with clear and relevant details are the best for teaching of composition. Discuss.
11. What are picture cut-outs? How are they prepared? Discuss their utility in the teaching of English?
12. Discuss the special role of audio-visual aids in foreign language. Discuss the precautions and principles of Teaching Aids.
13. Write short notes on:
   (a) Class magazine. (b) Projects

18. CO-CURRICULAR ACTIVITIES

1. What is the concept and importance of co-curricular activities?
2. Name various co-curricular activities. Explain any two in detail.
3. Discuss the role of teacher in organising co-curricular activities.

19.BASIC PRINCIPLES OF TESTING ENGLISH

Essay Type Questions

1. What is evaluation? What are the basic principles of evaluation?
2. What is the modern concept of evaluation? How does it differ from measurement?
3. Define the term 'measurement'. Enumerate its characteristics, functions and methods.
4. Discuss in detail the devices of evaluation which are used in the teaching of English?
5. Discuss the common flaws of traditional way of evaluation.
6. Differentiate between the terms examination and evaluation.
7. What are the basic principles of testing English?

Short Answer Type Questions

1. What is the importance of objective type questions and why is it called the best method?
2. What are the purpose of evaluation?
3. Discuss the importance of oral examination in teaching English.
4. Discuss the main functions of measurement.
5. What are the characteristics of good evaluation?

20. COMPREHENSIVE AND CONTINUOUS EVALUATION IN ENGLISH

Essay Type Questions

1. Only Continuous and Comprehensive Evaluation will improve the standards of English. Discuss.
2. 'What is the importance of Continuous and Comprehensive Evaluation of English?' Explain fully.
3. How can you evaluate the oral skills of students in English? Give any four useful methods.
4. What skills can be tested through the written technique? What type of questions can be prepared for testing reading?

Short Answer Type Questions

1. Write a short note on self-evaluation.
2. Write a short note on peer evaluation.
3. What are the limitations of Continuous and Comprehensive Evaluation?

21. DIGITAL PORTFOLIO: USE OF ICT

1. What do understand by Digital Portfolio? Discuss.
2. What is the difference between traditional approach to learning and technology supported learning? Explain the use of ICT in different ways.
3. What is multi-media presentation? How one can use world wide web?

22. CHARACTERISTICS OF GOOD TEXT BOOK

Essay Type Questions

1. As a teacher of English language, what will be your criteria in selecting a textbook for your school students?
2. Describe importance of textbooks. What are the characteristics of a good textbook in English?

23. DEVELOPMENT OF GOOD TEST ITEMS IN ENGLISH (OBJECTIVE TYPE, SHORT ANSWER TYPE AND ESSAY TYPE)

Essay Type Questions

1. Discuss the need of good test items in English. What are the qualities of a good test item?
2. What are the characteristics of a good test? Highlight some drawbacks of traditional ways of testing English.
3. Discuss the various types of objective type test.
4. Objective type tests are useful for some purposes but we need essay type also to test certain other language skills. Discuss and illustrate.
5. What are the various evaluation devices in English? Enumerate the various types of tests.

Short Answer Type Questions

1. Suggest 4 test items for judging the structure ability of VIII class students.
2. How can we judge the vocabulary of VI class students?

24. REMEDIAL AND ENRICHMENT CONTROL OF AURAL, ORAL, READING AND WRITING SKILLS

Essay Type Questions

1. "Remedial English has become a necessity in English teaching today." Keeping in view give five examples of incorrect English generally committed by learners at higher secondary level and suggest ways to correct them.
2. What do you understand by types of faults? State the sources of errors.
3. Suggest some programmes for remedial work in various areas?

Short Answer Type Question

1. Write short Notes on: (i) Contrastive analysis and (ii) Error Analysis.

25. PREPARATION OF AN ACHIEVEMENT TEST

Essay Type Questions

1. What is an achievement test? What are the different types of achievement tests? Also discuss the uses of such tests.
2. How will you prepare an achievement test? Discuss.
3. What are the characteristics of a good achievement test in English? What different types of questions would you use for assessing achievement in English grammar. Illustrate your answer with examples.

Short Answer Type Questions

1. What is an achievement test?
2. Discuss any two use of an achievement test.